P9-AZU-308

COMPLETE GUIDE
TO U.S.
CIVIL SERVICE JOBS

COMPLETE GUIDE

TO U.S.

CIVIL SERVICE JOBS

by DAVID R. TURNER, M.S. in Ed.

arco 219 Park Avenue South
New York, N.Y. 10003

Eighth Edition (B-1922)
First Printing, 1981

Published by Arco Publishing, Inc.
219 Park Avenue South, New York, N. Y. 10003

Library of Congress Catalog Card Number 81-65360
ISBN 0-668-05245-7

Printed in the United States of America

CONTENTS

HOW TO USE THIS INDEX
Slightly bend the right-hand edge
of the book. This will expose
the corresponding Parts
which match the index, below.

PART
1
2
3
4

PART ONE

HOW TO GET A FEDERAL JOB

PART TWO

THE EXAMS...AND HOW TO PREPARE FOR THEM

...continued on next page

CONTENTS continued

PART

1

2

3

4

PART THREE
THE JOBS IN CIVIL SERVICE

PART FOUR
AFTER YOU PASS THE TESTS

WHAT THIS BOOK WILL DO FOR YOU

ARCO Publishing, Inc. has followed testing trends and methods ever since the firm was founded in 1937. We specialize in books that prepare people for tests. Based on this experience, we have prepared the best possible book to help *you* score high.

To write this book we carefully analyzed every detail surrounding the forthcoming examination . . .
- the job itself
- official and unofficial announcements concerning the examination
- all the previous examinations, many not available to the public
- related examinations
- technical literature that explains and forecasts the examination

CAN YOU PREPARE YOURSELF FOR YOUR TEST?

You want to pass this test. That's why you bought this book. Used correctly, your "self-tutor" will show you what to expect and will give you a speedy brush-up on the subjects tested in your exam. Some of these are subjects not taught in schools at all. Even if your study time is very limited, you should:
- Become familiar with the type of examination you will have.
- Improve your general examination-taking skill.
- Improve your skill in analyzing and answering questions involving reasoning, judgment, comparison, and evaluation.

- Improve your speed and skill in reading and understanding what you read—an important part of your ability to learn and an important part of most tests.

This book will tell you exactly what to study by presenting in full every type of question you will get on the actual test.

This book will help you find your weaknesses. Once you know what subjects you're weak in you can get right to work and concentrate on those areas. This kind of selective study yields maximum test results.

This book will give you the *feel* of the exam. Almost all our sample and practice questions are taken from actual previous exams. On the day of the exam you'll see how closely this book follows the format of the real test.

This book will give you confidence *now*, while you are preparing for the test. It will build your self-confidence as you proceed and will prevent the kind of test anxiety that causes low test scores.

This book stresses the multiple-choice type of question because that's the kind you'll have on your test. You must not be satisfied with merely knowing the correct answer for each question. You must find out why the other choices are incorrect. This will help you remember a lot you thought you had forgotten.

After testing yourself, you may find that you are weak in a particular area. You should concentrate on improving your skills by using the specific practice sections in this book that apply to you.

YOUR GOVERNMENT JOB

The U.S. Civil Service Commission has been abolished since January 1, 1979 and its functions have been divided between two new agencies, the Office of Personnel Management (OPM) and the Merit Systems Protection Board (MSPB). The Office of Personnel Management has taken over many of the important responsibilities of the Civil Service Commission, including examinations and other employment matters, personnel investigations, personnel program evaluation, and training. The Merit Systems Protection Board is a separate and independent agency responsible for safeguarding both the merit system and the rights of individual employees in personnel matters. The addresses and telephone numbers for the new agencies remain the same as they had been under the Civil Service Commission.

FEDERAL CIVILIAN EMPLOYMENT

The executive branch includes the Office of the President, the 12 departments with cabinet representation, and a number of independent agencies, commissions, and boards. This branch is responsible for such activities as administering Federal laws; handling international relations; conserving natural resources; treating and rehabilitating disabled veterans; conducting scientific research; maintaining the flow of supplies to the Armed Forces; and administering other programs to promote the health and welfare of the people.

The Federal Government employs several million white-collar workers. Entrance requirements for white-collar jobs vary widely. Entrants into professional occupations are required to have highly specialized knowledge in a specified field, as evidenced by completion of a prescribed college course of study or, in many cases, the equivalent in experience. Occupations typical of this group are attorney, physicist, and engineer.

Entrants into administrative and managerial occupations usually are not required to have knowledge in a specialized field but rather, they must indicate by graduation from a 4-year college or by responsible job experience, that they have potential for future development. The entrant usually begins at a trainee level, and learns the duties of the job after he is hired. Typical jobs in this group are budget analyst, claims examiner, purchasing officer, administrative assistant, and personnel officer.

Technician, clerical, and aid-assistant jobs have entry level positions that usually are filled by persons having a high school education or the equivalent. For many of these positions, no prior experience or training is required. The entry level position is usually that of trainee, where the duties of the job are learned and skill is improved. Persons with junior college or technical school training, or those having specialized skills may enter these occupations at higher levels. Jobs typical of this group are engineering technician, supply clerk, clerk-typist, and nursing assistant.

Blue collar jobs — service, craft, and manual labor — provided employment to over 600,000 workers. The majority of these workers were in establishments such as naval shipyards, arsenals, air bases, or army depots; or they worked on construction, harbor, flood-control, irrigation, or reclamation projects.

The largest single group of blue-collar workers consists of mobile equipment operators and mechanics. Among these jobs are forklift operator, chauffeur, truckdriver and automobile mechanic. The next largest group of workers are general laborers, who perform a wide variety of manual jobs.

Many skilled occupations may be entered through apprenticeship programs. To qualify, experience normally is not required, but a test may be given to indicate whether an applicant has an aptitude for the occupation.

Federal employees are stationed in all parts of the United States and its territories and in many foreign countries. Although most Government departments and agencies have their headquarters in the Washington, D.C. metropolitan area, only 1 out of 11 Federal workers were employed there at the beginning of this year.

THE MERIT SYSTEM

The majority of Federal jobs in the United States are covered by the Civil Service Act. This act was passed by the Congress to hire Federal employees on the basis of individual merit and fitness. It provides for competitive examinations and the selection of new employees from among those who make the highest scores. The U.S. Civil Service Commission, which administers the Civil Service Act, examines applicants and refers eligible persons to Federal agencies.

Some Federal jobs are excepted from Civil Service requirements either by law or by action of the Civil Service Commission. However, most of the excepted positions are under separate merit systems of other agencies, such as the Foreign Service of the Department of State, the Department of Medicine and Surgery of the Veterans Administration, the Federal Bureau of Investigation, the Atomic Energy Commission, the Tennessee Valley Authority, and the Postal Service. These agencies establish their own standards for the selection of new employees.

In the United States, Civil Service competitive examinations may be taken by any resident. However, on the list of "Eligibles," priority will be given to U.S. citizens. To be eligible for appointment, an applicant must meet minimum age, training, and experience requirements for the particular position. A physical handicap will not in itself bar a person from a position if it does not interfere with his performance of the required duties. Examinations vary according to the types of positions for which they are held. Some examinations include written tests; others do not. Written examinations test the applicant's ability to do the job applied for, or his ability to learn how to do it. In nonwritten examinations, applicants are rated on the basis of the experience and training described in their applications and any supporting evidence required by the Commission.

The Commission notifies applicants whether they have achieved eligible or ineligible ratings, and enters the names of eligible applicants on a list in the order of their scores. When a Federal agency requests names of eligible applicants for a job vacancy, the Commission sends the agency the names at the top of the appropriate list. The agency can select any one of the top three available eligibles. Names of those not selected are restored to the list for consideration for other job openings.

Appointments to civil service jobs are made without regard to an applicant's race, color, religion, national origin, politics, or sex.

Pay rates of employees under the General Schedule are set by the Congress and are nation-wide. This General Schedule provides a pay scale for employees in professional, administrative, technical, and clerical jobs, and for employees such as guards and messengers. General Schedule jobs are classified and arranged in 18 pay grades according to difficulty of the duties, and the responsibilities, knowledge, experience, or skill required. Employees in all grades to GS-12 receive within-grade increases after they have completed the required service periods, if their work is determined to be of an acceptable level of competence. Within-grade increases also may be given in recognition of high-quality service.

High school graduates with no related work experience are usually appointed to GS-2 positions, but some with special skills begin at GS-3. Graduates of 2-year junior colleges and technical schools can often begin at the GS–4 level. Most young people appointed to professional and administrative positions enter at grades GS–5 or GS–7 depending on their academic record. Those who hold a master's degree or the equivalent in education or experience usually enter at grade GS–7; they may enter at grade GS–9 if they are well qualified. In addition, the Federal Government also appoints very well-qualified, experienced people at the GS–11 level and above. These appointments are for such positions as psychologist, statistician, economist, writer and editor, budget analyst, accountant, and physicist.

New appointments usually are made at the minimum rate of the salary range for the appropriate grade. However, appointments in hard-to-fill positions frequently are made at a higher rate.

Advancement depends upon ability, work performance, and generally, upon openings in jobs at higher grades. Employees frequently get promotions by qualifying for jobs at higher grades. Promotions also may be obtained when jobs are reclassified to a higher grade to reflect more difficult work assignments and increased responsibilities.

Craft, service, and manual workers employed by the Federal government are paid under the coordinated Federal wage system. Pay is fixed on the basis of prevailing rates paid by private employers for similar work.

Employees in agencies with separate merit systems are paid under acts other than those already mentioned.

The standard workweek for Federal Government employees is 40 hours, and the pay schedules are based on this workweek. If an employee is required to work overtime he is either paid overtime rates for the additional time worked or given compensatory time off at a later date. Most employees usually work 8 hours a day, 5 days a week, Monday through Friday, but in some cases, the nature of the work may call for a different workweek. Annual earnings for most full-time Federal workers are not affected by seasonal factors.

Federal employees earn 13 days of annual (vacation) leave during each of their first 3 years of service, then 20 days each year until they have completed 15 years; after 15 years, they earn 26 days of leave each year. In addition, they earn 13 days of paid sick leave a year. Nine paid holidays are observed annually. Employees who are members of military reserve organizations also are granted up to 15 days of paid military leave a year for training purposes. A Federal employee who is laid off is entitled to unemployment compensation similar to that provided for employees in private industry.

Other benefits available to most Federal employees include: A contributory retirement system; optional participation in low-cost group life and health insurance programs supported in part by the Government; and training programs to develop maximum job proficiency and help employees achieve their highest potential. These training programs may be conducted in Government facilities or in outside educational facilities at Government expense.

WHERE TO GO FOR MORE INFORMATION

Information on Federal employment opportunities is available from a number of sources. For college students, the college placement office is often a good source of such information. High school students in many localities may obtain information from their high school guidance counselors. Additional information may be obtained from State employment service offices.

Job Information Centers operated by the Office of Personnel Management are located in many large cities throughout the country. A complete listing of these offices appears in this book and you can get complete information concerning Federal jobs by calling, visiting, or writing to the office in your area.

Information about a specific agency also may be obtained by contacting the agency directly.

PART ONE

How To Get A Federal Job

CODE OF ETHICS
FOR FEDERAL EMPLOYEES

"Resolved by the House of Representatives (the Senate concurring), That it is the sense of the Congress that the following Code of Ethics should be adhered to by all Government employees, including office holders:

"Any person in Government service should:

"1. Put loyalty to the highest moral principles and to country above loyalty to persons, party, or Government department.

"2. Uphold the Constitution, laws, and legal regulations of the United States and of all governments therein and never be a party to their evasion.

"3. Give a full day's labor for a full day's pay: giving to the performance of his duties his earnest effort and best thought.

"4. Seek to find and employ more efficient and economical ways of getting tasks accomplished.

"5. Never discriminate unfairly by the dispensing of special favors or privileges to anyone, whether for remuneration or not; and never accept, for himself or his family, favors or benefits under circumstances which might be construed by reasonable persons as influencing the performance of his governmental duties.

"6. Make no private promises of any kind binding upon the duties of office, since a Government employee has no private word which can be binding on public duty.

"7. Engage in no business with the Government, either directly or indirectly, which is inconsistent with the conscientious performance of his governmental duties.

"8. Never use any information coming to him confidentially in the performance of governmental duties as a means for making private profit.

"9. Expose corruption wherever discovered.

"10. Uphold these principles, ever conscious that public office is a public trust."

APPLYING FOR FEDERAL JOBS

Note: The Civil Service Commission is now called the Office Of Personnel Management.

Since so many jobs must be filled, the Government cannot accept applications for all kinds of jobs all the time. Opportunities to apply for specific types of positions are announced when there is a need to fill such positions. The "announcement" tells about the jobs—what experience or education you must have before your application will be accepted, whether a written test is required, where the jobs are located, what the pay is, and so on. The announcement foreshadows your test.

KEEPING POSTED

Your Federal Job Information Center provides information about:

—All current job opportunities in any part of the United States.

—Specific vacancies in shortage categories

—Opportunities for overseas employment

—Employment advisory service

These centers are specially equipped to answer all inquiries about Federal employment opportunities. If you have any questions, write, visit, or phone your local Job Information Center.

To assist the Federal Job Information Center, many post offices also furnish information about current job opportunities and given out application forms. Your local post office can give you information about job opportunities or tell you the location of the nearest post office where this information can be obtained.

The following also have civil service information: State Employment Service Offices, national and State headquarters of veterans' organizations, placement officials at colleges, and personnel officers in Government agencies.

A newspaper such as the *Chief* (published in New York City) runs extensive listings of government job openings, including those abroad. The government itself uses newspapers and sometimes the radio for recruitment.

including those abroad. The government itself uses newspapers and sometimes the radio for recruitment.

As a special service to disabled veterans, the Civil Service Commission maintains a file of those who are interested in specific kinds of jobs. A ten-point veteran may write to the Commission in Washington, D.C., and ask that his name be placed in this file.

FEDERAL JOB INFORMATION CENTERS

The Interagency Board system, operated by the Civil Service Commission, consists of 65 boards of civil service examiners located in centers of Federal population throughout the country.

These boards announce and conduct examinations. They evaluate applicants' work experience, training, and aptitude. They refer the names of people who meet the requirements to Federal agencies who are seeking new employees. Each board also provides, through its **Federal Job Information Center,** a complete one-stop information service about Federal job opportunities in the area as well as in other locations.

Address Executive Officer, Interagency Board of U.S. Civil Service Examiners, at the location that serves your area. Telephone numbers may be found under the U.S. Government listing in the telephone director in cities where Federal Job Information Centers are located.

JOB INFORMATION CENTERS

The Office of Personnel Management offers Federal employment information through a nationwide network of Federal Job Information Centers.

For an answer to your questions about Federal employment, you can visit, write, or call the nearest Federal Job Information Center—the local address and telephone number are listed beside each city.

Some Job Information Centers provide information regarding jobs in other jurisdictions (city, county, or state). Those Intergovernmental Job Information Centers are identified below by a (●)

The Office of Personnel Management invites you to call and talk with our information specialists before writing a letter or filling out a job application. Information specialists can mail you job announcements, application forms, and pamphlets. A call can save you valuable time and effort.

Federal Job Information Centers are open to serve you Monday through Friday, except holidays.

Federal Job Information Centers

ALABAMA
Huntsville:
Southerland Building
806 Governors Dr, N.W. 35801
(205) 453-5070

ALASKA
Anchorage:
Federal Bldg. & U.S. Courthouse
701 C St., P.O. Box 22, 99513
(907) 271-5821

ARIZONA
Phoenix:
522 N. Central Ave. 85004
(602) 261-4736

ARKANSAS
Little Rock:
Federal Bldg. Rm. 1319
700 W. Capitol Ave. 72201
(501) 378-5842

CALIFORNIA
Los Angeles:
Linder Bldg.
845 S. Figueroa 90017
(213) 688-3360
Sacramento:
Federal Bldg., 650 Capitol Mall 95814
(916) 440-3441
San Diego:
880 Front St. 92188
(714) 293-6165
San Francisco:
Federal Bldg., Rm. 1001
450 Golden Ave. 94102
(415) 556-6667

COLORADO
● Denver:
1845 Sherman St., 80203
(303) 837-3506

CONNECTICUT
Hartford:
Federal Bldg., Rm. 717, 450 Main St. 06103
(203) 244-3096

DELAWARE
● Wilmington:
Federal Bldg., 844 King St. 19801
(302) 571-6288

DISTRICT OF COLUMBIA
Metro Area:
1900 E Street, N.W., 20415
(202) 737-9616

FLORIDA
● Miami:
1000 Brickell Ave., Suite 660, 33131
(305) 350-4725
● Orlando:
80 N. Hughey Ave. 32801
(305) 420-6148

GEORGIA
Atlanta:
Richard B. Russell Federal Bldg.,
75 Spring St. SW, 30303
(404) 221-4315

GUAM
Agana:
238 O'Hara St.
Room 308 96910
344-5242

HAWAII
Honolulu (and Island of Oahu):
Federal Bldg. Room 1310
300 Ala Moana Blvd. 96850
(808) 546-8600

IDAHO
Boise:
Box 035, Federal Bldg.,
550 W. Fort Street 83724
(208) 384-1726

ILLINOIS
Chicago:
Dirksen Bldg. Rm. 1322
219 S. Dearborn St. 60604
(312) 353-5136

INDIANA
Indianapolis:
46 East Ohio Street, Room 123, 46204
(317) 269-7161 or 7162

IOWA
Des Moines:
210 Walnut St., Rm. 191, 50309
(515) 284-4546

KANSAS
Wichita:
    One-Twenty Bldg., Rm. 101,
    120 S. Market St. 67202
    (316) 267-6311, ext. 106
In Johnson and Wyandott Counties dial 374-5702

KENTUCKY
Louisville:
    Federal Building
    600 Federal Pl. 40202
    (502) 582-5130

LOUISIANA
New Orleans:
    F. Edward Hebert Bldg.,
    610 South St., Rm 103 70130
    (504) 589-2764

MAINE
Augusta:
    Federal Bldg. Rm. 611
    Sewall St. & Western Ave. 04330
    (207) 622-6171 ext. 269

MARYLAND
Baltimore:
    Garmatz Federal Building
    101 W. Lombard St. 21201
    (301) 962-3822
DC Metro Area:
    1900 E St. N.W., 20415
    (202) 737-9616

MASSACHUSETTS
Boston:
    3 Center Plaza, 02108
    (617) 223-2571

MICHIGAN
Detroit:
    477 Michigan Ave, Rm. 595, 48226
    (313) 226-6950

MINNESOTA
Twin Cities:
    Federal Bldg.
    Ft. Snelling, Twin Cities, 55111
    (612) 725-3355

MISSISSIPPI
Jackson:
    100 W. Capitol St. (Suite 102) 39201
    (601) 969-4585

MISSOURI
Kansas City:
    Federal Bldg., Rm. 129
    601 E. 12th St. 64106
    (816) 374-5702
St. Louis:
    Federal Bldg., Rm. 1712,
    1520 Market St., 63103
    (314) 425-4285

MONTANA
Helena:
    Federal Bldg. & Courthouse
    301 S. Park, Rm. 153 59601
    (406) 449-5388

NEBRASKA
Omaha:
    U.S. Courthouse and Post Office Bldg.
    Rm. 1014, 215 N. 17th St. 68102
    (402) 221-3815

NEVADA
● Reno:
    Mill & S. Virginia Streets
    P.O. Box 3296 89505
    (702) 784-5535

NEW HAMPSHIRE
Portsmouth:
    Federal Bldg. Rm. 104,
    Daniel & Penhallow Streets, 03801
    (603) 436-7720 ext. 762

NEW JERSEY
Newark:
    Federal Bldg., 970 Broad St. 07102
    (201) 645-3673
In Camden, dial (215) 597-7440

NEW MEXICO
Albuquerque:
    Federal Bldg. 421 Gold Ave. SW, 87102
    (505) 766-2557

NEW YORK
Bronx:
    590 Grand Concourse, 10451
    (212) 292-4666
Buffalo:
    111 W. Huron St, Rm. 35, 14202
    (716) 846-4001
Jamaica:
    90-04 161st St., Rm. 200, 11432
    (212) 526-6192
New York City:
    Federal Bldg., 26 Federal Plaza, 10007
    (212) 264-0422
Syracuse:
    100 S. Clinton St. 13260
    (315) 423-5660

NORTH CAROLINA
Raleigh:
    Federal Bldg. 310 New Bern Ave.
    P.O. Box 25069, 27611
    (919) 755-4361

NORTH DAKOTA
Fargo:
    Federal Bldg, Rm. 202
    657 Second Ave. N. 58102
    (701) 237-5771 ext. 363

OHIO
Cleveland:
Federal Bldg., 1240 E. 9th St., 44199
(216) 522-4232
Dayton:
Federal Building Lobby
200 W 2nd St., 45402
(513) 225-2720 and 2854

OKLAHOMA
Oklahoma City:
200 NW Fifth St, 73102
(405) 231-4948

OREGON
Portland:
Federal Bldg., Lobby (North)
1220 SW Third St. 97204
(503) 221-3141

PENNSYLVANIA
● Harrisburg:
Federal Bldg., Rm. 168, 17108
(717) 782-4494
Philadelphia:
Wm. J. Green, Jr. Fed. Bldg,
600 Arch Street, 19106
(215) 597-7440
Pittsburgh:
Fed. Bldg. 1000 Liberty Ave., 15222
(412) 644-2755

PUERTO RICO
San Juan:
Federico Degetau Federal Bldg.
Carlos E. Chardon St.,
Hato Rey, P.R. 00918
(809) 753-4209, ext. 209

RHODE ISLAND
Providence:
Federal & P.O. Bldg., Rm. 310
Kennedy Plaza 02903
(401) 528-4447

SOUTH CAROLINA
Charleston:
Federal Bldg., 334 Meeting St., 29403
(803) 724-4328

SOUTH DAKOTA
Rapid City:
Rm. 201, Federal Building
U.S. Court House, 515 9th St. 57701
(605) 348-2221

TENNESSEE
Memphis:
Federal Bldg., 167 N. Main St. 38103
(901) 521-3956

TEXAS
Dallas:
Rm. 1C42, 1100 Commerce St., 75242
(214) 749-7721
El Paso:
Property Trust Bldg.—Suite N302
2211 E. Missouri Ave. 79903
(915) 543-7425
Houston:
702 Caroline Street, 77002
(713) 226-5501
San Antonio:
643 E. Durango Blvd., 78205
(512) 229-6600

UTAH
Salt Lake City:
350 South Main St. Rm 484, 84101
(801) 524-5744

VERMONT
Burlington:
Federal Bldg., Rm. 614
P.O. Box 489
Elmwood Ave. & Pearl St., 05402
(802) 862-6712

VIRGINIA
Norfolk:
Federal Bldg., Rm. 220,
200 Granby Mall, 23510
(804) 441-3355
D.C. Metro Area:
1900 E Street, N.W. 20415
(202) 737-9616

WASHINGTON
● Seattle:
Federal Bldg., 915 Second Ave. 98174
(206) 442-4365

WEST VIRGINIA
● Charleston:
Federal Bldg., 500 Quarrier St. 25301
(304) 343-6181, ext. 226

WISCONSIN
Milwaukee:
Plankinton Bldg., Rm. 205,
161 W. Wisconsin Ave. 53203
(414) 244-3761

WYOMING
Cheyenne:
2120 Capitol Ave., Rm. 304
P.O. Box 967 82001
(307) 778-2220, ext. 2108

Office of Personnel Management Regions

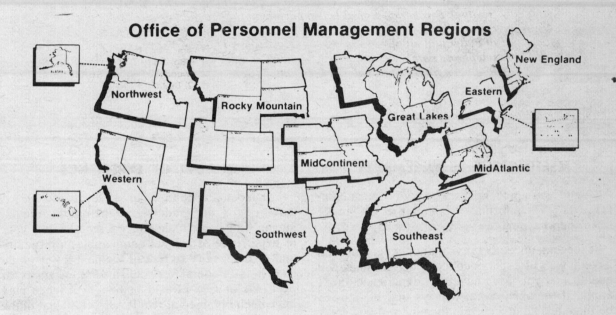

THE FEDERAL JOB ANNOUNCEMENT

The U.S. Civil Service Commission has been abolished since January 1, 1979 and its functions have been divided between two new agencies, the Office of Personnel Management (OPM) and the Merit Systems Protection Board (MSPB). The Office of Personnel Management has taken over many of the important responsibilities of the Civil Service Commission, including examinations and other employment matters, personnel investigations, personnel program evaluation, and training. The Merit Systems Protection Board is a separate and independent agency responsible for safeguarding both the merit system and the rights of individual employees in personnel matters. The addresses and telephone numbers for the new agencies remain the same as they had been under the Civil Service Commission.

MEETING THE REQUIREMENTS

Before you apply, read the announcement carefully. It gives information about the job to be filled and what qualifications you must have to fill it.

If the announcement says that only persons who have 1 year of experience along certain lines will qualify and you don't have that experience, don't apply. If the announcement says that the jobs to be filled are all in a certain locality and you don't want to work in that locality, don't file. Many disappointed applicants would have been saved time and trouble if they had only read the announcement carefully.

Credit will be given for unpaid experience or volunteer work such as in community, cultural, social service and professional association activities, on the same basis as for paid experience, that is, it must be of the type and level acceptable under the announcement. Therefore, you may, if you wish, report such experience in one or more of the experience blocks at the end of your personal qualifications statement, if you feel that it represents qualifying experience for the positions for which you are applying. To receive proper credit, you must show the actual time, such as the number of hours a week, spent in such activities.

QUALITY OF EXPERIENCE

For most positions, in order to qualify *on experience* for any grade above the entrance level, an applicant must have either 6 months or 1 year of experience at a level comparable in difficulty and responsibility to that of the next lower grade level in the Federal Service. In some instances for positions at GS–11 and below, experience may have been obtained at two levels below that of the job to be filled.

Depending on the type of position, the next lower level may be either one or two grades lower. If you were applying for a position as a Stenographer (single grade interval position), at grade GS–5, you should have at least 1 year of experience doing work equivalent to that done by a Stenographer at the GS–4 level. If you were applying for a two-grade interval position, however, such as Computer Specialist GS–7, you would need at least 1 year of experience equivalent to that of a GS–5 Computer Specialist in Federal Service, or 6 months equivalent to the GS–6 level. Where necessary, the announcement will provide more specific information about the level of experience needed to qualify.

5118

THE DUTIES

The words *Optional Fields* — sometimes just the word *Options* — may appear on the front page of the announcement. You then have a choice to apply for that particular position in which you are especially interested. This is because the duties of various positions are quite different even though they bear the same broad title. A public relations *clerk,* for example, does different work from a payroll *clerk,* although they are considered broadly in the same general area.

Not every announcement has options. But whether or not it has them, the precise duties are described in detail, usually under the heading: *Description of Work.* Make sure that these duties come within the range of your experience and ability.

SOME THINGS TO WATCH FOR

In addition to educational and experience requirements, there will be some general requirements you will have to meet.

Age. "How old are you?" There is no maximum age limit. The usual minimum age limit is 18, but for most jobs high school graduates may apply at 16.

If you are 16 or 17 and are out of school but not a high school graduate, you may be hired only (1) if you have successfully completed a formal Government or private training program preparing you for work, or (2) if you have been out of school at least 3 months, not counting the summer vacation and if school authorities sign a form agreeing with your preference for work instead of additional schooling. The form will be given to you by the agency that wants to hire you.

REMEMBER, JOB OPPORTUNITIES ARE BEST FOR THOSE WHO GRADUATE. IF YOU CAN, YOU SHOULD COMPLETE YOUR EDUCATION BEFORE YOU APPLY FOR FULL-TIME WORK.

If you are in high school, you may be hired for work during vacation periods if you are 16. (For jobs filled under the Summer Employment Examination, however, you must be 18 if still in high school.) You may also be hired for part-time work during the school year if you are 16 and meet all the following conditions:

(1) Your work schedule is set up through agreement with your school,
(2) Your school certifies that you can maintain good standing while working, and
(3) You remain enrolled in high school.

Some announcements may set a different minimum age limit. Be sure to check the announcement carefully before applying.

Citizenship. Are you an American citizen? Only citizens and people who owe permanent allegiance to the United States can receive competitive appointments.

Physical requirements. What is your physical condition? You must be physically able to perform the duties of the position, and must be emotionally and mentally stable. This does not mean that a handicap will disqualify an applicant so long as he can do the work efficiently without being a hazard to himself or to others.

For most positions, appointees must have good distant vision in one eye and be able to read without strain printed material the size of typewritten characters. They may use glasses to meet these requirements.

Persons appointed are usually required to be able to hear the conversational voice. They may use a hearing aid to meet this requirement. Blind persons and deaf persons may apply and be examined for positions with duties they can perform.

An amputation of an arm, hand, leg, or foot does not in itself bar a person from Federal employment. Here again the test is whether the person can do the duties of the position satisfactorily and without hazard to himself or others.

The Federal Government is the world's largest employer of handicapped people and has a strong program aimed at their employment. It recognizes that, in almost every kind of work, there are some positions suitable for the blind, the deaf, and others with serious impairments. If reading is necessary to perform duties, the blind person is permitted to provide a reader at no expense to the Government.

Of course, there are some positions — such as border patrolman, firefighter, and criminal investigator — that can be filled only by people in topnotch physical condition. Whenever this is the case, the physical requirements are described in detail in the announcements.

ABOUT THE TEST

The announcement also tells you about the kind of test you will be given. Several kinds of examinations are given by the Civil Service Commission. At the very beginning the job announcement states whether this is an assembled or unassembled examination. In the former, applicants assemble to take their test — usually a written one. The announcement always tells you the kind of examination you must take, and often sample questions are attached. The tests used in each examination are designed to measure the ability of the applicant to perform the duties of the position for which the examination is given. The amount of time required to take the test, and the method of rating — a scale of 100, with 70 as the passing grade — are also mentioned in the announcement.

CLOSING DATE

When an examination is announced, qualifications statements are accepted as long as the announcement is "open." In some instances, the closing date for acceptance of statements is stated in the announcement. In other instances, the closing date is not stated in the announcement; instead, public notice of the closing date is given later.

You must apply before the closing date. However, if you cannot apply on time because of military service, you may apply after the closing date, but not later than 120 days after honorable discharge. If you're working outside the United States for a government agency or for an international organization (such as the United Nations), you may also file late under certain conditions.

Persons who have been granted "10-point veteran preference" by the Civil Service Commission may also apply after the closing date.

If you think that you are entitled to apply after the closing date, write to the office that issued the announcement and describe the circumstances. That office will let you know whether your qualifications statement can be accepted.

One further fact: It is not necessary to pay anyone for helping you obtain a civil service position with the United States Government. No such intervention is possible.

THE APPLICATION FORM

The U.S. Civil Service Commission has been abolished since January 1, 1979 and its functions have been divided between two new agencies, the Office of Personnel Management (OPM) and the Merit Systems Protection Board (MSPB). The Office of Personnel Management has taken over many of the important responsibilities of the Civil Service Commission, including examinations and other employment matters, personnel investigations, personnel program evaluation, and training. The Merit Systems Protection Board is a separate and independent agency responsible for safeguarding both the merit system and the rights of individual employees in personnel matters. The addresses and telephone numbers for the new agencies remain the same as they had been under the Civil Service Commission.

FILLING OUT THE APPLICATION FORMS

If you are satisfied that you meet the requirements listed in the announcement, the next step is to fill out the application forms. At first you may have to fill out only a small card, but later you will have to fill out a 2- or 4-page personal qualifications statement. It is very important to do this carefully.

Answer every question in the statement. If you don't, the area office must write to you for the missing information. This will take time and delay action on your qualifications statement. You will ordinarily be given only one opportunity to send in this information. If you don't reply promptly, your statement will be canceled.

For many positions, written tests are not required, and civil service examiners rate applicants on their training and experience. Tell the whole story. You can't get credit for experience and training if you don't claim it on your statement.

Follow the instructions in the announcement as to when and where to send your statement. Be sure to send it to the right office before the closing date.

WHAT TO EXPECT ON
THE APPLICATION FORM

There are many different application forms. While there are minor differences in the questions asked, and the order in which they're presented, by and large this is what you can expect.

Name of examination, or kind of position applied for. This information appears in large type at the top of job announcements. All you have to do is to copy it .

Optional work (if mentioned in announcement)— Many examination announcements have options, that is, a choice of the kind of work you want to do. To answer this question you write the specific option of the job you are applying for, again copying it from the announcement form.

Place of Employment—The location of the position is contained in the announcement. You must consider, when you apply, whether you are certain you would care to work there. Many announcements list more than one federal establishment where the positions are open. If you would accept employment in any of the places, list them all; if you would rather not work in some of them, list only the places at which you would be willing to work.

Name—Give your full name, including your middle name if you have one. People who have changed their names often ask if this disqualifies them from Federal employment. If the change wasn't made for illegal purposes, it is no bar to a government job. A simple explanation attached to the application will save trouble later, for in the course of its investigation the Civil Service Commission or the Federal Bureau of Investigation is bound to discover the original name.

Your place of birth—The United States Government makes no distinction between people born abroad and those born in the United States in selecting workers for government positions.

Changes in the borders of many nations make it difficult for some foreign-born American citizens to know which country to list as the land of their birth. Federal personnel authorities understand this dilemma as well as anyone else. There is no set rule to follow in cases where a country or province has changed hands. One suggestion is to give the name of the town and the name of the nation which now controls it, together with an accompanying explanation, giving the name of the nation which held control at the time of the applicant's birth.

Your date of birth—Give the exact month, date, and year of your birth. Vanity has no business in a civil service application blank; this is not the place to take a few years off your age. Sometimes people who have given false ages elsewhere feel they must carry through with the Civil Service Commission; for example, young men who added a year or two to their ages in order to enlist in the armed forces. It isn't necessary. The Office of Personnel Management is interested in having the straight facts, and will determine itself whether a previous different statement about age is worth worrying about. It probably will not be.

When the government asks you to prove your age you will have to submit a copy of your birth certificate if one is available. You can get one from the Registrar of Vital Statistics in many states, from the State Board of Health in others; and in some cities, at City Hall or from the local Board of Health. In New York City the Health Department maintains birth records. You can find out where birth records are kept in your state by writing to your local newspaper, the county medical society, or the office of the state governor.

But many Americans have never had birth certificates; therefore the Civil Service Commission will accept other kinds of evidence, including: a valid baptismal record; a verified notation in an old family Bible, or other family record made at time of birth; a signed statement by the physician who attended at the birth; signed statements by substantial citizens who can vouch for the date of birth from personal knowledge; early school, Sunday school, and other local records which help reveal the age of the applicant; immigration records; newspaper clippings properly identified as to date; and census records. Since the census is taken every ten years, the United States Census Bureau should have a record of the applicant, containing his age, in the census following his birth. You can get one of these records from the Census Bureau by paying a small fee.

Height without shoes; weight. Height must be stated in feet and inches; weight, in pounds.

Legal or voting residence (state)—The state in which you vote is the one you list here. During and since the war Americans have moved a great deal. Many veterans consider their present homes temporary, and plan no permanent ties there. In some cases students take a deep interest in the community in which they are studying; other students look upon their college towns as merely places they are "passing through." The Civil Service Commission determines legal residence on these criteria: Where do you vote? If you are not a registered voter, what state do you consider to be your permanent residence, your home? A person who has moved from one state to another, and fully intends to make the second state his home, should consider himself—for civil service purposes—a resident of the second state. For certain "quota" jobs in Washington, the civil service law requires one year's residence in a state before it may be considered a legal residence. Sometimes close questions occur and there is real difficulty in determining legal residence. For most applicants, however, the test of voting—the state where you vote or where you intend to vote—is as good a test as any.

Have you ever been employed by the federal government? If you are now employed by the government, you must record your present grade and the date you were accorded that grade. If you have been formerly employed by the government it may be easier for you to get a new job.

Is your name currently on a list of eligibles for a Federal job? If so, you must give the name of the announcement and of the office maintaining the list. You must also give your rating and the date of your rating notice.

Although federal employees are not covered by social security benefits by virtue of their employment, you will be required to supply your social security number to the agency that employs you. This number will be used for identification purposes only.

THE "OMNIBUS" QUERY

We now reach the "omnibus" query. This consists of six parts and deals with specific information concerning certain preferences of yours about salary, length and location of employment. The information you provide in response to this question will enable the government to offer you a wider or narrower range of jobs and provide civil service authorities with an idea of your feelings about a short-term job if one should come up.

An important part of this question asks you *what is the lowest entrance salary you will accept?*

It may seem strange to find that question on the application form when the job-announcement specified the salary of the job so clearly. But there is good reason for this question; you may be eligible for a post paying (say) $8,005 a year, but before a job with this pay is open, another in the same occupation but carrying less responsibility may turn up at a basic entrance salary of $7,680. If you are willing to accept a position paying less than the amount listed on the announcement form, you can increase your opportunities for a job. Besides, if it is decided that you do not have all the qualifications for the better-paying post, but could fill a job in a lower grade, your name is placed on a list for the lower position. If you are interested only in the higher-salaried position, you will be disqualified if the examiners think you cannot fill it.

It doesn't, of course, inevitably follow that you will be considered only for the job at the lowest salary you are willing to accept. If you are qualified for a higher-paying position, and one of these comes along, you will usually be considered for it.

If you reject a lower-pay job, even after you have put down that you would take one, your name will still be on the list for the higher post. Under no circumstances will you be considered for a job paying less than the amount you give in answer to this question.

Another part of this question asks *if you would accept short-term appointment if offered for (a) 1 mo. or less, (b) 1 to 4 months, (c) 4 to 12 months?*

The Civil Service Commission wants a direct response now, on the application form, not after you have taken your examination. Temporary positions come up frequently and it is imperative to know whether you are available for a short-term post.

This question now proceeds to another subject: Your willingness to travel: *some; often; not at all.*

Many federal positions entail travel, and the government wants to know beforehand if you would be free to make the necessary trips. Be certain to answer this item as you really feel about it. It would be embarrassing if you stated that you were willing to travel frequently, and then, after being certified to a job, found that you could travel only occasionally.

As to preferred localities it inquires: *Would you accept appointment, if offered in Washington, D.C., any place in the U.S., any place outside the U.S., or only in specific localities?*

Here you must answer directly Yes or No. If you are free to work anywhere, the chances of obtaining government employment become much greater, because of the many federal establishments in all parts of the country and abroad.

It may be, of course, that you would not care to work in Washington, or "just anywhere" in the United States. Many people want to work only in certain places.

The final portion of the question asks if you will accept less than full time work.

VETERAN PREFERENCE

Note that you are asked (A) if you served on active duty, (B) if you were dishonorably discharged, (C) if you claim 5-point preference, (D) if you claim 10-point preference, and (E) to list dates, branch, and service or serial number of all active service.

Five-point preference is granted to honorably discharged veterans of: World War I; the period from December 7, 1941 to July 1, 1955; more than 180 consecutive days of active duty after January 31, 1955; and of service in a campaign for which a campaign badge has been authorized. An initial period of active training under the "six-month" Reserve or National Guard programs is discounted.

Ten-point preference is usually granted to disabled veterans, to veterans awarded the Purple Heart, to widows of veterans, and to mothers of deceased or disabled veterans.

If you claim five-point preference, you need only supply supporting records at the time of appointment. To claim 10-point preference, you must obtain Form 15 from a Civil Service office and attach it to your application.

EXPERIENCE

The "experience" item: This section consists of a series of blocks which you must fill in with the details of the positions you have held. The details which the Commission wants include: dates of employment, place of employment, name and address of employer, kind of business or organization (for example, dress manufacturing, wholesale grocer, service station, insurance agency), the number and kind of employees you supervised if you were in a supervisory position, the name and title of your immediate supervisor, the exact title of your position, the salary you earned when you started and your final salary, a description of your work. The government also wants to know your reason for desiring to change employment and the reasons for leaving your former positions.

If you were in the Armed Forces, list your military or merchant marine service and describe your major duty assignments.

Civil service examiners will check the answers you give here. This is stated as a strong warning against attempts to falsify or embroider the record. Let's take the point about the reasons you left your former positions. If you were fired, say so. It is better to have it that way than to state that you resigned and have the examiners find out a different story from your former employer.

Now it may be that the positions you held can't be fitted into tight compartments, one job between such and such dates, another job between such and such dates. You may have held down two part time jobs at the same time, then you may have had a period of unemployment, followed by a business for yourself. You may have worked for lots of people on a fee basis, been an interim salesman, taken time out for study, made money out of speculation in the stock market, or been a free-lance writer. Include any additional or supplemental information about your job on separate sheets of paper.

May inquiry be made of your present employer regarding your character and qualifications? The reason for this question is obvious; many persons applying for government jobs would jeopardize their present positions if their employers knew about the action. The government does not wish to put any applicant in this predicament. Your present employer will therefore not be consulted if you do not wish it.

HAVE YOU ANY SPECIAL APTITUDES?

Special Qualifications and Skills: This section is included so that you may cite any special qualifications not covered elsewhere in the application blank. It asks for a list of any special skills you possess, machines and equipment you can use, such as operation of shortwave radio, multilith, comptometer, keypunch, turret lathe, scientific or professional devices. Here, too, is a space in which you can list your typing and shorthand speed.

You are asked to list licenses or certificates you have held as a member of any trade or profession (such as pilot, electrician, radio operator, teacher, lawyer, CPA, etc.) and the states in which you

received them, as well as the year in which you received your most recent one.

You may mention any important publications you have written, your patents or inventions, public-speaking and public-relations experience, membership in professional or scientific societies.

Any occupational achievements which you feel might aid your case with the Civil Service Commission and with appointing officers should be included in a separate statement attached to the application form. Do you hold patents for inventions in your field of occupation? Have you won prizes for stenographic speed? Have you built up the circulation of a newspaper? Have you introduced efficiencies which saved money for your employer? Have you written reports or books in your field of activity? Tell the government officials. They'll be interested.

Education: This section queries you on the schools you attended. It gets specific, demanding to know when and where you attended. The application form has space, too, for a listing of college education, including the chief undergraduate subjects and semester hours in each. Other training which should be listed includes study courses given through the Armed Forces Institute, special courses at approved schools or colleges, and special vocational or business training. You must give the subject studied and the dates.

List any honors, awards, or fellowships you have received. This could help you get the job you want.

Indicate your knowledge of foreign languages. Such knowledge is often an important asset on a government job. The Civil Service Commission wants to know not only the foreign languages with which you are acquainted but how good your knowledge is of them. Thus you might have an excellent reading knowledge of French, a poor speaking ability and a good understanding of it when spoken by others. Each of these capacities must be listed separately.

References. The names of three persons, with their business or home addresses and occupations, are required. They must live in the United States or its territories, may not be related to you, and may not be supervisors whom you have mentioned in *Experience.* They must have what the Civil Service calls "definite" knowledge of your qualifications and fitness for the position for which you are applying. These individuals may later be consulted by government investigators, who will ask them a variety of questions about you, and may also ask them whom else they should contact to obtain additional information about you.

THE LAW AND FEDERAL EMPLOYMENT

LOYALTY QUERIES

The government asks two questions involving loyalty.

Are you now, or within the last ten years have you been, a member of the Communist Party, U.S.A., or any subdivision of the Communist Party, U.S.A.?

Are you now, or within the last ten years have you been, a member of an organization that to your present knowledge advocates the overthrow of the constitutional form of government of the U.S.A. by force or violence or other unlawful means?

If your answer to either question is "Yes," then you must list the name of the organization(s), the dates of your membership(s), and your understanding of the aims and purposes of the organization at the time of your membership.

DISABILITIES

Do you have, or have you had, heart disease, epilepsy, tuberculosis, or diabetes? Have you had a nervous breakdown? The government needs to know this to insure that you are not placed in a position which might impair your health, or which might be a hazard to you or others.

A "yes" or "no" answer is required from the applicant on these questions:

(A) *Have you been discharged from employment within the last five years?*

(B) *Have you resigned after being informed that your employer intended to discharge you within the last five years?*

If you were discharged from a civilian position, or resigned under pressure, you may as well list that fact. The Civil Service Commission knows it is dealing with human beings; many great Americans can point to a history of early dismissals from their jobs. A dismissal—in and of itself—will not bar you from a federal position if your qualifications measure up. However, a pattern of dismissals indicating incompetence, or a trait which might militate against the proper performance of duties on a federal post, or evidence of character delinquency, counts against the applicant. If you feel that your relationship with a former employer requires explanation, there is no objection to your stating the situation on a separate sheet of paper. The government is not interested in what happened between you and your former employers except as it demonstrates what kind of job you will do for the government.

Have you ever been convicted or have you for-feited bail? Are you now under charges for an offense? Omit anything that happened before your 21st birthday, adjudicated in a juvenile court or under a Youthful Offender Law. Also, omit traffic violations for which you were fined $30.00 or less.

While in military service were you ever convicted by general court martial? For each case, civil or military, you must give the date, charge, place, court, and action taken.

Of all questions asked this is probably the most troublesome. Many job applicants try to conceal dark—or just gray pages of their past, and almost invariably they are found out and barred from ever receiving federal employment. Yet an old conviction for a civil or criminal offense will not in itself prohibit an applicant from a federal job. During the war thousands of former "convicts" held and honorably performed jobs for the government. All circumstances are considered before a decision is made. Ordinarily a person who has been convicted of a felony must wait two years after release from prison or parole before his application will be considered by the Civil Service Commission. Exceptions are made, however, where unusual or meritorious circumstances appear to warrant special consideration. The Commission decides, upon the facts of the case, whether or not to accept applications from persons who have been convicted of misdemeanors, or who are under suspended sentence or on probation.

Does the United States employ in a civilian capacity, or in the armed forces, any relative of yours (by blood or marriage) with whom you live or have lived in the past 24 months?

The law forbids a Federal official to appoint any of his relatives or recommend them for appointment in his agency. A relative who is appointed in violation of this restriction cannot be paid.

The law forbids the appointment to the competitive civil service of any person if two or more members of his immediate family, living under the same roof, are employed by the government. The rule does not apply, however, to individuals entitled to veteran preference.

Do you receive an annuity or pension from the government—either civilian or military?

A veteran receiving compensation for service-connected disability may continue to receive it while in federal employ.

Some federal agencies have been authorized to hire their own personnel, especially for positions which present a recruitment problem. Therefore, it would be prudent for you to contact federal agencies directly when seeking federal employment, especially for positions which require special skills or training.

Standard Form 171

Personal Qualifications Statement

IMPORTANT
READ THE FOLLOWING INSTRUCTIONS CAREFULLY BEFORE FILLING OUT YOUR STATEMENT

- You must furnish all requested information. The information you provide will be used to determine your qualifications for employment. DO NOT SEND A RESUME IN LIEU OF COMPLETING THIS STATEMENT.

- If you fail to answer all questions on your Statement fully and accurately, you may delay consideration of your Statement and may lose employment opportunities. See the Privacy Act Information on the reverse of this sheet.

- So that it is understood that you did not omit an item, please write the letters "N/A" (Not Applicable) beside those items that do not apply to you, unless instructions indicate otherwise.

GENERAL INSTRUCTIONS

- If you are applying for a specific Federal civil service examination:

  —Read the examination announcement or the Qualifications Information Statement for the position to be certain that your experience and education are qualifying.

  —If a written test is required, follow the filing instructions on the admission card.

  —If no written test is required, mail this Statement to the Office of Personnel Management Area Office specified in the announcement or on the Qualifications Information Statement.

  —Be sure to include all other forms required.

  —If you have a change of name or address, notify the Office of Personnel Management Area Office with which you filed this Statement.

  —You may want to make a copy of this Statement for your personal use.

  —Please typewrite or write legibly or print clearly in dark ink.

INSTRUCTIONS RELATING TO SPECIFIC ITEMS

ITEM 13. Lowest Grade or Salary

- Enter the lowest grade or the lowest salary you will accept. You will not be considered for any lower grades or salary. You will be considered for any higher grades or salaries for which you qualify as specified in the examination announcement or the Qualifications Information Statement.

ITEM 16. Other Government and International Agencies

- The Office of Personnel Management is occasionally requested to refer for employment consideration the names of eligibles on competitive registers to State and local government agencies, congressional and other public offices, and public international organizations. Indicate your availability by checking the appropriate boxes. Your response to this question will not affect your consideration for other positions.

ITEM 18. Overnight Travel

- Indicate the number of nights per month you are willing to be away from home in a travel status. Some jobs require nearly constant travel of two or three weeks every month while others require infrequent, short or occasional extended periods of travel. You will be considered for positions requiring travel based on the number of nights per month for which you indicate travel availability.

ITEM 20. Active Military Service and Veteran Preference

- Five-point veteran preference is granted to veterans who receive an honorable or general discharge from the armed forces:

(a) after active duty during the periods April 6, 1917 to July 2, 1921 and December 7, 1941 to July 1, 1955;

(b) after more than 180 consecutive days of active duty, any part of which occurred after January 31, 1955 and before October 15, 1976.
NOTE—Service under an initial period of active duty for training under the "6-month" Reserve or National Guard programs is not creditable for veteran preference; and

(c) after service in a campaign for which a campaign badge has been authorized.

- Non-disabled veterans who retired at or above the rank of major or its equivalent are not eligible for veteran preference after October 1, 1980.

- You will be required to furnish records to support your claim for five-point preference only at the time of your appointment.

- Ten-point veteran preference is granted to:
(a) disabled veterans; and
(b) veterans awarded the Purple Heart.
Ten-point veteran preference is granted in certain cases to:
(a) unmarried widows and widowers of veterans;
(b) spouses of disabled veterans; and
(c) mothers of deceased or disabled veterans.
If you claim ten-point veteran preference, submit Standard Form 15, Claim for 10-Point Veteran Preference, and the required proof with this application. Obtain SF 15 and information on provisions of the Veteran Preference laws at any Federal Job Information Center.

- A clemency discharge does not meet the Veteran Preference Act requirement for discharge under honorable conditions. Accordingly, no preference may be granted to applicants with such discharge.

ITEM 21. Experience

- Fill in these experience blocks carefully and completely. A large part of your qualifications rating depends upon a thorough description of your experience and employment history.

- If you fail to give complete details, you may delay consideration of your Statement. Your description of duties may be verified with former employers.

- If you supervise or have supervised other employees, be sure to indicate the number and kind (and grades, if Federal Government) of employees supervised, and describe your duties as a supervisor under Description of Work.

- Volunteer Experience—You may receive credit for pertinent religious, civic, welfare service and organizational work performed with or without compensation. Show the actual amount of time spent in such work (for example, average hours per week or month). Complete all the items just as you would for a compensable position.

- Use separate blocks if your duties, responsibilities, or salary have changed materially while working for the same employer. Treat each such change as a separate position.

ITEM 21. Experience *(Continued)*

NOTE—Experience gained more than 15 years ago may be summarized in one block if it is not pertinent to the type of position you applied for.

- Include your military or merchant marine service in separate blocks in order and describe major duty assignments.

- Indicate in each block of Item 21 the name under which you were employed if it was different from the name in Item 6 of this Statement. Show former name in parentheses after "Description of duties and accomplishments in your work."

- Indicate any period of unemployment exceeding three months and your address at that time on the last line of the preceding experience block.

- Block A—Describe your present position in this block. Indicate if you are now unemployed or if you have never been employed.

- Blocks B and C—Describe in Block B the position you held just before your present position and continue to work backwards using Block C.

- Enter the average number of hours per week you work. If you work part time, indicate the average number of hours per week you work.

- Description of Work—Describe each job briefly, including required skills and abilities. Describe any specialties and special assignments, your authority and responsibility, your relationships to others, your accomplishments, and any other factors which help to describe the job.

- If your job contains experience in more than one type of work (for example: carpentry and painting, or personnel and budget) estimate and indicate the approximate percentage of time spent in each type of work. Place the percentages in parentheses at the end of the description of work.

- If you need additional experience blocks:
  —Use Standard Form 171-A, Continuation Sheet; or
  —A plain sheet of paper approximately 8 by 10½ inches in size. Be sure to include all of the information requested in Item 21.

  If you need additional space to describe a position held:
  —Continue in Item 34, Space for Detailed Answers; or
  —Continue on a plain sheet of paper.

- Identify each plain sheet of paper used by showing your name, birth date, examination or position title, and the block under Item 21 from which the description is continued.

- Attach all supplemental sheets to the top of page 3.

ITEM 32. Relatives Employed by the United States Government

- A Federal official (civilian or military) may not appoint any of his or her relatives or recommend them for employment in his or her agency, and a relative who is appointed in violation of this restriction cannot be paid. Therefore it is necessary to have information about your relatives who are working for the Federal Government. In listing relative(s) in answer to question 32 includes father; mother; son; daughter; brother; sister; uncle; aunt; first cousin; nephew; niece; husband; wife; father-in-law; mother-in-law; son-in-law; daughter-in-law; brother-in-law; sister-in-law; stepfather; stepmother; stepson; stepdaughter; stepbrother; stepsister; half brother, and half sister.

CERTIFICATION

- Be careful that you have answered all questions on your Statement correctly and considered all statements fully so that your eligibility can be decided on all the facts. Read the certification carefully before you sign and date your Statement.

- Sign your name in ink.

- Use one given name, initial or initials, and last name.

PRIVACY ACT INFORMATION

The Office of Personnel Management is authorized to rate applicants for Federal jobs under Sections 1302, 3301, and 3304 of Title 5 of the U.S. Code. We need the information you put on this form to see how well your education and work skills qualify you for a Federal job. We also need information on matters such as citizenship and military service to see whether you are affected by laws we must follow in deciding who may be employed by the Federal Government. We cannot give you a rating, which is the first step toward getting a job, if you do not answer these questions.

We must have your Social Security Number (SSN) to keep your records straight because other people may have the same name and birthdate. The SSN has been used to keep records since 1943, when Executive Order 9397 asked agencies to do so. The Office of Personnel Management may also use your SSN to make requests for information about you from employers, schools, banks, and others who know you, but only as allowed by law. The information we collect by using your SSN will be used for employment purposes and also for studies and statistics that will not identify you.

Information we have about you may also be given to Federal, State, and local agencies for checking on law violations or for other lawful purposes. We may also notify your school placement office if you are selected for a Federal job.

PLEASE DETACH THIS INSTRUCTION SHEET BEFORE SUBMITTING YOUR STATEMENT

Personal Qualifications Statement
Read instructions before completing form

Form Approved:
OMB No. 50-R0387

1. Kind of position *(job)* you are filing for *(or title and number of announcement)*

2. Options for which you wish to be considered *(if listed in the announcement)*

3. Home phone — Area Code / Number

4. Work phone — Area Code / Number / Extension

5. Sex *(for statistics only)* Male ☐ Female ☐

6. Other last names ever used

Name *(Last, First, Middle)*

Street address or RFD no. *(include apartment no., if any)*

City / State / ZIP Code

8. Birthplace *(City & State, or foreign country)*

9. Birth date *(Month, day, year)*

10. Social Security Number

11. If you have ever been employed by the Federal Government as a civilian, give your highest grade, classification series, and job title.

Dates of service in highest grade *(Month, day, and year)*
From / To

12. If you currently have an application on file with the Office of Personnel Management for appointment to a Federal position, list: (a) the name of the area office maintaining your application, (b) the position for which you filed, and (if appropriate) (c) the date of your notice of rating, (d) your identification number, and (e) your rating.

13. Lowest pay or grade you will accept: PAY $ per OR GRADE

14. When will you be available for work? *(Month and year)*

DO NOT WRITE IN THIS BLOCK
FOR USE OF EXAMINING OFFICE ONLY

Material ☐ Submitted ☐ Returned
Entered register:
Notations:
Form reviewed:
Form approved:

Option	Grade	Earned Rating	Preference	Aug. Rating

☐ 5 Points (Tent.)
☐ 10 Pts 30% or More Comp Dis
☐ 10 Pts Less Than 30% Comp Dis
☐ Other 10 Points
☐ Disallowed
☐ Being Investigated

Initials and date

ANNOUNCEMENT NO. / STATEMENT NO.

THIS SPACE FOR USE OF APPOINTING OFFICER ONLY
Preference has been verified through proof that the separation was under honorable conditions, and other proof as required.

☐ 5-Point ☐ 10 Points 30% or More Compensable Disability ☐ 10 Points Less Than 30% Compensable Disability ☐ 10-Point Other

Signature and title
Agency / Date

15. Are you available for temporary employment lasting: *(Acceptance or refusal of temporary employment will not affect your consideration for other appointments.)*
A. Less than 1 month? YES/NO
B. 1 to 4 months?
C. 5 to 12 months?

16. Are you interested in being considered for employment by: YES/NO
A. State and local government agencies?
B. Congressional and other public offices?
C. Public international organizations?

17. Where will you accept a job? YES/NO
A. In the Washington, D.C. Metropolitan area?
B. Outside the 50 United States?
C. Anyplace in the United States?
D. Only in *(specify locality)*

18. Indicate your availability for overnight travel:
A. Not available for overnight travel
B. 1 to 5 nights per month
C. 6 to 10 nights per month
D. 11 or more nights per month

19. Are you available for part-time positions *(fewer than 40 hours per week)* offering: YES/NO
A. 20 or fewer hours per week?
B. 21 to 31 hours per week?
C. 32 to 39 hours per week?

20. Veteran Preference. Answer all parts. If a part does not apply to you, answer "NO". YES/NO

A. Have you ever served on active duty in the United States military service? *(Exclude tours of active duty for training in Reserves or National Guard)*
B. Have you ever been discharged from the armed services under other than honorable conditions? *You may omit any such discharge changed to honorable or general by a Discharge Review Board or similar authority)*. If "YES", give details in item 34.
C. Do you claim 5-point preference based on active duty in the armed forces? If "YES", you will be required to furnish records to support your claim at the time you are appointed.
D. Do you claim 10-point preference? If "YES," check the type of preference claimed and complete and attach Standard Form 15, "Claim for 10-Point Veteran Preference," together with the proof requested in that form.

Type of Preference: ☐ Compensable Disability 30% or More ☐ Compensable Disability Below 30% ☐ Non-compensable Disability ☐ Purple Heart Recipient ☐ Spouse ☐ Widow(er) ☐ Mother

E. List dates, branch, and serial number of all active service *(enter "N/A" if not applicable)*
From / To / Branch of Service / Serial or Service Number

21. Experience: Begin with current or most recent job or volunteer experience and work back. Account for periods of unemployment exceeding three months and your residence address at that time on the last line of the experience blocks in order of occurrence.

May inquiry be made of your present employer regarding your character. qualifications. and record of employment?
(A "NO" will not affect your consideration for employment opportunities except for Administrative Law Judge positions.) ☐ YES ☐ NO

A

Name and address of employer's organization *(include ZIP code. if known)*	Dates employed *(give month and year)* From To	Average number of hours per week
	Salary or earnings Beginning $ per Ending $ per	Place of employment City State

Exact title of your position	Name of immediate supervisor	Area Code	Telephone number	Number and kind of employees you supervise
Kind of business or organization *(manufacturing. accounting. social services. etc.)*	If Federal service. civilian or military: series. grade or rank. and date of last promotion			Your reason for wanting to leave

Description of work *(Describe your specific duties. responsibilities and accomplishments in this job)*

For agency use *(skill codes. etc.)*

B

Name and address of employer's organization *(include ZIP code. if known)*	Dates employed *(give month and year)* From To	Average number of hours per week
	Salary or earnings Beginning $ per Ending $ per	Place of employment City State

Exact title of your position	Name of immediate supervisor	Area Code	Telephone number	Number and kind of employees you supervised
Kind of business or organization *(manufacturing. accounting. social services. etc.)*	If Federal service. civilian or military: series. grade or rank. and date of last promotion			Your reason for leaving

Description of work *(Describe your specific duties. responsibilities and accomplishments in this job)*

For agency use *(skill codes. etc.)*

C

Name and address of employer's organization *(include ZIP code. if known)*	Dates employed *(give month and year)* From To	Average number of hours per week
	Salary or earnings Beginning $ per Ending $ per	Place of employment City State

Exact title of your position	Name of immediate supervisor	Area Code	Telephone number	Number and kind of employees you supervised
Kind of business or organization *(manufacturing. accounting. social services. etc.)*	If Federal service. civilian or military: series. grade or rank. and date of last promotion			Your reason for leaving

Description of work *(Describe your specific duties. responsibilities and accomplishments in this job)*:

For agency use *(skill codes. etc.)*

If you need additional experience blocks, use Standard Form 171-A or blank sheets of paper
SEE INSTRUCTION SHEET

22. A. Special qualifications and skills *(skills with machines; patents or inventions; your most important publications [do not submit copies unless requested]; your public speaking and publications experience; membership in professional or scientific societies; etc.)*

B. Kind of license or certificate *(pilot, registered nurse, lawyer, radio operator, CPA, etc.)*	C. Latest license or certificate		D. Approximate number of words per minute	
	Year	State or other licensing authority	Typing	Shorthand

23. A. Did you graduate from high school or will you graduate within the next nine months, or do you have a GED high school equivalency certificate?

Yes	Month and Year	No	Highest grade completed	B. Name and location *(city and State)* of latest high school attended

C. Name and location *(city, State, and ZIP Code, if known)* of college or university. *(If you expect to graduate within nine months, give MONTH and YEAR you expect to receive your degree.*	Dates Attended		Years Completed		No. of Credits Completed		Type of Degree *(e.g., B.A.)*	Year of Degree
	From	To	Day	Night	Semester Hours	Quarter Hours		

D. Chief undergraduate college subjects	No. of Credits Completed		E. Chief graduate college subjects	No. of Credits Completed	
	Semester Hours	Quarter Hours		Semester Hours	Quarter Hours

F. Major field of study at highest level of college work

G. Other schools or training *(for example, trade, vocational, Armed Forces or business)*. Give for each the name and location *(city, State and ZIP Code, if known)* of school, dates attended, subjects studied, number of classroom hours of instruction per week, certificate, and any other pertinent data

24. Honors, awards, and fellowships received

25. Languages other than English: List the languages *(other than English)* in which you are proficient and indicate your level of proficiency by putting a check mark (✔) in the appropriate columns. **Candidates for positions requiring conversational ability in a language other than English may be given an interview conducted solely in that language.** Describe in item 34 how you gained your language skills and the amount of experience you have had *(e.g., completed 72 hours of classroom training, spoke language at home for 18 years, self-taught, etc.)*.

Name of Language(s)	PROFICIENCY							
	Can Prepare and Deliver Lectures		Can Converse		Have Facility to Translate Articles, Technical Materials, etc.		Can Read Articles, Technical Materials, etc., for Own Use	
	Fluently	With Difficulty	Fluently	Passably	Into English	From English	Easily	With Difficulty

26. References: List three persons who are NOT related to you and who have definite knowledge of your qualifications and fitness for the position for which you are applying. Do not repeat names of supervisors listed under Item 21, Experience.

Full Name	Present Business or Home Address *(Number, Street, City, State and ZIP Code)*	Telephone Number *(Include Area Code)*	Business or Occupation

Answer Items 27 through 33 by placing an "X" in the proper column.	YES	NO

27. Are you a citizen of the United States?.. ◄
   If "NO", give country of which you are a citizen.

NOTE: A conviction or a firing does not necessarily mean you cannot be appointed. The circumstances of the occurrence(s) and how long ago it (they) occurred are important. Give all the facts so that a decision can be made.

28. Within the last five years have you been fired from any job for any reason?.. ◄

29. Within the last five years have you quit a job after being notified that you would be fired?.. ◄
   If your answer to 28 or 29 above is "YES", give details in Item 34. Show the name and address (including ZIP Code) of employer, approximate date, and reasons in each case. This information should agree with your answers in Item 21. Experience

30. A. Have you **ever** been convicted, forfeited collateral, or are you now under charges for **any felony** or **any** firearms or explosives offense against the law? (A felony is defined as any offense punishable by imprisonment for a term exceeding one year, but does not include any offense classified under the laws of a State as a misdemeanor which is punishable by a term of imprisonment of two years or less.).. ◄
   B. During the past seven years have you been convicted, imprisoned, on probation or parole or forfeited collateral, or are you now under charges for any offense against the law not included in A above?.. ◄

NOTE: When answering A and B above, you may omit: (1) traffic fines for which you paid a fine of $50.00 or less; (2) any offense committed before your 18th birthday which was finally adjudicated in a juvenile court or under a youth offender law; (3) any conviction the record of which has been expunged under Federal or State law; and (4) any conviction set aside under the Federal Youth Corrections Act or similar State authority.

31. While in the military service were you ever convicted by a general court-martial?.. ◄
   If your answer to 30A, 30B, or 31 is "YES", give details in Item 34. Show for each offense: (1) date; (2) charge; (3) place; (4) court; and (5) action taken.

32. Does the United States Government employ in a civilian capacity or as a member of the Armed Forces any relative of yours (by blood or marriage)? (See Item 32 in the attached instruction sheet.)... ◄
   If your answer to 32 is "YES", give in Item 34 for such relatives: (1) name; (2) present address (including ZIP Code); (3) relationship; (4) department, agency, or branch of the armed forces.

33. Do you receive, or do you have pending, application for retirement or retainer pay, pension, or other compensation based upon military, Federal civilian, or District of Columbia Government service?.. ◄
   If your answer to 33 is "YES", give details in Item 34. If military retired pay, include the rank at which you retired.

Your Statement cannot be processed until you have answered all questions, including Items 27 through 33 above.
Be sure you have placed an "X" to the left of EVERY marker (◄) above, either in the "YES" or "NO" column.

34. Item No. | Space for detailed answers. Indicate Item numbers to which the answers apply.

If more space is required, use full sheets of paper approximately the same size as this page. Write on each sheet your name, birth date, and announcement or position title. Attach all sheets to this Statement at the top of page 3.

ATTENTION—THIS STATEMENT MUST BE SIGNED
Read the following paragraphs carefully before signing this Statement

A false answer to any question in this Statement may be grounds for not employing you, or for dismissing you after you begin work, and may be punishable by fine or imprisonment (U.S. Code, Title 18, Section 1001). All the information you give will be considered in reviewing your Statement.

AUTHORITY FOR RELEASE OF INFORMATION

I have completed this Statement with the knowledge and understanding that any or all items contained herein may be subject to investigation prescribed by law or Presidential directive and I consent to the release of information concerning my capacity and fitness by employers, educational institutions, law enforcement agencies, and other individuals and agencies, to duly accredited Investigators, Personnel Staffing Specialists, and other authorized employees of the Federal Government for that purpose

CERTIFICATION	SIGNATURE (sign in ink)	DATE
I certify that all of the statements made by me are true, complete and correct to the best of my knowledge and belief, and are made in good faith.		

CONTINUATION SHEET FOR STANDARD FORM 171
"PERSONAL QUALIFICATIONS STATEMENT"

Form Approved:
O.M.B. No. 50-R0367

INSTRUCTIONS—Fill out this form only when necessary for completion of Item 21 "EXPERIENCE," on Standard Form 171. Enclose with your Statement. Typewrite or print clearly in dark ink.

1. Name *(Last)* *(First)* *(Middle)*	2. Birth date *(Month, day, year)*	3. Kind of position applied for, or name of examination:

Name and address of employer's organization *(include ZIP Code, if known)*	Dates employed *(give month and year)* From To	Average number of hours per week
	Salary or earnings Beginning $ per Ending $ per	Place of employment City State

Exact title of your position	Name of immediate supervisor	Area Code	Telephone Number	Number and kind of employees you supervised
Kind of business or organization *(manufacturing, accounting, social services, etc.)*	If Federal service, civilian or military: series, grade or rank, and date of last promotion			Your reason for leaving

Description of work *(Describe your specific duties, responsibilities and accomplishments in this job.)*:

For agency use *(skill codes, etc.)*

Name and address of employer's organization *(include ZIP Code, if known)*	Dates employed *(give month and year)* From To	Average number of hours per week
	Salary or earnings Beginning $ per Ending $ per	Place of employment City State

Exact title of your position	Name of immediate supervisor	Area Code	Telephone Number	Number and kind of employees you supervised
Kind of business or organization *(manufacturing, accounting, social services, etc.)*	If Federal service, civilian or military: series, grade or rank, and date of last promotion			Your reason for leaving

Description of work *(Describe your specific duties, responsibilities and accomplishments in this job.)*:

For agency use *(skill codes, etc.)*

Name and address of employer's organization *(include ZIP Code, if known)*	Dates employed *(give month and year)* From To	Average number of hours per week
	Salary or earnings Beginning $ per Ending $ per	Place of employment City State

Exact title of your position	Name of immediate supervisor	Area Code	Telephone Number	Number and kind of employees you supervised
Kind of business or organization *(manufacturing, accounting, social services, etc.)*	If Federal service, civilian or military: series, grade or rank, and date of last promotion			Your reason for leaving

Description of work *(Describe your specific duties, responsibilities and accomplishments in this job.)*:

For agency use *(skill codes, etc.)*

THE FEDERAL GOVERNMENT IS AN EQUAL OPPORTUNITY EMPLOYER   171-203   Standard Form 171-A (rev. 12-77)
U.S. Civil Service Commission

Name and address of employer's organization *(include ZIP Code, if known)*		Dates employed *(give month and year)*	Average number of hours per week
		From To	
		Salary or earnings	Place of employment
		Beginning $ per	City
		Ending $ per	State

Exact title of your position	Name of immediate supervisor	Area Code Telephone Number	Number and kind of employees you supervised
Kind of business or organization *(manufacturing, accounting, social services, etc.)*	If Federal service, civilian or military: series, grade or rank, and date of last promotion		Your reason for leaving

Description of work *(Describe your specific duties, responsibilities and accomplishments in this job.)*:

For agency use *(skill codes, etc.)*

Name and address of employer's organization *(include ZIP Code, if known)*		Dates employed *(give month and year)*	Average number of hours per week
		From To	
		Salary or earnings	Place of employment
		Beginning $ per	City
		Ending $ per	State

Exact title of your position	Name of immediate supervisor	Area Code Telephone Number	Number and kind of employees you supervised
Kind of business or organization *(manufacturing, accounting, social services, etc.)*	If Federal service, civilian or military: series, grade or rank, and date of last promotion		Your reason for leaving

Description of work *(Describe your specific duties, responsibilities and accomplishments in this job.)*:

For agency use *(skill codes, etc.)*

Name and address of employer's organization *(include ZIP Code, if known)*		Dates employed *(give month and year)*	Average number of hours per week
		From To	
		Salary or earnings	Place of employment
		Beginning $ per	City
		Ending $ per	State

Exact title of your position	Name of immediate supervisor	Area Code Telephone Number	Number and kind of employees you supervised
Kind of business or organization *(manufacturing, accounting, social services, etc.)*	If Federal service, civilian or military: series, grade or rank, and date of last promotion		Your reason for leaving

Description of work *(Describe your specific duties, responsibilities and accomplishments in this job.)*:

For agency use *(skill codes, etc.)*

ARCO BUILDS CAREERS

2

PART TWO

*The Exams...and How
To Prepare For Them*

THE GOVERNMENT TESTS YOU

Note: The Civil Service Commission is now called the Office Of Personnel Management.

Most applicants for civil service jobs are worried by that awesome instrument called the test. Haunted by schoolday memories, applicants often approach the examination with fear, imagining that someone is going to give them a big list of trick questions, to trap them; or that they will have to sit down and laboriously work out the answers to difficult problems. The only factor that helps many people face the test is the knowledge that they aren't alone, that everybody else competing with them faces the same problems. Those who have any dealings with civil service applicants never cease to wonder how widespread this attitude is. If you are one of those who has this concept of a government test, change your opinion. It's all wrong!

You have found the position you'd like, filled out the application form, and sent it off to the Civil Service Commission.

What now?

KINDS OF TESTS

The announcement describes the kind of test given for the particular position. Please pay special attention to this section. It tells what areas are to be covered in the written test and lists the specific subjects on which questions will be asked. Sometimes sample questions are given.

The test and review material in this Arco book are based on the requirements as given in this section as well as on actual tests.

If the announcement said that a written test would be given, you will receive a notice through the mail telling you when and where to report for the test.

Special arrangements will be made for applicants who are blind, deaf, or otherwise handicapped who indicate the nature of their disability when they apply for the test.

The written test will be practical. It will test your ability to do the job that you applied for, or it will test your ability to learn how to do it.

If you fail a written test, you can usually take it again as long as applications are being accepted for it. If you pass it but want to try to improve your score, you can take it again after a year has passed provided it is still open.

Usually the announcement states whether the examination is to be assembled or unassembled. In an *assembled* examination applicants *assemble* in the same place at the same time to take a written or performance test. The *unassembled* examination is one where an applicant does not take a test; instead he is rated on his education and experience and whatever records of past achievement he is asked to provide.

If you apply for a position that does not involve a written test, your rating will be assigned on the basis of the experience and training you describe in your statement and any additional evidence secured by the Civil Service examiners. Your qualifications may also be verified with your former employers and supervisors.

If your examination is of the *unassembled* variety, the Commission may ask you to submit further evidence of your ability, in the form of work accomplished. In the meantime, the statements on your application form are being checked. When all this information is gathered, you are "rated" and the Commission will write to you, telling you how your qualifications look to the examiners. That's all there is to it, until you are called to the job.

In announcements that cover several grades or salary levels, you will be rated for those you qualify for, but you will not be rated for any grade if the pay for that grade is less than the minimum pay you state you will accept.

You will be notified whether you passed or failed the examination by the office that announced it. Be sure to notify that office of changes in essential information, such as address, name, availability, etc. When writing, give your full name, the title of the announcement, the rating you received, and your date of birth.

There are two main types of tests — competitive and non-competitive.

In a *competitive* examination all applicants for a position compete with each other; the better the mark, the better the chance of being appointed. In a *non-competitive* examination the applicant is tested solely to determine his qualification for a given position; he need only pass to become eligible for appointment.

The method of rating on all civil service written tests is on a scale of 100, with 70 as the usual passing mark.

The rating of the examination is usually done by the office which has issued the announcement.

RATING EXAMINATIONS

The rating of the examination is usually done by the office which has issued the announcement.

Written tests are most frequently rated by machine. In some written examinations, and for rating experience and training, two examiners work independently. In case of a protest about the rating a third examiner will be assigned to rate the exam again. Thus the chances of error, arbitrary grading, or bias are almost completely eliminated.

Evaluating Education. In evaluating the candidate's background, credit may be given for appropriate training received in the armed forces. A certificate of completion from an education instiution for a correspondence course is often counted as good background. Courses offered through the Armed Forces Institute are granted credit, too, in rating examinations. The announcement always tells the kind of education needed for the specific job, and the examiners give careful consideration to the entire educational background of the candidate as listed in the application form. Often courses which the candidate may not consider relevant are found by the examiners to be helpful for the post. They raise the total rating.

Evaluating Experience. When experience is a factor the examiners give credit for all kinds of valuable background, including experience gained in religious, civic, welfare, service, and organizational activities. Whether the experience was paid or unpaid makes no difference, but its length and quality do.

Veterans obtain special experience credit in one of the following ways, whichever would benefit the candidate more.

1. Military service may be considered an extension of the employment in which the applicant was engaged just before his entrance into the armed forces.

2. Duties performed while in military service may be considered on the basis of their value to the job for which the veteran is applying.

"Suitability." Investigations to determine an applicant's "suitability qualifications" with respect to character and loyalty are considered a part of the entire examining process, regardless of whether such investigations are conducted before or after appointment.

When all the parts of an examination have been rated the applicant is notified of his *numerical rating,* or mark.

If he has passed, he is now an *eligible,* that is, his name is placed on a list and is ready to be submitted, in due course, to a government department for appointment.

HOW TO BE A MASTER TEST TAKER

It's really quite simple. Do things right . . . right from the beginning. Make successful methods a habit by practicing them on all the exercises in this book. Before you're finished you will have invested a good deal of time. Make sure you get the largest dividends from this investment.

SCORING PAPERS BY MACHINE

A typical machine-scored answer sheet is shown below, reduced from the actual size of 8¼ x 11 inches. Since it's the only one that reaches the office where papers are scored, it's important that the blanks at the top be filled in completely and correctly

The chances are very good that you'll have to mark your answers on one of these sheets. Consequently, we've made it possible for you to practice with them throughout this book.

SAMPLE ANSWER SHEET

EXAM TITLE / TODAY'S DATE

SCHOOL OR BUILDING / ROOM NO. / SEAT NO.

YOUR SOCIAL SECURITY NO. / EXAM NO.

PRINT WITH SOFT PENCIL ONLY. Print, with pencil, your SOCIAL SECURITY NO. and the EXAM. NO. in the boxes at the tops of the columns. ONE NUMBER IN A BOX. In each column, darken (with pencil) the oval containing the number in the box at the top of the column. Only ONE OVAL in a COLUMN should be darkened. Then, using your pencil, print in the: Exam. Title, School or Building, Room No., Seat No., and Today's Date.

Follow the instructions given in the question booklet. Mark nothing ▶ but your answers in the ovals below.
SAMPLE QUESTION: When we add 5 and 3 we get: (A) 11 (B) 9 (C) 8 (D) 2. Since the answer is 8, your answer should be marked like this: ⊂A⊃ ⊂B⊃ ● ⊂D⊃
WARNING: Be sure that the oval you fill in is in the row numbered the same as the question you are answering. Use a No. 2 pencil (soft pencil).
BE SURE YOUR PENCIL MARKS ARE HEAVY AND BLACK. ERASE COMPLETELY ANY ANSWER YOU WISH TO CHANGE. DO NOT make stray pencil dots, dashes or marks ANYPLACE on this SHEET.

┌─ START HERE

1–25, 26–50, 51–75, 76–100, 101–125, 126–150 (answer ovals)

FOLLOW DIRECTIONS CAREFULLY

It's an obvious rule, but more people fail for breaching it than for any other cause. By actual count there are over a hundred types of directions given on tests. You'll familiarize yourself with all of them in the course of this book. And you'll also learn not to let your guard down in reading them, listening to them, and following them. Right now, before you plunge in, we want to be sure that you have nothing to fear from the answer sheet and the way in which you must mark it; from the most important question forms and the ways in which they are to be answered.

HERE'S HOW TO MARK YOUR ANSWERS ON MACHINE-SCORED ANSWER SHEETS:

Make only ONE mark for each answer. Additional and stray marks may be counted as mistakes. In making corrections, erase errors COMPLETELY. Make glossy black marks.

(a) Each pencil mark must be heavy and black. Light marks should be retraced with the special pencil.

(b) Each mark must be in the space between the pair of dotted lines and entirely fill this space.

(c) All stray pencil marks on the paper, clearly not intended as answers, must be completely erased.

(d) Each question must have only one answer indicated. If multiple answers occur, all extraneous marks should be thoroughly erased. Otherwise, the machine will give you *no* credit for your correct answer.

MULTIPLE CHOICE METHODS

Multiple choice questions are very popular these days with examiners. The chances are good that you'll get this kind on your test. So we've arranged that you practice with them in the following pages. But first we want to give you a little help by explaining the best methods for handling this question form.

You know, of course, that these questions offer you four or five possible answers, that your job is to select *only* the *best* answer, and that even the incorrect answers are frequently *partly* correct. These partly-true choices are inserted to force you to think . . . and prove that you know the right answer.

USE THESE METHODS TO ANSWER MULTIPLE CHOICE QUESTIONS CORRECTLY:

1. Read the item closely to see what the examiner is after. Re-read it if necessary.

2. Mentally reject answers that are clearly wrong.

3. Suspect as being wrong any of the choices which contain broad statements hinging on "cue" words like

absolute
absolutely
all
always
axiomatic
categorical
completely
doubtless
entirely
extravagantly
forever
immeasurably
inalienable
incontestable
incontrovertible
indefinitely
indisputable
indubitable
inevitable
inexorable
infallible
infinite
inflexible
inordinately
irrefutable
inviolable
never
only
peculiarly
positive
quite
self-evident
sole
totally
unchallenged
unchangeable
undeniable
undoubtedly
unequivocal
unexceptionable
unimpeachable
unqualified
unquestionable
wholly
without exception

If you're unsure of the meanings of any of these words, look them up in your dictionary.

4. A well-constructed multiple choice item will avoid obviously incorrect choices. The good examiner will try to write a cluster of answers, all of which are plausible. Use the clue words to help yourself pick the *most* correct answer.

5. In the case of items where you are doubtful of the answer, you might be able to bring to bear the information you have gained from previous study. This knowledge might be sufficient to indicate that some of the suggested answers are not so plausible. Eliminate such answers from further consideration.

6. Then concentrate on the remaining suggested answers. The more you eliminate in this way, the better your chances of getting the item right.

7. If the item is in the form of an incomplete statement, it sometimes helps to try to complete the statement before you look at the suggested answers. Then see if the way you have completed the statement corresponds with any of the answers provided. If one is found, it is likely to be the correct one.

8. Use your head! Make shrewd inferences. Sometimes with a little thought, and the information that you have, you can reason out the answer. We're suggesting a method of intelligence guessing in which you can become quite expert with a little practice. It's a useful method that may help you with some debatable answers.

NOW, LET'S TRY THESE METHODS OUT ON A SAMPLE MULTIPLE-CHOICE QUESTION.

1. Leather is considered the best material for shoes chiefly because
   (A) it is waterproof
   (B) it is quite durable
   (C) it is easily procurable
   (D) it is flexible and durable
   (E) it can be easily manufactured in various styles.

Here we see that every one of the answer statements is plausible: leather is waterproof if treated properly; it is relatively durable; it is relatively easily procurable; it bends and is shaped easily, and is, again, durable; it constantly appears in various styles of shoes and boots.

However, we must examine the question with an eye toward identifying the key phrase which is: *best* for shoes *chiefly*.

Now we can see that (A) is incorrect because leather is probably not the *best* material for shoes, simply because it is waterproof. There are far bet-

ter waterproof materials available, such as plastics and rubber. In fact, leather must be treated to make it waterproof. So by analyzing the key phrase of the question we can eliminate (A).

(B) seems plausible. Leather is durable, and durability is a good quality in shoes. But the word *quite* makes it a broad statement. And we become suspicious. The original meaning of *quite* is completely, wholly, entirely. Since such is the case we must reject this choice because leather is *not completely* durable. It does wear out.

(C) Leather is comparatively easy to procure; but would that make it *best* for shoes? And would that be the *chief* reason why it is used for making shoes? Although the statement in itself is quite true, it does not fit the key phrase of the question and we must, reluctantly, eliminate it.

(D) is a double-barreled statement. One part, the durability, has been suggested in (B) above. Leather is also quite flexible, so both parts of the statement would seem to fit the question.

(E) It is true that leather can be manufactured in various styles, but so can many other materials. Again, going back to the key phrase, this could be considered one, but not the *chief* reason why it is *best* for shoes.

So, by carefully analyzing the *key* phrase of the question we have narrowed our choices down to (D). Although we rejected (B) we did recognize that durability is a good quality in shoes, but only one of several. Since flexibility is also a good quality, we have no hesitation in choosing (D) as the correct answer.

The same question, by slightly altering the answer choices, can also call for a *negative* response. Here, even more so, the identification of the key phrase becomes vital in finding the correct answer. Suppose the question and its responses were worded thus:

2. Leather is considered the best material for shoes chiefly because
   (A) it is waterproof
   (B) it is easily colored
   (C) it is easily procurable
   (D) it can easily be manufactured in various styles
   (E) none of these.

We can see that the prior partially correct answer (B) has now been changed, and the doubly-correct answer eliminated. Instead we have a new response possibility (E), "none of these."

We have analyzed three of the choices previously and have seen the reason why none of them are the *chief* reason why leather is considered the *best* material for shoes. The two new elements are (B) "easily colored," and (E) "none of these."

If you think about it, leather *can* be easily colored and often is, but this would not be the chief reason why it is considered *best*. Many other materials are just as easily dyed. So we must come to the conclusion that *none* of the choices are *completely* correct—none fit the key phrase. Therefore, the question calls for a negative response (E).

We have now seen how important it is to identify the key phrase. Equally, or perhaps even more important, is the identifying and analyzing of the key *word*—the qualifying word—in a question. This is usually, though not always, an adjective or adverb. Some of the key words to watch for are: *most, best, least, highest, lowest, always, never, sometimes, most likely, greatest, smallest, tallest, average, easiest, most nearly, maximum, minimum, chiefly, mainly, only, but* and *or*. Identifying these key words is usually half the battle in understanding and, consequently, answering all types of exam questions.

Rephrasing the Question

It is obvious, then, that by carefully analyzing a question, by identifying the key phrase and its key words, you can usually find the correct answer by logical deduction and, often, by elimination. One other way of examining, or "dissecting," a question is to restate or rephrase it with each of the suggested answer choices integrated into the question.

For example, we can take the same question and rephrase it.

(A) The chief reason why leather is considered the best material for shoes is because it is waterproof.

or

(A) Because it is waterproof, leather is considered the best material for shoes.

or

(A) Chiefly because it is waterproof, leather is considered the best material for shoes.

It will be seen from the above three new versions of the original statement and answer that the question has become less obscure because it has been, so to speak, illuminated from different angles. It becomes quite obvious also in this rephrasing that the statement (A) is incorrect, although the *original* phrasing of the question left some doubt.

The rules for understanding and analyzing the key phrase and key words in a question, and the way to identify the *one* correct answer by means of intelligent analysis of the important question-answer elements, are basic to the solution of all the problems you will face on your test.

In fact, perhaps the *main* reason for failing an examination is failure to *understand the question*. In many cases, examinees *do* know the answer to a particular problem, but they cannot answer correctly because they do not understand it.

METHODS FOR MATCHING QUESTIONS

In this question form you are actually faced with multiple questions that require multiple answers. It's a difficult form in which you are asked to pair up one set of facts with another. It can be used with any type of material . . . vocabulary, spatial relations, numbers, facts, etc.

A typical matching question might appear in this form:

Directions: Below is a set of words containing ten words numbered 3 to 12, and twenty other words divided into five groups labeled Group A to Group E. For each of the numbered words select the word in one of the five groups which is most nearly the same in meaning. The letter of that group is the answer for that numbered item.

Although this arrangement is a relatively simple one for a "matching" question, the general principle is the same for all levels of difficulty. Basically, this type of question consists of two columns. The elements of one of the columns must be matched with some or all of the elements of the second column.

3. fiscal

4. deletion

5. equivocal

6. corroboration

7. tortuous

8. predilection

9. sallow

10. virtuosity

11. scion

12. tenuous

Group A
indication ambiguous
excruciating thin

Group B
confirmation financial
phobia erasure

Group C
fiduciary similar
yellowish skill

Group D
theft winding
receive procrastination

Group E
franchise heir
hardy preference

Correct Answers

3. B	6. B	9. C	10. C
4. B	7. D	8. E	11. E
5. A			12. A

There are numerous ways in which these questions may be composed, from the simple one shown to the most difficult type of arrangement. In many cases the arrangement of the question may be so complicated that more time may be spent upon the comprehension of the instructions than on the actual question. This again, points up the importance of fully and quickly understanding the instructions before attempting to solve any problem or answer any question.

Several general principles apply, however, when solving a matching question. Work with one column at a time and match each item of that column against all the items in the second column, skipping around that second column looking for a proper match. Put a thin pencil line through items that are matched so they won't interfere with your later selections. (This is particularly important in a test that tells you to choose any item only once. The test gets real tricky, however, when you are asked to choose an item more than once.)

Match each item very carefully—don't mark it unless you are certain—because if you have to change any one, it may mean changing three or four or more, and that may get you hopelessly confused. After you have marked all your *certain* choices, go over the unmarked items again and make a *good* guess at the remaining items, if you have time.

USE CONTROLLED ASSOCIATION when you come to an item which you are not able to match. Attempt to recall any and all facts you might have concerning this item. Through the process of association, a fact recalled might provide a clue to the answer.

TRUE-FALSE TACTICS

True-false questions may appear on your test. Because they are easier to answer they are used less frequently than multiple-choice questions. However, because examiners find that they are easier to prepare, here are some suggestions to help you answer them correctly.

I. Suspect the truth of broad statements hinging on those *all or nothing* "cue" words we listed for you in discussing multiple-choice questions.

II. Watch out for "spoilers" . . . the word or phrase which negates an otherwise true statement.
Vegetation is sparse on the Sahara desert where the climate is hot and humid.   T   F

III. Statements containing such modifiers as *generally, usually, most,* and similar words are usually true.

IV. If the scoring formula is "Rights minus Wrongs", don't guess. If you know it's true, mark it T. If you don't know it's true, ask yourself "What have I learned that would make it false?" If you can think of nothing on either side, omit the answer. Of course, if the R-W formula is not being used it is advisable to guess if you're not sure of an answer.

V. Your first hunch is usually best. Unless you have very good reason to do so, don't change your first answer to true-false questions about which you are doubtful.

Single-Statement Question

The basic form of true-false question is the "single-statement" question; i.e., a sentence that contains a single thought, such as:

1. The Statue of Liberty is in New York
         T   F

The same statement becomes slightly more difficult by including a negative element

2. The Statue of Liberty is not in New York
         T   F

or, more subtly:
3. The Statue of Liberty is not in Chicago
         T   F

or, by adding other modifiers:
4. The Statue of Liberty is sometimes in New York   T   F

5. The Statue of Liberty is always in New York   T   F

Even from these very simple and basic examples of a "single-statement" true-false question it can be seen that a *complete understanding* of the subject area as well as of the phrasing of the question is essential before you attempt to answer it. Careless or hasty reading of the statement will often make you miss the *key* word, especially if the question appears to be a very simple one.

An important point to remember when answering this type of question is that the statement must be *entirely true* to be answered as "true"; if even just a *part* of it is false, the answer must be marked "false."

Composite-Statement Question

Sometimes a true-false question will be in the form of a "composite statement," a statement that contains more than one thought, such as:

6. The Statue of Liberty is in New York, and Chicago is in Illinois   (T) F

Some basic variations of this type of composite-statement question are these:

7. The Statue of Liberty is in New York, and Chicago is in Michigan   T F
8. The Statue of Liberty is not in New York and Chicago is in Illinois   T F
9. The Statue of Liberty is not in New York and Chicago is in Michigan   T F

Of the four questions above, only question 6 is true. Each of the other statements (7 , 8 , 9), is false because each contains at least *one* element that is false.

It can be seen from the above that in a composite statement *both* elements, or "substatements," must be true in order for the answer to be "true." Otherwise, the answer must be "false."

This principle goes for all composite statements that are, or can be, connected by the word "and," even if the various "thoughts" of the statement seem to be entirely unrelated.

We have seen how to handle a composite statement that consists of *unrelated* substatements. Finally, we will examine a composite true-false statement which consists of *related* elements:

10. The Golden Gate Bridge is in San Francisco, which is not the capital of California.
      (T) F
11. The Golden Gate Bridge is in San Francisco, the capital of California.
      T F
12. The Golden Gate Bridge is not in San Francisco, the capital of California.
      T F
13. The Golden Gate Bridge is not in San Francisco, which is not the capital of California.
      T F

Again, only the first composite statement (10) is true. All the rest are false because they contain at least one false substatement.

EXAMINATION FORECAST

Note: The Civil Service Commission is now called the Office Of Personnel Management.

If you want a preview of your exam, look these questions over carefully. We did . . . as we compiled them from official announcements and various other sources. A good part of this book is based on these prophetic questions. Practice and study material is geared closely to them.

A look at the following questions is the easiest, quickest, most important help you can get from this book. These predictive questions give you foresight by providing an "overview" with which to direct your study. They are actual samples of the question types you may expect on your test.

A portion of the standard answer sheet is provided after each test for marking your answers in the way you'll be required to do on the actual exam. At the right of this answer sheet, to make the scoring job simpler (after you have derived your own answers), you'll find our correct answers.

TESTS AND TESTING METHODS

MANY examinations make use of an answer sheet which is scored by machine, and the examiner gives you a special pencil which must be used in order to have the machine work properly.

We have gathered a variety of typical government tests in this chapter to show you the *kinds* of questions that are asked. The tests shown here are divided into seven classes:

1. Tests of verbal abilities.
2. Tests of reasoning.
3. Clerical tests.
4. Stenographer and typist tests.
5. Tests for the postal service.
6. Knowledge tests for professional and semi-professional positions.
7. Mechanical and non-verbal tests.

The examples of test questions in this chapter do not represent all of the kinds of sample questions which the U.S. Civil Service Commission provides for applicants. When you apply in response to a job announcement, the examining office will send you, without charge, sample questions showing the nature of the written test required for that particular job. There are only a few tests for which no samples are available and, in such cases, the announcement or other information sent to applicants tells them so.

TESTS OF VERBAL ABILITIES

Tests of verbal abilities (often referred to in Civil Service usage as "general tests") are designed to test a wide range of abilities, including the ability to understand words, interpret the meaning of sentences and paragraphs, and recognize and apply the rules of grammar and spelling. There are many kinds of questions which could be used for this purpose; the ones most commonly used are shown on this page and the next three.

Vocabulary

These words are not limited only to words actually used on the job. Vocabulary questions are a good measure of a competitor's general ability, as well as his aptitude for work requiring skill with words.

There is no printed list of all words whose meanings are tested in civil service examinations. No study of a selected list of words is likely to help in preparing for an examination. The general improvement of your vocabulary will help, however, and you will find that this improvement will make other kinds of questions more understandable also.

Directions: In each of the following questions you are to find which one of five words or phrases offered as choices has most nearly the same meaning as the word or phrase in CAPITAL LETTERS or *italics*. On the answer sheet mark the letter of the suggested answer which you think is the best.

1. If a report is VERIFIED it is
   A) changed
   B) confirmed
   C) replaced
   D) discarded
   E) corrected

Since "confirmed," lettered B, means most nearly the same as "verified," the space under B is marked on the answer sheet for question 1.

2. A clerk who shows FORBEARANCE TOWARD THE OPINION OF OTHERS shows
   A) severity
   B) hypercriticism
   C) tolerance
   D) quietness
   E) thankfulness

3. A *controversy* between two persons is
   A) an agreement
   B) a dispute
   C) a partnership
   D) a plot
   E) an understanding

4. To say that a condition is *generally or extensively existing* means that it is
   A) artificial   D) timely
   B) prevalent   E) transient
   C) recurrent

5. *Authentic* means most nearly
   A) detailed   D) technical
   B) reliable   E) practical
   C) valuable

6. *The two farms lie close to each other, but are not in actual contact.* This sentence means most nearly that the two farms are
   A) adjoining
   B) abutting
   C) touching
   D) adjacent
   E) united

The space under D is marked for this question because "adjacent" best describes the meaning of the sentence in italics. The other choices all indicate that the farms are in contact in some degree or are touching each other.

Word Relations

In each of the following questions the first two words in capital letters go together in some way. Find how they are related. Then select from the last five words the one that goes with the third word in capital letters in the same way that the second word in capital letters goes with the first. The answer sheet is marked to show the correct choice of answers for these two questions.

7. FOOD is to HUNGER as SLEEP is to
   A) night   D) health
   B) dream   E) rest
   C) weariness

Food relieves hunger and sleep relieves weariness. Therefore, C, the letter before "weariness," is marked on the answer sheet for this question.

8. SPEEDOMETER is related to POINTER as WATCH is related to
   A) case   D) spring
   B) hands   E) numerals
   C) dial

On the answer sheet the space under B has been blackened to show that *watch* and *hands* are related in most nearly the same way as *speedometer* and *pointer*.

	A	B	C	D	E
1		▮			
2			▮		
3		▮			
4		▮			
5		▮			
6				▮	
7			▮		
8		▮			

VERBAL ABILITIES

Interpretation of Paragraphs

Each question consists of a quotation followed by a series of five statements. Among the five statements there is only one that *must* be true if the quotation is true. Other statements among the five may or may not be true, but they are not necessary conclusions from the quotation. You are to select the *one* statement which is *best supported* by the quotation.

1. (*Reading*) "The application of the steam engine to the sawmill changed the whole lumber industry. Formerly the mills remained near the streams; now they follow the timber. Formerly the logs were floated downstream to their destination; now they are carried by the railroads."

What besides the method of transportation does the quotation indicate has changed in the lumber industry?
A) speed of cutting timber
B) location of market
C) type of timber sold
D) route of railroads
E) source of power

The quotation says nothing about the speed of steam-powered sawmills, location of the market for lumber, the type of timber sold, or the route of railroads. It does, however, mention "the application of the steam engine to the sawmill"—which gave a new source of power for sawmill operations. E is therefore the answer, and the space under E is blackened for question 1.

2. (*Reading*) "More patents have been issued for inventions relating to transportation than for those in any other line of human activity. These inventions have resulted in a great financial saving to the people and have made possible a civilization that could not have existed without them."

Select the alternative that is best supported by the quotation. Transportation
A) would be impossible without inventions
B) is an important factor in our civilization
C) is still to be much improved
D) is more important than any other activity
E) is carried on through the Patent Office

The space on the Answer Sheet under B is marked for question 2 because the statement lettered B is implied in the quotation. A is not strictly true, since manpower without inventions could supply transportation of a sort; C is probably true but is not in the quotation; D is exaggerated; E is not implied in the information given.

3. (*Reading*) "There exists a false but popular idea that a clue is some mysterious fact which most people overlook, but which some very keen investigator easily discovers and recognizes as having, in itself, a remarkable meaning. The clue is most often an ordinary fact which an observant person picks up—something which gains its significance when, after a long series of careful investigations, it is connected with a network of other clues."

According to the quotation, to be of value, clues must be
A) discovered by skilled investigators
B) found under mysterious circumstances
C) discovered soon after the crime
D) observed many times
E) connected with other facts

The quotation does not say that the clue must be (A) discovered by an investigator in order to make it of value; it does not mention (B) the circumstances under which a clue must be found; nothing in the paragraph implies that the value of a clue depends upon the (C) time of its discovery, nor upon the (D) number of times it is observed. E is the answer, because the quotation does say that a clue gains its significance, or value, when *connected with other clues or facts*.

4. (*Reading*) "Just as the procedure of a collection department must be clear-cut and definite, the steps being taken with the sureness of a skilled chess player, so the various paragraphs of a collection letter must show clear organization, giving evidence of a mind that, from the beginning, has had a specific end in view."

The quotation best supports the statement that a collection letter should always
A) show a spirit of sportsmanship
B) be divided into several paragraphs
C) express confidence in the debtor
D) be brief, but courteous
E) be carefully planned

	A	B	C	D	E
1	‖	‖	‖	‖	▌
2	‖	▌	‖	‖	‖
3	‖	‖	‖	‖	▌
4	‖	‖	‖	‖	▌

Proverbs

These questions test ability to understand meanings and apply generalizations. The answer is the sentence which means the same thing as the saying quoted.

1. The saying "Many hands make light work" means most nearly
   A) Most people prefer easy jobs.
   B) When several work together, each finds his task easy.
   c) Much light work can be done by hand.
   D) There are often too many to help.
   E) One does his best work when working alone.

2. The saying "To know the road, ask of those who have traveled it" means most nearly
   A) Know your destination before you start.
   B) Seek counsel of experienced persons.
   c) When in doubt, stop.
   D) The traveled road is the easiest route.
   E) If you would advance, profit by your past.

The statement lettered B means most nearly the same as "Many hands make light work." Therefore the space under B is blackened for question 1.

Judgment

These questions are based on a variety of facts, sometimes on facts with which the candidate would be expected to be familiar, sometimes on facts explained in the question itself. The questions are of various degrees of difficulty. In some cases judgment items may pertain to a particular field of subject-matter, knowledge of which is necessary for the job.

3. Hospital beds are usually higher than beds in private homes. Which of the following is the BEST reason for this fact?
   A) Hospital beds are in use all day, instead of at night only.
   B) Many hospital patients are children.
   c) Private homes seldom have space enough for high beds.
   D) The care of patients is less difficult when the beds are high.
   E) The danger of falling out of bed is greater where there are no nurses.

The suggestion lettered D is the answer and is marked on the answer sheet. Of all the suggestions given as possible reasons why hospital beds are higher than other kinds, the one lettered D is clearly the most reasonable and best.

4. Objects are visible because
   A) they are opaque
   B) they are partially in shadow
   c) they absorb light from the sun
   D) light falls on them and is reflected to the eye
   E) light rays penetrate their surfaces

On the section of the answer sheet at the right, the space under D is marked for question 4 because the statement lettered D is the only one that explains why objects are visible. The other statements may be true, but they do not account for the visibility of objects.

5. In starting a load, a horse has to pull harder than he does to keep it moving, because
   A) the load weighs less when it is moving
   B) there is no friction after the load is moving
   c) the horse has to overcome the tendency of the wagon to remain at rest
   D) the wheels stick to the axles
   E) the horse becomes accustomed to pulling the load

6. Which of the following would be the *surest* indication that a druggist may have violated the legal requirement that narcotic drugs be dispensed only on a physician's prescription?
   A) A number of people known to have purchased other drugs from him are believed to possess narcotics, but no prescriptions issued to these persons are in the druggist's file.
   B) He is himself an addict.
   c) His wholesaler refuses to sell him narcotics.
   D) The total of his present narcotics stock and the amount legally accounted for is much less than his purchases.
   E) The supply of narcotics in stock is less than the amount which he recently reported.

The facts related in A do not indicate that these customers have secured their narcotics from this druggist—the narcotics may have been obtained from some other druggist on a proper prescription; B is no indication that prescriptions did not cover all the narcotics he has dispensed, either for his own use or for other people; c might be true for many reasons—for example, his credit may be bad; and E could be explained by legal sales made since his last report. The answer is D, because violation of the requirement mentioned is a likely explanation of the large difference; therefore D is marked on the answer sheet.

VERBAL ABILITIES

Grammar and English Usage

In each of questions 1 and 2, select the sentence that is preferable with respect to grammar and good usage in a formal letter or report.

1. A) They do not ordinarily present these kind of reports in detail like this.
   B) Reports like this is not generally given in such great detail.
   C) A report of this kind is not hardly ever given in such detail as this one.
   D) This report is more detailed than what such reports ordinarily are.
   E) A report of this kind is not ordinarily presented in such detail as this one.

2. A) Although that statement is true, I did not leave it influence my decision.
   B) My decision is not effected by that statement, even though it is true.
   C) Although true, I have not let that statement influence my decision.
   D) That statement is true, but it does not affect my decision.
   E) Because that statement is true does not have any effect on my decision.

In questions 3 and 4, four words or phrases have been underlined and lettered A, B, C, and D. If there is an error in usage in one of the underlined words or phrases, mark on the answer sheet the letter of the one in which the error occurs. If there is no error, mark the E space.

3. The gasoline tank bust and escaping gasoline became ignited in an unknown manner.
              A   B   C   D

4. The truck was in good mechanical condition when examined ten hours before the accident occurred.
        A   B   C   D

Spelling

5. Select the one misspelled word.
   A) reliable   D) accurrate
   B) detailed   E) sanctioned
   C) different

In questions like the following, find the correct spelling of the word and blacken the proper space on your answer sheet. If none of the suggested spellings is correct, blacken space D on your answer sheet.

6. A) occassion   C) ocassion
   B) occasion   D) none of these

The correct spelling of the word is *occasion*. Since the B spelling is correct, the space under B is marked for this question.

Look at each word in the following list and decide whether the spelling is *all right* or *bad*. On the answer sheet blacken space
    A if the spelling is ALL RIGHT
    B if the spelling is BAD

7. running A
8. indien B
9. skool B

In questions like 10, a sentence is given in which one word, which is underlined, is spelled as it is pronounced. Write the correct spelling of the word in the blank. Then decide which one of the suggested answers, A, B, C, or D, is the correct answer to the question. (Sometimes the question will refer to one letter in the word, sometimes to a combination of letters.)

10. The new treasurer uses the same system that his pred-eh-sess'-urr did.
    In the correct spelling, _____, what is the tenth letter?

    A) s
    B) e
    C) o
    D) none of these

The correct spelling of the underlined word is *predecessor*. Since the tenth letter is "o," which is given as answer C, the space under C has been blackened.

	A	B	C	D	E
1					▊
2				▊	
3	▊				
4					▊
5				▊	
6		▊			
7	▊				
8		▊			
9		▊			
10			▊		

TESTS OF REASONING

In some jobs, it is necessary to understand, interpret, and apply rules and principles. In others, it is necessary also to discover principles from available data or information. These types of reasoning ability can be tested by different kinds of tests—for example, questions on the relationship of words, understanding of paragraphs, or solving of numerical problems.

Other types of questions that have been found useful in testing reasoning abilities are illustrated on these two pages. Here the competitor is asked to find relationships between elements (numbers, letters, or patterns), to find the rule by which they are bound together in groups or arranged in a certain order, and to select or arrange other elements according to that rule.

Number Series

Each of these three questions gives a series of six numbers. Each series of numbers is made up according to a certain rule or order. You are to find what the next number in the series should be; then blacken the space on the answer sheet that is lettered the same as the correct suggested answer

1. 2 4 6 8 10 12
   A) 14
   B) 16
   c) 18
   D) 20
   E) none of these

In question 1, the rule is to add 2 to each number (2+2=4; 4+2=6; etc.). The next number in the series is 14 (12+2= 14). Since *14* is lettered A among the suggested answers, the space lettered A is blackened on the answer sheet for question 1.

2. 7 8 6 7 5 6
   A) 2
   B) 3
   C) 4
   D) 5
   E) none of these

In question 2, the rule is to add 1 to the first number, subtract 2 from the next, add 1, subtract 2, and so on. The next number in the series is 4. On the answer sheet, the letter c should be blackened for question 2.

3. 3 6 9 12 15 18
   A) 39
   B) 40
   c) 45
   D) 59
   E) none of these

In question 3, the rule is to add 3, making 21 the next number in the series. The correct answer to question 3 is *none of these*, since 39, 40, 45, and 59 are all incorrect answers; therefore E is marked on the answer sheet.

The next two questions are more difficult. In these, the arrangement is more complicated, and the answer is chosen from groups of two numbers, of which one group gives the next two numbers in the series.

4. 1 1 2 1 3 1 4 1
   A) 1 5   D) 5 5
   B) 4 1   E) 6 1
   c) 5 1

The series consists of 1's alternating with numbers in ascending numerical order. The next two numbers would be 5 and 1; therefore c is the correct answer.

5. 2 8 3 7 5 6 8 5
   A) 10 6   D) 12 4
   B) 11 3   E) 12 6
   c) 11 4

This series consists of a subseries for which the rule is to add 1, add 2, add 3, add 4, alternating with another subseries in descending numerical order. The next number in the first subseries would be 8+4, or 12; and the next number in the descending series would be 4. Therefore D is the correct choice.

Letter Series

In each of these questions there is a series of letters which follow some definite order, and at the right there are five sets of two letters each. Look at the letters in the series and determine what the order is; then from the suggested answers at the right, select the set that gives the next two letters in the series in their correct order. Mark the space that has the same letter as the set you have chosen.

6. X C X D X E X   A) F X   B) F G   c) X F   d) E F   E) X G

The series consists of X's alternating with letters in alphabetical order. The next two letters would be F and X; therefore, A is the correct answer.

7. A B D C E F H   A) G H   B) I G   c) G I   d) K L   E) I H

If you compare this series with the alphabet, you will find that it goes along in pairs, the first pair in their usual order and the next pair in reverse order. The last letter given in the series is the second letter of the pair G—H, which is in reverse order. The first missing letter must, therefore, be G. The next pair of letters would be I—J, in that order; the second of the missing letters is I. The alternative you look for, then, is G I, which is lettered c.

REASONING

Symbol Series

Questions 1 and 2 consist of a series of five symbols at the left and five other symbols labeled A, B, C, D, and E at the right.

In each question, first study the series of symbols at the left; then from the symbols at the right, labeled A, B, C, D, and E, select the one which continues the series most completely. Next to the question number on the answer sheet blacken the space lettered the same as the symbol which you have chosen.

1.

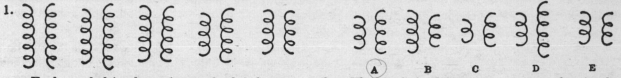

Each symbol in the series at the left has two coils. The symbols differ from one another in the number of loops that each coil has. In the first symbol, each coil has five loops; in the second, the left-hand one has four and the right-hand one has five; in the third, each coil has four. In this series, first the left-hand coil loses a loop and then the right-hand coil loses one.

Since the fifth symbol has three loops in each coil, the next symbol in this series must have two loops in the left-hand coil and three in the right-hand coil. Since symbol A is the only one which has two loops in the left-hand coil and three in the right-hand coil, A is the answer, and you should blacken space A for question 1 on the answer sheet.

2.

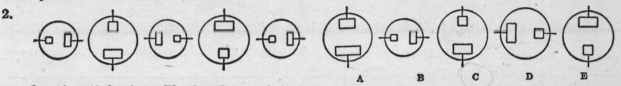

Question 2 is harder. The first five symbols show an alternation from small to large to small; and a quarter-turn in a counterclockwise direction each time. The answer should be a large circle, therefore (which eliminates B from the alternatives), with the larger rectangle at the bottom of the circle (which eliminates D and E). A second look at A shows that the rectangles within it are larger than any of the rectangles in the other circles; this change has no basis in the series. Thus C is left as the correct answer.

Symbol Classification

Each of the next two questions has two boxes at the left. The first box has three symbols, and the second box has two symbols with one missing symbol represented by a question mark. There is always some difference between the symbols in the first box and the symbols in the second box. You are to decide what the difference between the symbols in the first box and the symbols in the second box is, and choose the symbol lettered A, B, C, D, or E, which can best take the place of the missing symbol in the second box.

(NOTE.—Do not confuse this type of question with the type above. The symbols in each box are simply a *group* and not a series with a definite progression.)

3.

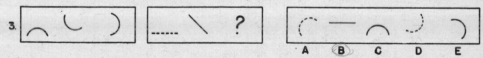

In question 3 all the symbols in the first box are curved, while the symbols in the second box are straight. Of the lettered symbols in the third box, only B is straight, so B has been marked on the answer sheet. (Note that although one symbol in the second box is made of dashes, the other is not. The type of line, therefore, is not the feature that distinguishes the second box from the first.)

4.

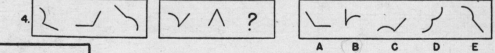

In question 4 the given symbols consist of two lines making an angle. There are curved lines and straight lines in each box; therefore the difference that must be found cannot be the difference between curved and straight. The angles formed in the first box are *obtuse*; those in the second box are *acute*. Now a check of the alternatives shows that only one of them consists of lines making an acute angle; the correct answer B is therefore marked.

CLERICAL TESTS

Clerk

The following sample questions show the types and approximate difficulty of the questions that will be used in the written examination. They show also how the questions are to be answered by those who take the examination. Read the directions below, then look at these sample questions and try to answer them. Record your answers on the Sample Answer Sheet. Then check your answers with those given on the Correct Answers to Sample Questions.

Each question has several suggested answers lettered A, B, C, etc. Decide which one is the best answer to the question. Then, on the Sample Answer Sheet, find the answer space numbered to correspond with the number of the question, and blacken the space between the lines with the same letter as the best suggested answer.

NAME AND NUMBER COMPARISONS: In each line across the page there are three names or numbers that are much alike. Compare the three names or numbers and decide which ones are exactly alike. On the answer sheet, blacken the space lettered

    A if ALL THREE names or numbers are exactly ALIKE
    B if only the FIRST and SECOND names or numbers are exactly ALIKE
    C if only the FIRST and THIRD names or numbers are exactly ALIKE
    D if only the SECOND and THIRD names or numbers are exactly ALIKE
    E if ALL THREE names or numbers are DIFFERENT

1.	Davis Hazen	David Hozen	David Hazen
2.	Lois Appel	Lois Appel	Lois Apfel
3.	June Allan	Jane Allan	Jane Allan
4.	10235	10235	10235
5.	32614	32164	32614

Sample Answer Sheet / Correct Answers to Sample Questions

ALPHABETIZING: In each of the following questions there is a name enclosed in a box, followed by a series of four names in proper alphabetic order. The spaces between the names are lettered A, B, C, D, and E. Decide in which space the boxed name belongs in that series; then blacken the proper space on the answer sheet.

6. | Kessler, Neilson |

  A) →
    Kessel, Oscar
  B) →
    Kessinger, D. J.
  C) →
    Kessler, Karl
  D) →
    Kessner, Lewis
  E) →

7. | Olsen, C. C. |

  A) →
    Olsen, C. A.
  B) →
    Olsen, C. D.
  C) →
    Olsen, Charles
  D) →
    Olsen, Christopher
  E) →

8. | Robeson, Carl |

  A) →
    Robey, Clarke
  B) →
    Robinette, Claude
  C) →
    Robinson, Claude
  D) →
    Robinton, Charles
  E) →

COMPUTATIONS: Work each problem and compare your answer with suggested answers A, B, C, and D. On the Sample Answer Sheet, blacken the proper space. If your answer does not agree with any of the first four suggested answers, blacken space E on the answer sheet.

9. Add:

    9 6 3
    2 5 7
    4 1 6
   ————

Answers
A) 1,516
B) 1,526
C) 1,636
D) 1,726
E) none of these

10. Divide:

   2 7 / 4 3 7 9 . 4

A) 160.2
B) 160.22
C) 1,620.2
D) 1,622
E) none of these

11. From a shipment of supplies, an inspector accepts 32 boxes and rejects 8 boxes. What percentage of the boxes of supplies is accepted?

A) 20   D) 80
B) 25   E) none of these
C) 75

VERBAL ABILITIES: Each sample question has suggested answers lettered A, B, C, etc. Decide which one is the best answer to the question. Then blacken the proper space on the answer sheet.

12. *Authentic* means most nearly

A) detailed   D) technical
B) reliable   E) practical
C) valuable

For each question like samples 13 and 14, find the correct spelling of the word and blacken the proper space on your answer sheet. If no suggested spelling is correct, blacken space D on your answer sheet.

13. A) occassion   C) ocassion
    B) occasion   D) none of these

14. A) amature   C) amatuer
    B) amatur   D) none of these

15. (*Reading*) "Just as the procedure of a collection department must be clear-cut and definite, the steps being taken with the sureness of a skilled chess player, so the various paragraphs of a collection letter must show clear organization, giving evidence of a mind that, from the beginning, has had a specific end in view."

The quotation best supports the statement that a collection letter should always

A) show a spirit of sportsmanship
B) be divided into several paragraphs
C) express confidence in the debtor
D) be brief, but courteous
E) be carefully planned

The following question contains five sentences. Decide which one of the sentences is preferable with respect to grammar and usage such as would be suitable in a formal letter or report. Then blacken the proper space on the answer sheet.

16. A) They don't ordinarily present these kind of reports in detail like this.
B) Reports like this is not generally given in such great detail.
C) A report of this kind isn't hardly ever given in such detail as this one.
D) This report is more detailed than what such reports ordinarily are.
E) A report of this kind is not ordinarily presented in such detail as this one.

Sample Answer Sheet					Correct Answers to Sample Questions				
A	B	C	D	E	A	B	C	D	E
9					9		■		
10 A B C D E					10 A B C D ■				
11 A B C D E					11 A B C D ■				
12 A B C D E					12 A ■ C D E				
13 A B C D E					13 A ■ C D E				
14 A B C D E					14 A B C D ■				
15 A B C D E					15 A B C D ■				
16 A B C D E					16 A B C D ■				

Accounting Clerk

The following sample questions show the types of questions that will be used in the written tests. They show also how the questions in the tests are to be answered. Read the directions below; then answer the sample questions. Record your answers on the Sample Answer Sheet on these pages. Then compare your answers with those given on the Correct Answers to Sample Questions.

Each sample question has a number of suggested answers lettered A, B, C, D, and E. Decide which one is the best answer to the question. Then, on the Sample Answer Sheet, find the answer space numbered to correspond with the number of the question and blacken the space between the lines lettered the same as the best suggested answer.

For each question like 1 and 2, choose the one of the five suggested answers that means most nearly the same as the word or group of words in *italics*.

1. A small crane was used to *raise* the heavy parts. *Raise* means most nearly
   A) drag
   B) unload
   C) deliver
   D) lift
   E) guide

2. The reports were *consolidated* by the secretary. *Consolidated* means most nearly
   A) combined
   B) concluded
   C) distributed
   D) protected
   E) weighed

3. (*Reading*) "What constitutes skill in any line of work is not always easy to determine; economy of time must be carefully distinguished from economy of energy, as the quickest method may require the greatest expenditure of muscular effort, and may not be essential or at all desirable."
   The quotation best supports the statement that
   A) energy and time cannot both be conserved in the performing of a single task
   B) the most efficiently executed task is not always the one done in the shortest time
   C) if a task requires muscular energy, it is not being performed economically
   D) skill in performing a task should not be acquired at the expense of time
   E) a task is well done when it is performed in the shortest time

Regulation (on which Questions 4 and 5 are based):
   Full-time employees shall earn and be credited with sick leave at the rate of 1¼ days per calendar month.

Directions (for Questions 4 and 5):
   The following table gives the sick-leave records of two full-time employees for the calendar year 1950. For each of these employees, the workweek consisted of five 8-hour days. For each question, determine the balance of accumulated sick leave to the credit of the employee at the end of December 1950. At the right side of the table are four suggested answers, designated by A, B, C, and D at the top of the columns. If one of these suggested answers is correct, blacken the proper space on the Sample Answer Sheet. If the correct answer is not given under A, B, C, or D, blacken the space under E on the Sample Answer Sheet.

Questions:

Employee	Accumulated Sick Leave 12/31/49 Days – Hours	Sick Leave Used in 1950 Days – Hours	Balance of Accumulated Leave 12/31/50				
			A Days – Hours	B Days – Hours	C Days – Hours	D Days – Hours	E
4. No. 4	8 – 4	2 – 1	6 – 3	7 – 5	17 – 5	21 – 3	None of these
5. No. 5	60 – 0	8 – 7	51 – 1	51 – 7	60 – 0	66 – 3	

6. A voucher contained the following items:

   6 desks @ $89.20 . . . $525.20
   8 chairs @ $32.50 . . . 260.00
   _____
   Total $885.20

   The terms were given on the voucher as 3%, 10 days; net, 30 days. Verify the computations, which may be incorrect, and calculate the correct amount to be paid. If payment is made within the discount period, the amount to be paid is
   A) $761.64   D) $858.64
   B) $771.34   E) none of these
   C) $795.20

Sample Answer Sheet

1 A B C D E
2 A B C D E
3 A B C D E
4 A B C D E
5 A B C D E
6 A B C D E

Questions 7 and 8 are based on the following portion of a withholding tax table:

If the payroll period with respect to an employee is MONTHLY:

And wages are—		And number of withholding exemptions claimed is—				
At least	But less than	0	1	2	3	4
		The amount of income tax to be withheld shall be				
$172	$176	$31.30	$21.30	$11.30	$1.30	0
176	180	32.00	22.00	12.00	2.00	0
180	184	32.80	22.80	12.80	2.80	0

7. K received a monthly wage of $176.40 the first 3 months of the year and $182.50 the remaining 9 months. He claimed 3 exemptions for the first 4 months and 4 for the remaining 8 months. What was the total income tax withheld during the year?

A) $0.00
B) $6.00
C) $8.80
D) $11.20
E) none of these

8. L, who has 2 exemptions, receives a monthly wage of $175.50. If no amounts other than income tax were withheld, his monthly take-home pay would be

A) $154.20
B) $164.20
C) $174.20
D) $175.50
E) none of these

Correct Answers to Sample Questions

	A	B	C	D	E
1	‖	‖	‖	▮	‖
2	▮	‖	‖	‖	‖
3	‖	▮	‖	‖	‖
4	‖	‖	‖	▮	‖
5	‖	‖	‖	‖	▮
6	‖	▮	‖	‖	‖
7	‖	‖	▮	‖	‖
8	‖	▮	‖	‖	‖

Storekeeping Clerk

The following sample questions show the kinds of questions in the examination and the way to answer the questions.

Answers to questions are to be marked on the Sample Answer Sheet. The answer sheet has numbers matching the numbers of the test questions. Beside each number on the answer sheet are spaces lettered A, B, C, D, and E. The suggested answers to each question are also lettered. Select the correct answer to each question and mark the answer sheet in the space under the letter of the correct answer to that question.

In each question like sample I, select the *one* of the five suggested answers that means most nearly the same as the word or the group of words that is *in italics*. Mark the space on the Sample Answer Sheet under the letter that is the same as the letter of the answer you have selected.

I. *An innovation* in office procedure is always
   A) a conventional practice
   B) an improvement
   C) a new method
   D) an inadequate change
   E) a preliminary trial

   The space under C is marked for this question because *a new method* is the one of the five suggested answers that means most nearly the same as *an innovation*.

II. (*Reading*) "Just as the procedure of a collection department must be clear-cut and definite, the steps being taken with the sureness of a skilled chess player, so the various paragraphs of a collection letter must show clear organization, giving evidence of a mind that, from the beginning, has had a specific end in view."

   The quotation best supports the statement that a collection letter should always
   A) show a spirit of sportsmanship
   B) be divided into several paragraphs
   C) express confidence in the debtor
   D) be brief, but courteous
   E) be carefully planned

In each question like the following, find the correct spelling of the word and blacken the proper space on your answer sheet. If no suggested spelling is correct, blacken space D on your answer sheet.

III. A) athalete   C) athlete
    B) athelete   D) none of these

   The correct spelling of the word is *athlete*. Since the C spelling is correct, the space under C is marked for this question.

Work each problem and compare your answer with suggested answers A, B, C, and D. On the Sample Answer Sheet, blacken the proper space. If your answer does not agree with any of the first four suggested answers, blacken space E on the answer sheet.

IV. Add: Answers
     9 6 3   A) 1,516
     2 5 7   B) 1,526
     4 1 6   C) 1,636
     ———   D) 1,726
                    E) none of these

V. From a shipment of supplies, an inspector accepts 32 boxes and rejects 8 boxes. What percent of the boxes of supplies are accepted?
    A) 20
    B) 25
    C) 75
    D) 80
    E) none of these

In each line across the page there are three names or numbers that are much alike. Compare the three names or numbers and decide which ones are exactly alike. On the Sample Answer Sheet, blacken the space lettered

A   if ALL THREE names or numbers are exactly ALIKE
B   if only the FIRST and SECOND names or numbers are exactly ALIKE
C   if only the FIRST and THIRD names or numbers are exactly ALIKE
D   if only the SECOND and THIRD names or numbers are exactly ALIKE
E   if ALL THREE names or numbers are DIFFERENT

VI.   Davis Hazen   David Hozen   David Hazen
VII. Lois Appel   Lois Appel   Lois Apfel
VIII. June Allan   Jane Allan   Jane Allan
IX.   10235   10235   10235
X.   32614   32164   32614

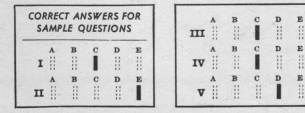

SAMPLE ANSWER SHEET				

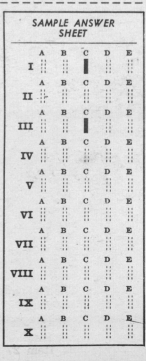

Answer questions like XI through XVII in the following way.

Assume that a stockroom floor is divided into three sections—West, Central, and East. There are a number of bins in each of these sections. Each bin is numbered and holds one particular type of stock item which has the same number as the bin in which it is kept. For example, bin number 3 holds a supply of stock item number 3. The bins and stock items are located in the three sections as follows:

LOCATION PLAN

Section	Bin and Item Numbers
West	1–10
Central	11–20
East	21–30

Each question contains several numbers, which are the stock numbers of the items to be taken from the bins to fill an order. To answer each question, decide which section or sections contain the bins from which the items are to be taken. On the answer sheet, mark

A   if the order is filled from only ONE section
B   if the order is filled from the WEST and CENTRAL sections only
C   if the order is filled from the WEST and EAST sections only
D   if the order is filled from the CENTRAL and EAST sections only
E   if the order is filled from ALL THREE sections

Now do the following sample questions and mark your answers on the Sample Answer Sheet.

Sample Answer Sheet

	A	B	C	D	E
XI					
XII					
XIII					
XIV					
XV					
XVI					
XVII					

XI. 26, 28, 29   A
The answer to question XI is A, because all three items in this order are found in only ONE section.

XII. 2, 12, 25, 29   E
The answer here is E, because items must be taken from ALL THREE sections to fill this order.

XIII. 12, 15, 27   D
Here D is the answer, because items must be taken from the CENTRAL and EAST sections.

XIV. 2, 8, 21, 25   C

XV. 19, 20, 21   D

From time to time bins, with the items they hold, will be moved from one section to another. Also, items may become unavailable and other items will have to be substituted for them. Write the Location Plan on scratch paper, and make a record of all changes in the Plan.

Change I. The following shifts are made in the stock:

Bins and items 11 and 12 are moved from the Central section to the West section.

Bin and item 21 are moved from the East section to the Central section.

The following substitutions are to be made:

Discontinued	Replaced by
Item 15	Item 25
Item 27	Item 3

Your changed Location Plan should read:

Section	Bin and Item Numbers		
West	~~1–10~~	1–12	
Central	~~11–20~~	13–21	For 15 use 25
East	~~21–30~~	22–30	For 27 use 3

After you have made these changes, answer questions XVI and XVII on the basis of the changed Location Plan.

XVI. 2, 11, 22, 23   C

XVII. 15, 24, 29   A

The answer to question XVI is C, because, in accordance with the above changes, the order will be filled from the WEST and EAST sections.

The answer to question XVII is A, because Item 25 will be used for Item 15 and the order will, therefore, be filled from only ONE section.

Now compare your answers with the Correct Answers for Sample Questions.

Correct Answers for Sample Questions

	A	B	C	D	E
XI	■				
XII					■
XIII				■	
XIV			■		
XV				■	
XVI			■		
XVII	■				

Archives Assistant and Library Assistant

The following sample questions show the types and approximate difficulty of the questions that will be used in the written examination. They show also how the questions are to be answered by those who take the examination. Read the directions below; then look at these sample questions and try to answer them. Record your answers on the Sample Answer Sheets. Then compare your answers with those given on the Correct Answers to Sample Questions.

Each question has several suggested answers lettered A, B, C, etc. Decide which one is the best answer to the question. Then, on the Sample Answer Sheet, find the answer space numbered to correspond with the number of the question, and blacken the space between the lines with the same letter as the best suggested answer.

NAME AND NUMBER COMPARISONS: In each line across the page there are three names or numbers which are much alike. Compare the three names or numbers and decide which ones are exactly alike. On the answer sheet, blacken the space lettered

A   if ALL THREE names or numbers are exactly ALIKE
B   if only the FIRST and SECOND names or numbers are exactly ALIKE
C   if only the FIRST and THIRD names or numbers are exactly ALIKE
D   if only the SECOND and THIRD names or numbers are exactly ALIKE
E   if ALL THREE names or numbers are DIFFERENT

1.	Davis Hazen	David Hozen	David Hazen
2.	Lois Appel	Lois Appel	Lois Apfel
3.	June Allan	Jane Allan	Jane Allan
4.	10235	10235	10235
5.	32614	32164	32614

Sample Answer Sheet

	A	B	C	D	E
1					
2					
3					
4					
5					
6					
7					
8					

Correct Answers to Sample Questions

	A	B	C	D	E
1					■
2		■			
3				■	
4	■				
5			■		
6					■
7	■				
8		■			

ALPHABETIZING: In each of the following questions there is a name enclosed in a box, and a series of four other names in proper alphabetic order. The spaces between the names are lettered A, B, C, D, and E. Decide in which space the boxed name belongs in that series. Then blacken the proper space on the answer sheet.

6. | JONES, JANE |

A) →
   Goodyear, G. L.
B) →
   Haddon, Mary
C) →
   Jackson, Harry
D) →
   Jenkins, William
E) →

7. | ROBESON, CARL |

A) →
   Robey, Clarke
B) →
   Robinette, Claude
C) →
   Robinson, Claude
D) →
   Robinton, Chas.
E) →

8. | OLSEN, C. C. |

A) →
   Olsen, C. A.
B) →
   Olsen, C. D.
C) →
   Olsen, Charles
D) →
   Olsen, Christopher
E) →

In question 6 the name in the box follows "Jenkins, William" when all five names are in alphabetic order; therefore the space under E should be blackened for question 6.

9. *Authentic* means most nearly

  A) detailed   D) technical
  B) reliable   E) practical
  C) valuable

For sample 10, read the paragraph and answer the question that follows it.

10. (*Reading*) "Just as the procedure of a collection department must be clear-cut and definite, the steps being taken with the sureness of a skilled chess player, so the various paragraphs of a collection letter must show clear organization, giving evidence of a mind that, from the beginning, has had a specific end in view."

The quotation best supports the statement that a collection letter should always

  A) show a spirit of sportsmanship
  B) be divided into several paragraphs
  C) express confidence in the debtor
  D) be brief, but courteous
  E) be carefully planned

For each question like samples 11 and 12, find the correct spelling of the word. If none of the spellings is correct, blacken the space under D on the answer sheet.

11. A) occassion   C) ocassion
    B) occasion   D) none of these

12. A) amature   C) amatuer
    B) amatur   D) none of these

All competitors will take the three tests having questions similar to samples 1 through 12. In addition, some competitors will take a test having questions similar to samples 13 and 14. The examination announcement will indicate which tests will be given for various positions.

For each question like samples 13 and 14, decide which one of the suggested answers is the best answer to the question. Then blacken the proper space on the answer sheet.

13. In general, the most important advantage of good employee morale is that it results in

  A) high production
  B) decreased work for the supervisor
  C) increased ease in rating workers' efficiency
  D) high standing for the supervisor with management
  E) less desire for wage increases among employees

14. Which one of the following types of information would be most useful to a supervisor in determining which employee should lose his job in case lay-offs are necessary?

  A) length of service with the supervisor
  B) marital status
  C) education
  D) age
  E) job performance rating

Office Machine Operator

The following sample questions show the types and approximate difficulty of the questions that will be used. They also show how the questions are to be answered by those who take the tests.

Read the directions; then look over the sample questions and try to answer them. For your answers to the samples, use the Sample Answer Sheets. (For the actual examination, you will be given separate answer sheets on which your answers can be scored by an electric machine.) Each number on the answer sheet stands for the question with the same number. For each question, make a solid black mark in the space between the dotted lines below the letter that is the same as the letter of the answer you select. After you have marked all your answers, compare your answers with those given in the Correct Answers to Sample Questions.

In the test that has questions like 1 through 10 below, each question is a line of three names or three numbers that are much alike. Compare the three names or numbers and decide which ones are exactly alike. On the Sample Answer Sheet, blacken the space lettered

    A   if ALL THREE names or numbers are exactly ALIKE
    B   if only the FIRST and SECOND names or numbers are exactly ALIKE
    C   if only the FIRST and THIRD names or numbers are exactly ALIKE
    D   if only the SECOND and THIRD names or numbers are exactly ALIKE
    E   if ALL THREE names or numbers are DIFFERENT

1.	Davis M. Hazen	David M. Hozen	David M. Hazen
2.	Lois Berger Appel	Lois Berger Appel	Lois Berger Apfel
3.	June McPherson Allan	Jane McPherson Allan	Jane McPherson Allan
4.	Annabel K. Dove	Annabel H. Dove	Annabel K. Dove
5.	J. Menninger Baxter	J. Menninger Baxter	J. Menninger Baxter
6.	3449212	3449212	3449112
7.	2153107	2153017	2153117
8.	1023576	1023576	1023576
9.	32614513	32164513	32614513
10.	412893778	412893378	412893378

Sample Answer Sheet

	A	B	C	D	E		A	B	C	D	E
1						6					
2						7					
3						8					
4						9					
5						10					

Correct Answers to Sample Questions

	A	B	C	D	E		A	B	C	D	E
1					■	6		■			
2		■				7					■
3				■		8	■				
4			■			9			■		
5	■					10				■	

Questions like the Sample Test List below are to show how well your eyes and hand work together. You will be given a list like the one below, and an answer sheet. The list consists of several columns of numbers with letters. The numbers in the list refer to the numbers on the Sample Answer Sheet. The letters refer to the answer positions A, B, C, D, and E. For each number and letter in the list, find the same number on the answer sheet and mark the space for the letter. Thus, the first question is 52 E, and 52 on the answer sheet is marked in space E to show you how an answer should be marked. The next question is 26 B, so find 26 on the answer sheet and mark space B.

Continue with the other questions in the same way, marking the space for the letter that goes with the question number. For some of the numbers on the answer sheet you will be told to mark more than one letter and for some numbers you will not mark any letter at all.

It will help you to notice how the answer sheet is arranged. (For these sample questions, the center of the sheet is omitted.) Each column has spaces for 25 numbers, so the second column begins with 26, the third with 51, and so forth.

Sample Test List

52	E	70	C	21	A	123	C
26	B	122	A	2	C	49	C
98	D	72	B	52	B	21	C
27	A	26	D	74	E	27	E
120	C	50	B	1	D	96	E
72	E	76	D	25	B	125	B
101	B	121	D	46	C	97	A
121	B	23	D	101	A	71	C
46	B	100	C	95	D	51	B
25	D	124	D	22	E	45	A
73	B	47	E	20	D	23	A
102	E	45	E	24	B	20	A
95	B	48	A	47	B	74	C
22	C	99	D	2	E	96	B
77	E	75	A	48	D	99	E

Work as fast as you can without making errors. Do the questions down one column before you go to the next column. Do not skip around the list.

In this test, do not waste time going over the marks you make. Once over with firm pressure is enough as long as the mark is clear and almost fills the space. If you make an error, erase it completely, because actual test papers will be scored by electric scoring machines.

Sample Answer Sheet

All competitors will take the two tests having questions like the samples shown on pages 62 and 63. In addition, some competitors will take a typing test of somewhat the same type as the one shown below. Some competitors will take another test having questions like the samples given on page 65. The examination announcement will indicate which tests will be given for various positions.

In the typewriting test you are to show how well you know the alphabetic keyboard.

Set your *marginal stop* for a left-hand margin of about 2½ inches. You will type only *one column, down the center* of your page.

Set your machine to *double space* between lines. Allow one space between words; use the space bar for this purpose.

If you notice that you have made an error, double space and begin the same line again. *Do not make any erasures* or other corrections.

As soon as you have typed a line correctly, double space and begin the next line. When taking the examination, if you finish all the lines before time is called, begin copying the list a second time.

Since the machines that some appointees will operate do not make any difference between capital letters and small letters, it makes *no difference whether you use capitals* in this test. You may type a line all in capitals or all in small letters, or in any combination. Similarly, although there is no punctuation in the list, you will not be charged with an error if you happen to type a comma or a period.

If you were copying from a list like the Practice List at the bottom of this page and you abandoned incorrect lines, you would be credited for having the first three lines of the list correctly typed if your paper looked like this—

Nesbit ED ELECTRICIAN Transit Belmont

Foley Jno survv

Foley John

foley jno surveyor bayside co. norfolk

Lewis Don lineman HydroPower B

LEWIS DON LINEMAN HYDRO POWER BEDFORD

PRACTICE LIST

Nesbit Ed electrician Transit Belmont	Proctor S drycleaning service manager
Foley Jno surveyor Bayside Co Norfolk	Adam Fred assembler and bench grinder
Lewis Don lineman Hydro Power Bedford	Brown Cal automobile mechanic skilled
Burkert T miner Penn Colliery Glencoe	Wetmore S demonstrator office devices
Nesbitt F welder United Steel Phoenix	Loman Leo calculating machine repairs

In the examination, you will be given these directions and time to copy the Practice List in order to exercise your fingers and to see that your machine is working properly. For the actual test, you will be given a longer list and be allowed 10 minutes for making correct copies of as many lines as you can.

Some competitors will take a test having questions similar to those shown below. Each question has five suggested answers, lettered A, B, C, D, and E. For each question, decide which one of the suggested answers is the best answer to the question. Then, on the Sample Answer Sheet, find the number that is the same as the number of the question and blacken the space between the dotted lines just below the letter that is the same as the letter of your answer.

1. A supervisor is planning a discussion with his workers as part of a training course. To which one of the following factors should he give most attention?

   A) preparing in advance questions that will promote the discussion of important matters
   B) getting as many men as possible to attend the meeting
   C) inviting only those workers who do not hesitate to speak in a group
   D) making certain that the meeting will not drag out too long
   E) selecting about six men to make speeches which they will prepare in advance

2. A group of employees has recently been hired to perform simple, routine tasks. The use of which one of the following statements in the training of the group would be most likely, in general, to create interest in this work?

   A) emphasis upon the pleasant working conditions and special services which the company offers its employees
   B) explanation of the inspection system by which all work is reviewed in order to make certain that it conforms with requirements
   C) demonstration that the work is extremely simple and therefore there can be no excuse for failure to perform it properly
   D) a frank statement that the work is monotonous but must be done even if it is not interesting
   E) explanation of the relationship and the importance of the work to the total work of the organization

SAMPLE ANSWER SHEET							CORRECT ANSWERS TO SAMPLE QUESTIONS				
	A	B	C	D	E		A	B	C	D	E
1	‖	‖	‖	‖	‖	1	▌	‖	‖	‖	‖
	A	B	C	D	E		A	B	C	D	E
2	‖	‖	‖	‖	‖	2	‖	‖	‖	‖	▌

Electronic Computer Operator

The following sample questions show the kinds of questions in the examination and the way to answer the questions.

Answers to questions are to be marked on the Sample Answer Sheet. The answer sheet has numbers matching the numbers of the test questions. Beside each number on the answer sheet are spaces lettered A, B, C, D, and E. The suggested answers to each question are also lettered. Select the correct answer to each question and mark the answer sheet in the space under the letter of the correct answer to that question.

In each of the two following questions, at the left there is a series of seven letters which follow some definite order or pattern, and at the right there are five sets of two letters each. Look at the letters in the series and determine what the order is; then, from the suggested answers at the right, select the set that gives the next two letters in the series. Next to the question number on the Sample Answer Sheet blacken the space that has the same letter as the set you have chosen.

1. X C X D X E X   A) F X   B) F G   c) X F   D) E F   E) X G

In question 1 only A could be the answer because the series consists of X's alternating with letters in alphabetical order. Sample question 2 is done in the same way.

2. A R C S E T G   A) H I   B) H U   c) U J   D) U I   E) I V

Each of the next three questions has two boxes at the left. The symbols in the first box are like each other in some way, and the symbols in the second box are like each other in some way. But whatever it is that makes the symbols alike in one box makes them different from those in the other box. There is a question mark in the second box to indicate that a symbol is missing. You are to choose from the lettered symbols in the third box the one which best fits into the second box.

3.

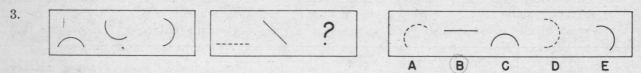

Look at question 3. In this question, all the symbols in the first box are curved lines; in the second box they are straight lines. Of the answer choices, only B is straight, so B should be marked on the Sample Answer Sheet. (Note that some of the lines are "dotted"; but this is not the *difference* between the two boxes, for if it were it would also be the *likeness* between the symbols in the second box—they would both be dotted lines.) Now do questions 4 and 5.

4.

5.

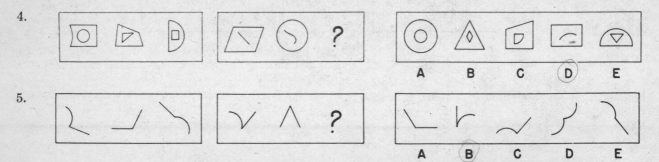

	Sample Answer Sheet		

	A	B	C	D	E
1					
2					
3					
4					
5					

	Correct Answers to Sample Questions		

	A	B	C	D	E
1	▮				
2				▮	
3		▮			
4				▮	
5		▮			

NOTE: There is not supposed to be a *series* or progression in these symbol questions. If you look for a progression in the first box and try to find the missing figure to fill out a similar progression in the second box, you will be wasting time. For example, look at question 3. A competitor who saw that both boxes had a horizontal figure followed by an oblique one might try to find a vertical figure to match the last one in the first box. If he chose D he would be missing the real point of the question. Remember, look for a *likeness* within each box and a *difference* between the two boxes.

Answer questions like 6 through 12 in the following way:

Assume that a stockroom floor is divided into three sections—West, Central, and East. There are a number of bins in each of these sections. Each bin is numbered and holds one particular type of stock item which has the same number as the bin in which it is kept. For example, bin number 3 holds a supply of stock item number 3. The bins and stock items are located in the three sections as follows:

LOCATION PLAN

Section	Bin and Item Numbers
West	1–10
Central	11–20
East	21–30

Each question contains several numbers, which are the stock numbers of the items to be taken from the bins to fill an order. To answer each question, decide which section or sections contain the bins from which the items are to be taken. On the answer sheet, mark

- A if the order is filled from only ONE section
- B if the order is filled from the WEST and CENTRAL sections only
- C if the order is filled from the WEST and EAST sections only
- D if the order is filled from the CENTRAL and EAST sections only
- E if the order is filled from ALL THREE sections

Now do the following sample questions and mark your answers on the Sample Answer Sheet.

6. 26, 28, 29
The answer to question 6 is A, because all three items in this order are found in only ONE section.

7. 2, 12, 25, 29
The answer here is E, because items must be taken from ALL THREE sections to fill this order.

8. 12, 15, 27
Here D is the answer, because items must be taken from the CENTRAL and EAST sections.

9. 2, 8, 21, 25

10. 19, 20, 21

From time to time bins, with the items they hold, will be moved from one section to another. Also, items may become unavailable and other items will have to be substituted for them. Write the Location Plan on scratch paper, and make a record of all changes in the Plan.

Change I. The following shifts are made in the stock:

Bins and items 11 and 12 are moved from the Central section to the West section.

Bin and item 21 are moved from the East section to the Central section.

The following substitutions are to be made:

Discontinued	Replaced by
Item 15	Item 25
Item 27	Item 3

Your changed Location Plan should read:

Section	Bin and Item Numbers		
West	~~1–10~~	1–12	
Central	~~11–20~~	13–21	For 15 use 25
East	~~21–30~~	22–30	For 27 use 3

After you have made these changes, answer questions 11 and 12 on the basis of the changed Location Plan.

11. 2, 11, 22, 23

12. 15, 24, 29

The answer to question 11 is C, because, in accordance with the above changes, the order will be filled from the WEST and EAST sections.

The answer to question 12 is A, because Item 25 will be used for Item 15 and the order will, therefore, be filled from only ONE section.

Now compare your answers with the Correct Answers to Sample Questions.

Sample Answer Sheet

	A	B	C	D	E
6					
7					
8					
9					
10					
11					
12					

Correct Answers to Sample Questions

	A	B	C	D	E
6	■				
7					■
8				■	
9			■		
10			■		
11			■		
12	■				

Telephone Operator

The following sample questions show the types and approximate difficulty of the questions that will be used in the written tests. They show also how the questions are to be answered by those who take the tests.

Read the directions below; then look over the sample questions carefully and try to answer them. Each question has five suggested answers lettered A, B, C, D, and E. Decide which one is the best answer to the question. Then, on the Sample Answer Sheet, find the number that is the same as the number of the question and make a solid black mark in the space between the dotted lines just below the letter that is the same as the letter of the answer you have selected.

In each question like samples 1 and 2, find the one city name, if any, that is spelled correctly. On the Sample Answer Sheet, blacken the space between the dotted lines under the letter that is the same as the letter of your choice. If none of the suggested spellings is correct, blacken space E.

1. A) Mobile, Ala.
   B) Brocton, Mass.
   C) Yeork, Pa.
   D) Sou Falls, S. Dak.
   E) none of these

2. A) Brookelin, N. Y.
   B) Alambra, Calif.
   C) Attlanta, Ga.
   D) Joplinn, Mo.
   E) none of these

Since none of the city names in 2 is spelled correctly, your answer should be E.

Each question like sample 3 contains five sentences. Decide which one of the sentences is preferable with respect to grammar and usage such as would be suitable for a telephone operator. Then blacken the proper space on the answer sheet.

3. A) I haven't no report on your call yet.
   B) I had ought to receive a report on your call soon.
   C) Can I ring you when I have a report on your call?
   D) Do you want for me to ring as soon as I receive a report on your call?
   E) I do not have any report on your call yet.

For each question like sample 4, read the paragraph and then answer the question that follows it.

4. (*Reading*) "Alertness and attentiveness are qualities essential for success as a telephone operator. The work the operator performs often takes careful attention under conditions of stress."

The quotation best supports the statement that a telephone operator

   A) always works under great strain
   B) cannot be successful unless she memorizes many telephone numbers
   C) must be trained before she can render good service
   D) must be able to work under difficulties
   E) performs more difficult work than do Office Machine Operators

---

Compare your answers with those given in the Correct Answers for Sample Questions, at the right.

Sample Answer Sheet						Correct Answers to Sample Questions 1–4				
	A	B	C	D	E	A	B	C	D	E
1						▮				
2										▮
3										▮
4									▮	

Questions like samples 5 through 15 are to test the accuracy with which you hear numbers like telephone numbers and make correct connections for the numbers that you hear. The examiner will give you a number as the first question, then pause for you to answer the question, then give you a number as the second question, and so on. For almost every number that the examiner gives, you have that number, below, together with three wrong numbers. You are to pick out the number you hear and make a check mark at the right of it. If the number is not one of the four listed for the question, check "none of these."

Do not ask the examiner to repeat any number. If you miss one, try to get the next question. In the first sample, the answer has been checked for you.

Part of a list such as the examiner would use in reading these sample questions is shown at the right.

SAMPLE QUESTIONS

5. A) 1 3 4 4
    B) 3 1 3 4
    C) 3 1 4 4 ∨
    D) 4 1 3 3
    E) none of these

6. A) 2 6 8 7 ✓
    B) 2 7 6 8
    C) 2 8 6 7
    D) 2 8 7 6
    E) none of these

7. A) 1 0 0 9 3
    B) 1 0 9 0 3
    C) 1 9 0 0 3
    D) 1 9 3 0 0 ✓
    E) none of these

8. A) 6 2 3 7 5
    B) 6 7 2 3 5 ✓
    C) 6 7 2 5 3
    D) 7 6 2 3 5
    E) none of these

9. A) 1 5 5 9 6
    B) 5 1 1 6 9
    C) 5 1 9 9 6
    D) 5 5 1 9 6
    E) none of these ∨

10. A) 3 2 8 9 7
    B) 3 8 2 9 7 ✓
    C) 3 8 9 2 7
    D) 8 3 2 9 7
    E) none of these

11. A) 4 1 3 6 2
    B) 4 1 6 2 3
    C) 4 1 6 3 2 ✓
    D) 4 6 1 3 2
    E) none of these

12. A) 6 6 8 1
    B) 8 1 6 6
    C) 8 8 6 1
    D) 8 0 6 6 1
    E) none of these ✓

13. A) 5 7 6 8 5
    B) 5 7 6 8 9 ✓
    C) 5 7 8 6 9
    D) 7 5 6 8 9
    E) none of these

14. A) 4 7 2 8 ✓
    B) 4 7 8 2
    C) 4 0 7 2 8
    D) 4 7 2 0 8
    E) none of these

15. A) 3 6 2 8
    B) 3 8 2 8
    C) 3 8 2 6 8
    D) 8 3 6 2 8 ✓
    E) none of these

Sample Examiner's List

The rates at which the examiner is to read are shown by the 10-second markings at the right. He should read each number as rapidly as he would tell an operator what phone number he wants, and then he should pause before reading the next. For example, in the first 10 seconds he should read 3144, pause, read 2687, pause, and be ready to begin 19300.

3 1 4 4
2 6 8 7   10 sec.

1 9 3 0 0
6 7 2 3 5   20 sec.

5 1 1 9 6
3 8 2 9 7
4 1 6 3 2   30 sec.

8 6 6 1
5 7 6 8 9
4 7 2 8
8 3 6 2 8   40 sec.

Sample Answer Sheet | Correct Answers to Sample Questions 5 – 15

On the Sample Answer Sheet on the right, you are to show what answer you chose for each question. Do this by blackening the space between the dotted lines under the letter that is the same as the letter of your choice. Be accurate, because a check mark beside a correct answer on the test booklet will not do you any good unless you blacken the same answer on the answer sheet. The answer for sample 5 has been blackened to show you how it is done.

Questions like the Sample Test List below are to show how well your eyes and hand work together You will be given a list like the one below, and an answer sheet. The list consists of several columns of numbers with letters. The numbers in the list refer to the numbers on the Sample Answer Sheet. The letters refer to the answer positions A, B, C, D, and E. For each number and letter in the list, find the same number on the answer sheet and blacken the space for the letter. Thus, the first question is 5 2 E, and 52 on the answer sheet is blackened in space E as a sample. The next question is 2 6 B, so find 26 on the answer sheet and blacken space B.

Continue with the other questions in the same way, marking on the Sample Answer Sheet below the space for the letter that goes with the question number. For some of the numbers on the answer sheet you will be told to mark more than one letter and for some numbers you will not mark any letter at all.

It will help you to notice how the answer sheet is arranged. (For these sample questions, the center of the sheet is omitted.) Each column has spaces for 25 numbers, so the second column begins with 26, the third with 51, and so forth.

Work as fast as you can without making errors. Do the questions down one column of the list before you go to the next column. Do not skip around the list.

Do not waste time going over the marks you make. Once over with firm pressure is enough as long as the mark is clear and almost fills the space. If you make an error, erase it completely, because papers will be scored by an electric scoring machine.

Sample Test List

5 2	E		7 3	B		7 6	D
2 6	B		1 0 2	E		1 2 1	D
9 8	D		9 5	B		2 3	D
2 7	A		2 2	C		1 0 0	C
1 2 0	C		7 7	E		1 2 4	D
7 2	E		2 6	D		4 7	E
1 0 1	B		1 2 2	A		4 5	E
1 2 1	B		7 2	B		4 8	A
4 6	B		7 0	C		9 9	D
2 5	D		5 0	B		7 5	A

Sample Answer Sheet

	A B C D E		A B C D E		A B C D E		A B C D E		A B C D E
1		26		51		76		101	
2		27		52		77		102	

	A B C D E		A B C D E		A B C D E		A B C D E		A B C D E
20		45		70		95		120	
21		46		71		96		121	
22		47		72		97		122	
23		48		73		98		123	
24		49		74		99		124	
25		50		75		100		125	

TESTS FOR STENOGRAPHER
AND TYPIST EXAMINATION

GENERAL TEST *(Both Typists and Stenographers take this):*

The following samples show the kinds and approximate difficulty of questions that will be used in the General Test; they show also how the questions are to be answered by those who take the examination. Look over the questions carefully and try to answer them. Record your answers on the Sample Answer Sheet below. Then compare them with the Answers to Sample Questions.

Each sample question has several suggested answers, lettered A, B, C, etc. Decide which one is the best answer to the question. Then, on the Sample Answer Sheet, find the number that is the same as the number of the question and blacken the space between the dotted lines just below the letter that is the same as the letter of the answer you have selected.

1. *Authentic* means most nearly
   A) detailed
   B) reliable ✓
   C) valuable
   D) technical
   E) practical

For sample 2, read the paragraph and answer the question that follows it.

2. *(Reading)* "Just as the procedure of a collection department must be clear-cut and definite, the steps being taken with the sureness of a skilled chess player, so the various paragraphs of a collection letter must show clear organization, giving evidence of a mind that, from the beginning, has had a specific end in view."

The quotation best supports the statement that a collection letter should always
   A) show a spirit of sportsmanship
   B) be divided into several paragraphs
   C) express confidence in the debtor
   D) be brief, but courteous
   E) be carefully planned ✓

For each question like samples 3 and 4, find the correct spelling of the word. If none of the spellings is correct, blacken the space under D on the answer sheet.

3. A) occassion
   B) occasion ✓
   C) ocassion
   D) none of these

4. A) amature
   B) amatur
   C) amatuer
   D) none of these ✓

Select the sentence that is preferable with respect to grammar and usage such as would be suitable in a formal letter or report.

5. A) They do not ordinarily present these kind of reports in detail like this.
   B) Reports like this is not generally given in such great detail.
   C) A report of this kind is not hardly ever given in such detail as this one.
   D) This report is more detailed than what such reports ordinarily are.
   E) A report of this kind is not ordinarily presented in such detail as this one.

If the sample questions are correctly answered, the Sample Answer Sheet will be marked as shown in the Answers to Sample Questions.

Sample Answer Sheet						Answers to Sample Questions				
	A	B	C	D	E	A	B	C	D	E
1							■			
2										■
3							■			
4									■	
5										■

(For PLAIN COPY, which is also taken by both Typists and Stenographers, see page 74.)

STENOGRAPHY *(Only Stenographers take this):*

A practice dictation and a test exercise will be dictated at the rate of 80 words a minute.

The sample printed on page 72 shows the length and the difficulty of material to be used by the examiner in giving the dictation. If each pair of lines is dictated in exactly 10 seconds, the dictation will be at the rate of 80 words a minute. Have someone dictate the exercise to you at the rate shown, so that you may have some idea as to how well prepared you are to take the examination. The periods should be dictated; the commas should not be dictated, but the passage should be read with the expression that the commas indicate.

Sample Dictation:

In recent years there has been a great increase in the need for capable stenographers,	10 sec.
not only in business offices but also in public service agencies, both	20 sec.
governmental and private. (Period) The high schools and business schools in many parts of	30 sec.
the country have tried to meet this need by offering complete commercial courses. (Period)	40 sec.
The increase in the number of persons who are enrolled in these courses shows that	50 sec.
students have become aware of the great demand for stenographers. (Period) A person	1 min.
who wishes to secure employment in this field must be able to take dictation	10 sec.
and to transcribe the notes with both speed and accuracy. (Period) The rate of	20 sec.
speed at which dictation is given in most offices is somewhat less than that of	30 sec.
ordinary speech. (Period) Thus, one who has had a thorough training in shorthand	40 sec.
should have little trouble in taking complete notes. (Period) Skill in taking dictation	50 sec.
at a rapid rate is of slight value if the stenographer cannot also type her notes	2 min.
in proper form. (Period) A businessman sometimes dictates a rough draft of the ideas	10 sec.
he wishes to have included in a letter, and leaves to the stenographer the task	20 sec.
of putting them in good form. (Period) For this reason, knowledge of the essentials	30 sec.
of grammar and of composition is as important as the ability to take	40 sec.
dictation. (Period) In addition, a stenographer should be familiar with the sources of	50 sec.
general information that are most likely to be used in office work. (Period)	3 min.

On page 73, the TRANSCRIPT and WORD LIST for part of the above dictation are similar to those each competitor will receive for the dictation exercise. Many words have been left out of the TRANSCRIPT.   Compare your notes with it and, when you come to a blank space in the TRANSCRIPT, decide what word (or words) belongs in the space.   For example, you will find that the word "there" belongs in blank No. 1.

Look at the WORD LIST to see whether you can find the missing word.   Notice what letter (A, B, C, or D) is printed beside it, and write that letter in the blank.   For example, the word "there" is listed, followed by the letter *C*.   We have already written *C* in blank No. 1 to show you how you are to record your choice.   Now decide what belongs in each of the other blanks.   You are to write *E* if the exact answer is NOT listed.   You may also write the word (or words), or the shorthand for it, if you wish.   The same choice may belong in more than one blank.

ALPHABETIC WORD LIST

Write *E* if the answer is NOT listed.

advertising—A	many—D
agencies—D	marked—A
almost—C	met—A
also—C	most—C
and—D	need—D
business—B	offering—D
but—A	only—B
claimed—B	opening—A
colleges—C	parts—A
complete—B	private—C
country—A	schools—D
demand—B	sections—B
especially—D	the need—A
even—B	their—D
government—B	there—C
great—C	to complete—C
has been—D	to meet—C
high schools—A	to offer—B
in—C	trained—C
in government—A	tried—A

TRANSCRIPT

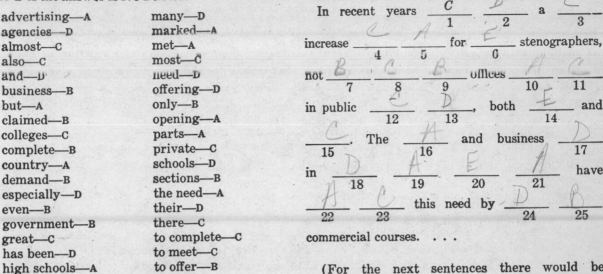

In recent years ___C___ ___D___ a ___C___
              1   2   3

increase ___C___ ___A___ for ___E___ stenographers,
        4   5   6

not ___B___ ___C___ ___B___ offices ___A___ ___C___
     7   8   9   10   11

in public ___E___ ___D___, both ___E___ and
         12   13   14

___C___. The ___A___ and business ___D___
 15   16   17

in ___D___ ___A___ ___E___ ___A___ have
    18   19   20   21

___A___ ___C___ this need by ___D___ ___B___
 22   23   24   25

commercial courses. . . .

(For the next sentences there would be another word list, if the entire sample dictation were transcribed.)

You will be given a special answer sheet like the sample at the left, below, on which your answers can be scored by an electric machine. Each number on the answer sheet stands for the blank with the same number in the transcript. Blacken the space between the dotted lines below the letter that is the same as the letter you wrote in the transcript. If you have not finished writing letters in the blanks in the transcript, or if you wish to make sure that you have lettered them correctly, *you may continue to use your notes after you begin marking the answer sheet.*

Answer Sheet for Sample Transcript

Correct Answers for Sample Transcript

COPYING FROM PLAIN COPY (*Both Typists and Stenographers take this*):

The sample given below shows the kind of material that competitors must copy. See whether you can copy it twice in 10 minutes and how many errors your copies contain. Competitors will be required to meet a certain minimum in accuracy as well as in speed. Above the minimum speed and accuracy requirements, accuracy counts twice as much as speed in determining whether the competitor is eligible on Copying from Plain Copy.

Space, paragraph, spell, punctuate, capitalize, and begin and end each line precisely as shown in the exercise.

In the examination you will have 10 minutes in which to make copies of the test exercise, keeping in mind that your eligibility will depend upon accuracy as well as speed. Each time you complete the exercise, simply double space once and begin again. Use both sides of the paper.

Your typing must go a little over halfway through a second copy of the exercise to make you eligible in speed. With that minimum speed, your paper must not have more than 9 errors. The number of errors permitted increases with the amount typed.

> This practice exercise is similar in length and diffi-
> culty to the one that you will be required to typewrite for
> the Plain Copy Test. You are to space, capitalize, punctu-
> ate, spell, and begin and end each line precisely as in the
> copy. Directions regarding erasures will be given when you
> take the Plain Copy Test. Follow carefully all directions
> given at the time of the examination. Practice typewriting
> this material on scratch paper until the examiner tells you
> to stop, remembering that for this examination it is more
> important to typewrite accurately than to typewrite rapidly.

> There are several ways in which a typist can prepare
> herself to be an efficient worker in a business office.
> First of all, she should know her typewriter thoroughly, the
> location of all the keys, even those used infrequently, and
> the use of the marginal stops and extra devices furnished on
> modern typewriters. In addition to being completely familiar
> with the typewriter, she should be equipped with knowledge
> of the correct spellings and correct use of a large number
> of words. Although a letter has been typewritten neatly,
> without omissions or insertions, it will still be considered
> unsatisfactory if it contains any misspellings whatsoever.

TESTS FOR THE POSTAL SERVICE

Postal Service employees are under civil service competitive regulations, but they have a separate classification scale as to hours, pay rates, days of leave, and so on. Most postal employees receive time-and-a-half for overtime and a 10 percent differential for night work. The salaries of full-time employees, and the hourly rates of substitutes, are fixed according to duties performed and length of service. Promotions in grade are given regularly for satisfactory service.

Written examinations are given for many Postal Service positions, including Substitute Clerk-Substitute Carrier. Employees normally enter the Postal Service as substitutes. Tests for the positions mentioned are illustrated on the next two pages.

A general test like those described earlier in the "Examination Forecast" may be given for other Postal Service positions, except that the questions deal with Postal Service duties. Examples of a reading question based on Postal Service rules, and an arithmetic question dealing with postal clerk's duties, are given here.

1. (*Reading*) "Postmasters may authorize their assistants to sign their names to such reports, letters, and papers as are not specially required to be signed by the postmaster himself. The signature should be: 'John Doe, postmaster, by Richard Roe, assistant postmaster.' The name of the postmaster may be written or stamped, but the signature of the assistant shall be in ink."

According to the quotation,

A) an assistant postmaster who signs for the postmaster should include his own title in the signature ✓

B) any postmaster's assistant has authority to sign official papers for him

C) no authority delegated to the assistant postmaster can be redelegated by him

D) requisitions must bear the personal signature of the postmaster

E) the assistant postmaster must write the postmaster's signature with pen and ink when he signs for the postmaster

B is not the answer because these instructions indicate that the postmaster may not have given any such authority. C is not the answer because there is nothing in these instructions to show that an assistant postmaster cannot delegate authority to perform other tasks. D is not the answer because these instructions do not indicate that requisitions are among those papers which are "specially required to be signed by the postmaster himself." Since these instructions indicate that the postmaster's name may be stamped, E is not the answer. A is the answer because the illustration of the proper form to be used includes the words "assistant postmaster," the title of the signer in this case; so the answer sheet is marked under A.

2. If a patron offered a $20 bill in payment of postage on one parcel for which the charge is $2.31 and on two other parcels on each of which the charge is $5.08, how much change should he receive?
A) $7.39
B) $7.53 ✓
C) $9.70
D) $10.30
E) none of these

On the next two pages are practice tests like those given in the examinations for Substitute Clerk-Substitute Carrier. Completely new lists of addresses, sorting schemes, and keys are used on the examination itself.

These tests are strictly timed by the person giving the examination and the score depends on the *number* of *correct* answers within the time allowed. Some tests are purposely made long enough so that not every competitor can finish, in order to see which competitors work fastest.

POSTAL SERVICE

Address Test

This is a sample of the test in which you will be given addresses to compare.

Mark each answer on the Sample Answer Sheet in the row that has the same number as the number of the question.

For Part I of the test, mark the space on your answer sheet under A if the two addresses are exactly *alike* in every way. Mark the space under B if they are NOT *alike* in every way.

For Part II, go back to number 1 on the answer sheet, but this time mark the space under D if the two addresses are exactly *alike* in every way and mark the space under E if they are NOT *alike* in every way.

When you have finished the test, you should have marks in columns A and B filled in for Part I and columns D and E filled in for Part II. There should be no marks in column C.

The answers to these sample questions are shown on the Sample Answer Sheet at the right.

PART I

1. . . . . . 2134 S 20th St   2134 S 20th St

Since the first two addresses are exactly alike, A is marked on the Sample Answer Sheet.

2. . . . . 4608 N Warnock St   4806 N Warnock St
3. . . . . 1202 W Girard Dr   1202 W Girard Rd
4. . . . . 3120 S Harcourt St   3120 S Harcourt St
5. . . . . 4618 W Addison St   4618 E Addison St
6. . . . . 39–B Parkway Rd   39–D Parkway Rd
7. . . . . 6425 N Delancey   6425 N Delancey
8. . . . . 5407 Columbia Rd   5407 Columbia Rd
9. . . . . 2106 Southern Ave   2106 Southern Ave
10. . . . . Highfalls N C   Highlands N C
11. . . . . 2873 Pershing Dr   2873 Pershing Dr
12. . . . . 1329 N H Ave NW   1329 N J Ave NW
13. . . . . 1316 N Quinn St Arl   1316 N Quinn St Alex
14. . . . . 7507 Wyngate Dr   7505 Wyngate Dr
15. . . . . 2918 Colesville Rd   2918 Colesville Rd
16. . . . . 2071 Belvedere Dr   2071 Belvedere Dr
17. . . . . Palmer Wash   Palmer Mich
18. . . . . 2106 16th St SW   2106 16th St SW

PART II

1. . . . . 2207 Markland Ave   2207 Markham Ave
2. . . . . 5345 16th St NW   5345 16th St NE
3. . . . . 239 Summit Pl   239 Summit Pl
4. . . . . 152 Continental Bldg   152 Continental Blvd
5. . . . . 8092 13th Rd S Aberdeen   8029 13th Rd S Aberdeen
6. . . . . 3906 Queensbury Rd   3906 Queensbury Rd
7. . . . . 4719 Linnean Ave NW   4719 Linnean Ave NW
8. . . . . Bradford Me   Bradley Me
9. . . . . Parrott Ga   Parrott Va
10. . . . . K–42 Lowell House   K–42 Lowell House
11. . . . . 6929 W 135 Place   6929 W 135 Plaza
12. . . . . 5143 Somerset Cir   5143 Somerset Cir
13. . . . . 8501 Kennedy St   8501 Kennedy St
14. . . . . 2164 W McLean Ave   2164 W McLean Ave
15. . . . . 7186 E St NW   7186 F St NW
16. . . . . 2121 Beechcrest Rd   2121 Beechcroft Rd
17. . . . . 3609 E Montrose St   3609 E Montrose St
18. . . . . 324 S Alvadero St   324 S Alverado St

The material on the next page is reprinted from the sample questions that are given in the examination room. If you apply for a Postal Service examination that uses this test, you will receive a form containing a longer practice test similar to this.

FOLLOWING INSTRUCTIONS—SAMPLE TEST

Directions: Read carefully.

Follow the directions in this sample carefully so that when you take the examination you will remember *how* to do the test.

Finding train numbers:

Below is a SORTING SCHEME and KEY. In the SORTING SCHEME is a list of post offices. Each post office is followed by a letter. (For example, after "Guilford" is the letter "F." This "F" refers to the KEY at the right which reads "F Atlantic 6." Mail for Guilford is sent by way of Atlantic on Train 6.) Always begin with a post office in the SORTING SCHEME and find the train number in the KEY.

SORTING SCHEME

Atlantic	F	Melfa	G	Shields	J			
Bloxam	T	Nandua	M	Silva	O			
Greta	O	Nelson	F	Tangier	J			
Groton	K	Oak Hill	H	Tasley	G			
Guilford	F	Onley	S	Withams	P			
Hopeton	K	Painter	I					
Hopkins	I	Parksley	S					
Kane	G	Paulson	H					
Keller	J	Quimby	U					
Mears	U	Sanford	S					

KEY

Mail sent by way of—

F	Atlantic	6
G	Melfa	2
H	Oak Hill	7
I	Hopkins	3
J	Tangier	8
K	Hopeton	5
M	Painter	
O	Greta	9
P	Keller	
S	Sanford	4
T	Groton	
U	Parksley	

Do not make any marks in this SORTING SCHEME or KEY before you read the directions below.

BEGIN HERE. Do not skip any part of these directions. Work with a pencil so that if you want more practice you can erase the work.

Completing the KEY:

Look at "Painter" in the KEY. It is not followed by a number. Write after it the letter which you find after Painter in the SORTING SCHEME. Your KEY should now read "M Painter I." Find the letters after Keller, Groton, and Parksley in the SORTING SCHEME and write them after those offices in the KEY.

Recording Answers:

In each question below a post office name is followed by five train numbers. Use the SORTING SCHEME and KEY to find the correct train number. Then see what column (A, B, C, D, E) the correct train number is in, and mark this letter on your Sample Answer Sheet on the next page.

For Example.—For the first post office below, Painter, you are to find the correct train number. In the SORTING SCHEME, Painter is followed by the letter "I." This tells you to look at "I" in the KEY, which reads "Hopkins 3," and means that mail for Painter is routed by way of Hopkins on Train 3. The number 3 after Painter, below, is in column B, so, to mark your answer, you should blacken the space under B for question 1 on the Sample Answer Sheet.

Question No.	Post Office	A	B	C	D	E	(Sample Answer Sheet columns)
1	Painter	2	3	5	7	9	(Train numbers)
2	Paulson	3	4	5	7	8	
3	Mears	2	3	4	5	7	
4	Kane	2	3	4	5	6	

Mail for Mears is sent by way of U Parksley through S Sanford on Train 4, which is in column C, so you should blacken the space under C on the Sample Answer Sheet for question 3.

Making Changes in the SORTING SCHEME and KEY:

Never put numbers in the SORTING SCHEME. Make changes from the Bulletins *exactly* as they direct you to.

Never cross out names in the SORTING SCHEME.

> **Bulletin No. 1:**
> ### CHANGES IN ROUTING
> (When changing SORTING SCHEME change KEY. too, if the name is in KEY. Note that the names in the SORTING SCHEME are in alphabetical order, but those in the KEY are not.)
>
> | | |
> |---|---|
> | Silva by way of I. | Painter by way of K. |
> | Shields by way of O. | Change KEY G to read: G Train 10. |
> | Guilford by way of P. | Melfa by way of H. |

To make the change for Silva, cross out the "O" after Silva in the SORTING SCHEME and write "*I.*" Now your SORTING SCHEME for Silva should read "Silva Ø I." This means that mail for Silva is now sent by way of I, that is, through Hopkins on Train 3.

To make the change for Painter, cross out the I after Painter in the SORTING SCHEME and write "*K.*" Then find Painter in the KEY and change the I after it to K. Mail for Painter will now go through K, that is, through Hopeton on Train 5. To change KEY G, cross out "Melfa 2" and write "*Train 10.*" Make the other changes ordered.

Mark on your Sample Answer Sheet the space for the letter showing the train on which you should put mail for:

Question No.		A	B	C	D	E
5	Tasley	2	3	7	8	10
6	Nandua	2	3	5	8	9
7	Withams	4	6	8	9	10

In answering question 6 for Nandua, did you start to mark C for *question* 5 because you were thinking of *Train 5*? Be sure to mark the right question on the answer sheet.

> **Bulletin No. 2:**
>
> | OFFICES ESTABLISHED (Add to SORTING SCHEME) | CHANGES IN ROUTING (When changing SORTING SCHEME change KEY, too, if the name is in KEY.) |
> |---|---|
> | | |
> | Saxis by way of F. | Paulson by way of G. |
> | Talbot by way of H. | Parksley by way of O. |
> | | Change KEY J to read: J Tangier 2. |

To add Saxis to the SORTING SCHEME, write "*Saxis F*" on the first line at the end of the SORTING SCHEME. To change KEY J, cross out 8 after J Tangier and write "*2.*"

Make the other changes ordered.

Mark on your Sample Answer Sheet the space for the letter showing the train on which you should put mail for:

Question No.		A	B	C	D	E
8	Mears	4	5	7	9	10
9	Silva	2	3	5	7	9
10	Guilford	2	6	8	9	10
11	Painter	2	3	4	5	6
12	Parksley	3	4	5	7	9
13	Shields	2	3	5	7	9
14	Talbot	3	4	7	9	10
15	Melfa	2	3	5	7	10

NOTE.—If you have chosen 4 for Mears, you have not made the change for Parksley in both SORTING SCHEME and KEY. Mail for Mears should be sent through U Parksley O by way of O Greta on Train 9.

Bulletin No. 3:

OFFICES ESTABLISHED (Add to SORTING SCHEME)	CHANGES IN ROUTING (When changing SORTING SCHEME change KEY, too, if the name is in KEY.)
Somerset by way of G. Elkton by way of W.	Oak Hill by way of W. (Be sure to change Oak Hill in the KEY.) Add to KEY: W Train 12. Parksley by way of K. Change KEY F to read: F Atlantic 3.

To make the addition to the KEY, write *"W Train 12"* on the first line at the end of the KEY.

Mark on your Sample Answer Sheet the space for the letter showing the train on which you should put mail for:

Question No.		A	B	C	D	E
16	Parksley	4	5	7	8	9
17	Talbot	3	6	7	10	12
18	Somerset	2	4	8	10	12
19	Saxis	3	4	5	6	8
20	Paulson	2	4	7	10	12
21	Elkton	2	4	7	10	12

Bulletin No. 4:

CHANGES IN ROUTING (When changing SORTING SCHEME change KEY, too, if the name is in KEY.)	
Painter by way of O. Hopkins by way of J. Kane by way of P.	Change KEY S to read: S Melfa. (Cross out Sanford 4 in the KEY.) Sanford by way of H.

To complete the change for KEY S, you must refer to the SORTING SCHEME to find the letter which should be written after Melfa.

Mark on your Sample Answer Sheet the space for the letter showing the train on which you should put mail for:

Question No.		A	B	C	D	E
22	Sanford	2	4	7	10	12
23	Nandua	3	5	8	9	10
24	Hopkins	2	3	4	6	8
25	Kane	2	4	6	8	10

NOTE.—If you have chosen Train 5 for Nandua, you have not made the change for Painter in both SORTING SCHEME and KEY.

When you have completed the sample questions, check your work with the completed SORTING SCHEME and KEY, and Correct Answers to Sample Questions.

SORTING SCHEME

Atlantic	F	Melfa	S H	Shields	Y O
Bloxam	T	Nandua	M	Silva	G I
Greta	O	Nelson	F	Tangier	H
Groton	K	Oak Hill	R W	Tasley	G
Guilford	Y P	Onley	S	Withams	P
Hopeton	K	Painter	E H O	Sadie	F
Hopkins	P J	Parksley	E O K	Talbot	H
Kane	S P	Paulson	H G	Somerset	G
Keller	J	Quinby	U	Elkton	W
Mears	U	Sanford	S H		

KEY

Mail sent by way of—

F Atlantic	K 3
G Melfa	2 Train 10
H Oak Hill	Y W
I Hopkins	S J
J Tangier	E 2
K Hopeton	5
M Painter	E H O
O Greta	9
P Keller	J
S Sanford	4 Melfa H
T Groton	K
U Parksley	E G K
W Train 12	

Rural Carrier and Fourth Class Postmaster

TABLE OF POSTAL RATES

You will need to refer to these rates to answer the questions on Computation of Postal Charges. The rates are not necessarily those in effect. Base all answers on the rates given.

First Class (limit 70 pounds):

Letters and written and sealed matter, 4 cents for each ounce or fraction thereof, local and nonlocal.

Government postal cards, 3 cents each.

Private mailing or post cards, 3 cents each.

Air Mail, other than parcel post (limit 8 ounces):

Letters, 7 cents for each ounce or fraction thereof.

Postal cards and private mailing or post cards, 5 cents each.

Second Class.— Transient (no weight limit):

Newspapers, magazines, and other periodicals containing notice of second-class entry, sent by other than the publisher, 2 cents for the first 2 ounces or fraction thereof, and 1 cent for each additional ounce or fraction thereof, or the fourth-class rate, whichever is lower.

Third Class (up to but not including 16 ounces):

Circulars and other miscellaneous printed matter, and merchandise; books and catalogs of 24 or more pages; and seeds, cuttings, bulbs, roots, and plants; 3 cents for the first 2 ounces or fraction thereof, plus 1½ cents for each additional ounce or fraction thereof.

Fourth Class (16 ounces and over):

See "Rates for Fourth-Class matter" at end of this table.

Special-Handling Fees. Fourth-class matter only. Fees are in addition to regular postage and secure transportation with first-class mail:

Up to and including 2 pounds	$0.25
Over 2 pounds but not over 10 pounds	.35
Over 10 pounds	.50

Special-Delivery Fees (Fees are in addition to regular postage):

Up to and including 2 pounds	$0.30	$0.55
Over 2 pounds but not over 10 pounds	.45	.65
Over 10 pounds	.60	.80

Registered Mail (Fees are in addition to regular postage): Fees for liability limited to—

$ 10	$0.60	$400	$1.35	$ 800	$1.85
100	.85	600	1.60	1,000	2.00
200	1.10				

Mail without intrinsic value (no liability), fee 50 cents.

Insured Mail (third- and fourth-class matter). (Fees are in addition to regular postage): Fees for liability limited to—

$10	$0.10	$100	$0.30
50	.20	200	.40

Money-Order Fees (limit for each order $100):

For orders from—	Fee	For orders from—	Fee
$0.01 to $5	$0.15	$10.01 to $100	$0.30
5.01 to 10	.20		

Rates for Fourth-Class matter:

Fourth-class matter includes merchandise, printed matter, and all other mailable matter not first- or second-class or second-class transient, in packages weighing 16 ounces and over. The same matter in packages weighing up to but not including 16 ounces is third-class. Rates for fourth-class matter are calculated by the pound (a fraction of a pound counting as 1 pound) and the distance or zone to which it is to go. The table below gives the cost of sending a package of the weight shown in the left-hand column to the different zones shown at the heads of the other columns.

Weight, 1 pound and not exceeding	Local delivery	Zones 1-2	Zone 3	Zone 4	Zone 5	Zone 6
2 pounds	$0.29	$0.40	$0.42	$0.46	$0.52	$0.59
3 pounds	.31	.46	.49	.55	.64	.73
4 pounds	.33	.51	.55	.64	.75	.88
5 pounds	.35	.57	.62	.72	.87	1.02
6 pounds	.37	.62	.68	.80	.97	1.15

For the examination itself, competitors will be given a table of postal rates and weights for all zones.

Questions

Each sample question has five suggested answers lettered A, B, C, D, and E. Decide which one is the best answer to the question. Then, on the Sample Answer Sheet below blacken the space lettered the same as your answer for the question. After you have answered all the questions, compare your answers with those given in the Correct Answers to Sample Questions.

Computation of Postal Charges

Assume that you are a rural carrier assigned to a route out of Washington, D. C. Weights of articles and zones are given in each problem where they are needed. By "package" is meant in every case an unsealed package of merchandise. All mail matter except letters is sent unsealed, unless otherwise described.

Base all your answers wholly on the information contained in the questions and in the "TABLE OF POSTAL RATES" at the left, which contains all the information you will need.

1. What is the total amount you should receive from a patron for:
   Three 4-cent stamps, and
   Two 3-pound packages to Dayton, Ohio, zone 4?
   A) $0.59   D) $1.22
   B) $0.77   E) none of these
   C) $0.83

   EXPLANATION.—The charge for three 4-cent stamps is 12 cents. The "TABLE OF POSTAL RATES" shows you that postage for a 3-pound package to zone 4 is 55 cents; the postage for two such packages is $1.10. The sum of 12 cents and $1.10 is $1.22; therefore D is marked for question 1 on the Sample Answer Sheet.

2. What is the total amount you should receive from a patron for:
   A money order for $10, and
   A 2-ounce letter to Duluth, Minnesota, via air mail?
   A) $10.21   D) $10.37
   B) $10.25   E) none of these
   C) $10.31

   EXPLANATION.—The patron must pay the face value of the money order, $10, and the "TABLE OF POSTAL RATES" shows that the fee for a $10 money order is 20 cents; therefore, the total cost of the money order is $10.20. Air-mail postage for the letter is 8 cents an ounce, or 16 cents for the two ounces. The sum of $10.20 and 16 cents is $10.36. None of the suggested answers is the sum, so blacken space E.

3. What is the total amount you should receive from a patron for:
   Two letters, 1 ounce each, special delivery to New York City, registered and of no intrinsic value, and
   Fifty separate circulars, weight 3 ounces each, to addresses in Baltimore, Maryland?
   A) $1.82   D) $4.90
   B) $2.06   E) none of these
   C) $2.31

   EXPLANATION.—According to the "TABLE OF POSTAL RATES," special delivery up to and including 2 pounds is 30 cents, and all special delivery rates are in addition to regular postage. Regular postage for letters is 5 cents for each ounce. Therefore, the rate for one special delivery 1-ounce letter to New York City is 35 cents. Registered mail of no intrinsic value is 60 cents. Thus the cost for a 1-ounce special delivery letter to New York City which is registered and has no intrinsic value is 35 cents plus 60 cents, or 95 cents. Two of these letters would be $1.90. Circulars are sent by third class which, according to the "TABLE OF POSTAL RATES," is 4 cents for the first 2 ounces or fraction thereof and 2 cents for each additional ounce or fraction thereof. 3-ounce circulars would be 6 cents apiece; fifty of them would total $3.00.

General Questions

4. The kind of postal service that mail-order firms use most is
   A) air mail   D) lockbox
   B) parcel post   E) special delivery
   C) postal savings

5. Letters are delivered promptly by the post office so that the
   A) office can be closed on time   D) letters will not be damaged
   B) inclosures will not be lost   E) public may not be inconvenienced
   C) mail will not be heavy

6. Mail which is *sent from an addressee's old address to his new address* is said to be
   A) returned   D) received
   B) canceled   E) detained
   C) forwarded

7. A *fundamental* point is one that is
   A) final   D) emphasized
   B) essential   E) difficult
   C) drastic

8. (*Reading*) "In the business districts of cities collections from street letter boxes are made at stated hours, and collectors are required to observe these hours exactly. Any businessman using these boxes can rely with certainty upon the time of the next collection."

   According to the quotation, an important characteristic of mail collections is their
   A) cheapness   D) speed
   B) extent   E) regularity
   C) safety

CORRECT ANSWERS TO SAMPLE QUESTIONS

1. D	3. D	5. E	7. B
2. E	4. B	6. C	8. E

KNOWLEDGE TESTS FOR PROFESSIONAL
AND SEMIPROFESSIONAL POSITIONS

Supervision

1. In general, the most important advantage of good employee morale is that it results in
   A) high production
   B) decreased work for the supervisor
   C) increased ease in rating workers' efficiency
   D) high standing for the supervisor with management
   E) less desire for wage increases among employees

Since A is the best answer, the space under A is marked on the sample answer sheet.

2. Which one of the following types of information would be most useful to a supervisor in determining which employee should lose his job in case lay-offs are necessary?
   A) length of service with the supervisor   D) age
   B) marital status   E) job performance rating
   C) education

Since E is the best answer, the space under E is marked on the sample answer sheet.

Administration

3. A number of national organizations require the approval of the headquarters office on all actions originating in the field offices, instead of following the alternate procedure of delegating authority for such actions. This requirement of headquarters' review and approval is frequently unsatisfactory to the headquarters office itself. In general, the most frequent reason for the *dissatisfaction* in the headquarters office is that
   A) headquarters may lack the information necessary for approving these cases
   B) field offices resent the review
   C) the review causes delay
   D) it is felt that authority should be commensurate with responsibility
   E) clearance through a large number of divisions is required in most headquarters offices

Since A is the best answer to question 3, the space under A is marked on the sample answer sheet.

Occupational Analysis

4. In the machine shop of a manufacturing firm, a job with the title of Foreman has the following duties: "Installs cutting tools in various types of semiautomatic machinery. Adjusts the guides, stops, working tables of machines, and other controls to handle the size of stock to be machined. Operates and adjusts machine until accurate production (based on blueprint specifications, patterns, or templates) has been achieved. Checks production with precision gages, often to tolerances of 0.0005 inch. Turns machine over to regular operator when it is producing satisfactorily."
Which of the following would be the most descriptive title for this job?
   A) cutting-machine mechanic   D) machinist
   B) dimensional checker   E) tool and die maker
   C) job setter

Since C is the best answer to question 4, the space under C is marked on the sample answer sheet.

Public Affairs

5. The most important way in which geographic factors influence rural community structure is by
   A) influencing the size of the farms and thus the density of the population
   B) influencing the birth rate
   C) dictating the habits of the people
   D) influencing the temperament of the people in such a way as to make them cooperative or noncooperative
   E) being the most important determinants of community boundaries

Since A is the best answer to question 5, the space under A is marked on the sample answer sheet.

6. The following table indicates the distribution, by type of economic activity, of those employed in a country. Which of the following five countries most probably has the occupational distribution indicated in this table?

Employment by Activity

Agriculture and Fishing	655, 190
Mining	51, 449
Manufacturing	926, 997
Construction	257, 466
Transport and Communications	296, 737
Commerce, Banking, Insurance	447, 242
Domestic Service	243, 555
Total Employment	3, 185, 816

A) Bulgaria   D) Portugal
B) Hungary   E) Turkey
C) Netherlands

Since C is the best answer to question 6, the space under C is marked on the sample answer sheet.

Engineering and Other Physical Sciences

Engineers and scientists hired by the Government at the lower professional grades are sometimes given a written test covering their branch of science, as well as the aptitude tests appropriate for the type of work. The written test nearly always requires a knowledge of whatever branch of mathematics is involved in the scientific field.

1. A plane figure consists of a square 10 inches on a side and an isosceles triangle whose base is the left edge of the square and whose altitude dropped from the vertex opposite the 10-inch base of the triangle common to the square is 6 inches. Approximately how far in inches from the left side of the square is the center of gravity of the whole figure located?

   A) 2.92   D) 3.75
   B) 3.15   E) 4.28
   C) 3.38

   In the Sample of the Answer Sheet, the space under c has been marked for Sample 1, as 3.38 is the correct answer.

2. The stiffness of a rectangular beam varies
   A) as the depth
   B) inversely as the depth
   C) as the square of the depth
   D) as the cube of the depth
   E) inversely as the cube of the depth

3. At atmospheric pressure, steam at 100° C. is passed into 400 grams of water at 10° C. until the temperature of the water rises to 40° C. It is then found that the weight of the water has increased to 420 grams due to the condensing steam. The heat of vaporization of steam in calories per gram at 100° C. is
   A) 60   D) 600
   B) 300   E) none of these
   C) 540

4. The addition of HCl to a solution of sodium acetate causes
   A) the precipitation of sodium chloride
   B) a decrease in the concentration of acetate ion
   C) an increase in the concentration of sodium ion
   D) an increase in the concentration of hydroxide ion
   E) no change in the concentration of hydroxide ion

Psychology

5. In experiments on the localization of sound in space, the sounds which can be most accurately located by the hearer are those sounds originating at points
   A) in the plane equidistant from the two ears of the hearer
   B) in front of the hearer
   C) above and below the hearer
   D) to the left and to the right of the hearer
   E) behind the hearer

Statistics

7. If 4 is added to every observation in a sample, the mean is
   A) increased by 4
   B) increased by 4 times the number of observations
   C) increased by 4 divided by the number of observations
   D) decreased by 4
   E) not affected

8. A distribution for which one of the following variables would constitute a discrete series?
   A) weight of eighth-grade pupils
   B) width of the visual field
   C) "items right" score on a history test
   D) auditory reaction time
   E) age at marriage of 850 charwomen
   Since C is the best answer to the question, the space under C has been marked.

6. In the field of measurement of interests, the Preference Record is associated with the name of
   A) Remmers   D) Viteles
   B) Kuder   E) Bell
   C) Bingham

9. Of the following measures, which one is the most stable under conditions of random sampling?
   A) mode   D) harmonic mean
   B) median   E) geometric mean
   C) arithmetic mean

10. The standard deviation is a measure of which one of the following characteristics of a population
   A) skewness   D) randomness
   B) symmetry   E) variability
   C) normality

Geologist

1. The fumaroles of The Valley of Ten Thousand Smokes, Katmai region, Alaska, exhaled notable amounts of
   A) He and Ne
   B) Br_2 and C_2H_4
   C) HCl and HF
   D) $Al(OH)_3$ and H_2SO_4
   E) CsCl and RbCl

2. Listed below are major periods in geologic time:

   Cambrian to Silurian
   Devonian
   Mississippian to Permian
   Triassic to Cretaceous

   Which one of the following forms of animal life was *not* dominant during any of the above periods?
   A) fishes
   B) mammals
   C) marine invertebrates
   D) reptiles and ammonites
   E) amphibians

3. Which one of the following topographic features can be formed by either erosional or depositional agencies?
   A) river terrace
   B) sea stack
   C) esker
   D) roches moutonnees
   E) barchan

4. Symmetrical ripple marks are most likely to be developed in deposits formed in which one of the following environments?
   A) a sand-dune region
   B) along a river flood plain
   C) in a bay at the mouth of a big river
   D) in a large lake
   E) on a playa

5. Which one of the following methods is considered the most reliable for determining the strike of a formation shown on a geologic map?
   A) topographic relief from top to bottom of formation
   B) width of outcrop between upper and lower contacts
   C) direction of the contact–V up or down a stream valley traversed by the contact
   D) determination of fold axes of adjacent formations
   E) two or more contact points of the same elevation

Sample Answer Sheet						Correct Answers for Sample Questions				
A	B	C	D	E		A	B	C	D	E
1		■			1			■		
2					2		■			
3					3	■				
4					4			■		
5					5					■

KNOWLEDGE TESTS

Accounting

An accounting position in the Federal Government may involve one or more of the following activities, with varying degrees of responsibility: Cost accounting, tax accounting, auditing, bookkeeping, analysis and interpretation of financial statements, constructive accounting, and fund or governmental accounting. Very few positions require a specialized knowledge of governmental accounting; most positions require experience or training in commercial accounting principles and practices.

Examinations may be announced for accountants or for accountants and auditors in general; the test in such cases will be based on principles generally applicable to all accounting activities. Occasionally, an examination for a specialized position will test the accounting principles more directly applicable to the duties of that position.

1. An operating mining company properly charged $1,200 to expense to reflect the wear and tear on its equipment. The corresponding credit should have been made to
   A) reserve for contingent liability
   B) reserve for depletion
   C) reserve for depreciation
   D) surplus reserve
   E) earned surplus

2. The Jones Company had a merchandise inventory of $24,625 on January 1, 1950. During the year the company purchased $60,000 worth of goods, sales were $85,065, and the cost of goods sold was $28,060. The inventory on December 31, 1950, was
   A) $25,065.00
   B) $28,500.00
   C) $49,690.00
   D) $57,005.00
   E) none of these

The answer to question 2 is $56,565, which is not given as A, B, C, or D. The answer sheet is marked under E, therefore.

Weather Forecasting

Weather forecasting is an increasingly important science, which uses many skilled workers, both professional and subprofessional. Ordinarily the persons selected for trainee jobs are given aptitude tests containing mechanical and physical problems. A knowledge of algebra and physics is sometimes required. Professional tests contain questions in the science of weather, or meteorology.

3. Particles of dust, smoke, or microbes often cause the air to be
   A) hazy
   B) clear
   C) humid
   D) dry
   E) cold

4. Helium, neon, krypton, and xenon are
   A) never found in the atmosphere
   B) found in place of hydrogen in the upper atmosphere
   C) found in the atmosphere in very small quantities
   D) found in the Arctic region in largest proportion
   E) found only over the ocean

5. The air is warmed to the greatest extent by
   A) the sun's rays directly
   B) only conduction from the earth
   C) hot vapors
   D) dust particles
   E) both convection and conduction from the earth

Safety

Examinations for the position of safety inspector or foreman in dangerous occupations, such as mining, stress knowledge of safety devices, rules, and precautions. The correct answers for the two following questions are marked on the section of the Answer Sheet.

6. An electrical detonator is
   A) an instrument used to measure electrical energy
   B) a part of an electrical signaling apparatus
   C) a device used for detecting sound
   D) a device used to fire explosives
   E) a part of an electric-light bulb

7. Most authorities in the field of safety planning agree that the ultimate success of any safety program depends on the
   A) individual worker
   B) foreman
   C) management
   D) state government
   E) safety instructor

Aircraft Mechanics

1. A propeller that has blades which may be modified in flight to get the most advantageous blade angle is called a
   A) controllable pitch propeller
   B) feathered propeller
   c) variable speed propeller
   D) counter-rotating propeller

2. A hinged section of an airplane wing that is used to reduce airspeed for landing is called
   A) a rudder
   B) an elevator
   c) a flap
   D) a rib

Radio Maintenance

3. The symbol at the right represents a
   A) fixed resistance
   B) rheostat
   c) rectifier tube
   D) variable condenser

4. The symbol at the right represents
   A) current
   B) an amplifier
   c) a battery
   D) a transformer

5. A device used for point to point analysis of either voltage or resistance is known as a
   A) volt-ohm-milliammeter
   B) ballistic galvanometer
   c) chanalyst
   D) vacuum tube voltmeter with external probe
   E) megger

Mathematics

   In some positions, even at the trainee level, a working knowledge of algebra or geometry is needed to perform the duties of the job or to complete the training course. For Junior Scientist and Engineer positions, candidates are tested on their ability to work out formulas from information supplied. Mathematicians are given more difficult material, including trigonometry, differential equations, and other branches.

6. The product of $(3m-n)$ and $3m$ is
   A) $9m^2-3mn$
   B) $9m^2-mn$
   c) $9m-3n$
   D) $9m^2-n^2$
   E) $3m^2-3mn$

   Since $9m^2-3mn$ is the answer, the Sample Answer Sheet at the right has been marked to show that A is the answer to question 6.

7. The length l of a spiral spring supporting a pan is increased c centimeters for x grams of weight placed on the pan. What is the length of the spring if w grams are placed on the pan?
   A) $lc+\dfrac{x}{w}$
   B) $l+\dfrac{w}{cx}$
   c) $l+\dfrac{cw}{x}$
   D) $\dfrac{l+cw}{x}$
   E) $\dfrac{l+cx}{w}$

8. Find the total differential of $(x^2+y^2)^{\frac{1}{2}}$.
   A) $x(x^2+y^2)-\frac{1}{2}$
   B) $y(x^2+y^2)-\frac{1}{2}$
   c) $xdx+ydy$
   D) $\dfrac{xdx}{\sqrt{x^2+y^2}}+\dfrac{ydy}{\sqrt{x^2+y^2}}$
   E) $xdx-ydy$

   Sometimes the use of a slide rule is permitted in examinations which contain problems that could be worked with its aid. If there is a statement in the announcement of examination, or in the card of admission to the examination room, that the use of a slide rule, protractor, scale, or any other device is permitted, the applicant must furnish the instrument himself if he wishes to use it. If any instrument or device is *required* to be furnished by the applicant, the announcement or admission card will say so. If it is not required but simply permitted, it is up to the applicant to decide whether he will use it or not.

	A	B	C	D	E
1	▮				
2			▮		
3			▮		
4			▮		
5	▮				
6	▮				
7			▮		
8				▮	

MECHANICAL AND NONVERBAL TESTS

As used in this booklet, "nonverbal" describes tests that do not depend on knowledge of language or understanding of words, so much as on the ability to work with numbers, diagrams, and other symbols.

Shop Arithmetic

In each of the following machine-scored problems, five different answers are suggested. Sometimes the last one is "none of these." In question 9, none of the figures given is the correct answer; hence the proper letter to choose is E, which is the letter preceding the answer "none of these."

1. When 100, 125, 75, and 20 are added the answer is
(A)220 (B)270 (C)325 (D)320 (E)420
The sum of these numbers is 320. Look at the choices given and you will find the number 320 after the letter (D). Therefore, to answer question 1, the space under the letter D on the answer sheet should be blackened.

2.
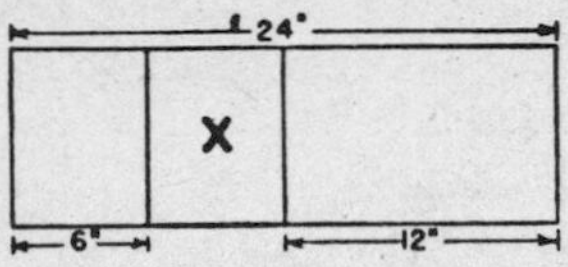

X is what part of the whole sheet?
(A)$\frac{1}{6}$ (B)$\frac{1}{3}$ (C)$\frac{1}{4}$ (D)$\frac{1}{5}$
(E) none of these

3.
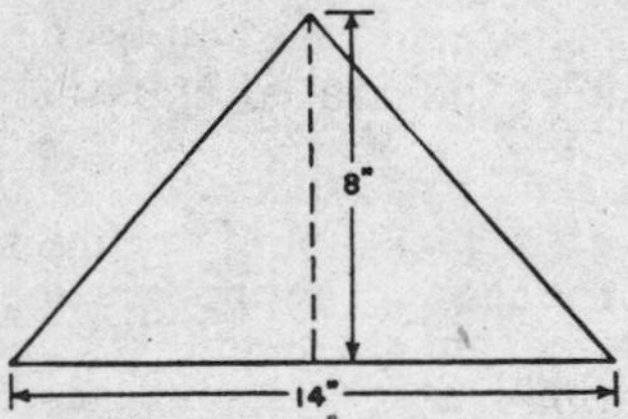

The area of the triangle in square inches is
(A)56 (B)112 (C)122 (D)22 (E)448

4.
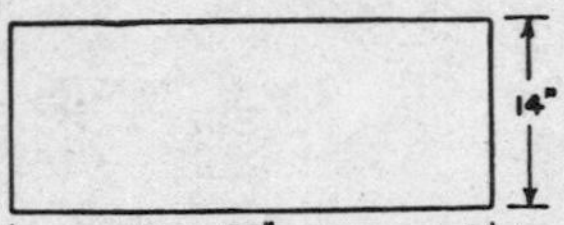

What is the greatest number of pieces 9″ x 2″ that could be cut from the given sheet of metal?
(A)18 (B)21 (C)26 (D)80 (E)28

5.
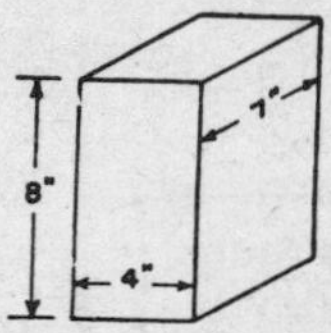

The volume of the rectangular solid in cubic inches is
(A)224 (B)28 (C)896 (D)56 (E)32

6. $\frac{1}{2}$ of $\frac{1}{4}$ is
(A)$\frac{1}{12}$ (B)$\frac{1}{8}$ (C)$\frac{1}{2}$ (D)$\frac{1}{4}$ (E)8

7. A circular saw cuts 8 boards per minute. If there are 1,440 boards to be cut, the number of *hours* required to cut these boards is
(A)$2\frac{1}{3}$ (B)$2\frac{2}{3}$ (C)4 (D)$3\frac{2}{3}$ (E)3

8. A drawing of a certain building is 10 inches by 15 inches. On this drawing 1 inch represents 5 feet. If the same drawing had been made 20 inches by 30 inches, 1 inch on the drawing would represent
(A)$7\frac{1}{2}$ feet (B)5 feet (C)10 feet
(D)$3\frac{1}{3}$ feet (E)$2\frac{1}{2}$ feet

9. During his first 8-hour day, an apprentice earned 40 percent as much as a master mechanic. If the master mechanic earned $28.00, what was the apprentice's average *hourly* earning?
(A)$1.60 (B)$2.40 (C)$1.68
(D)$1.12 (E) none of these

10. An opening 6 yards long and 3 feet wide is to be covered by sheathing. Enough lumber is available to cover two-thirds of the area of the opening. How many square feet will remain uncovered?
(A)2 (B)4 (C)6 (D)12
(E) none of these

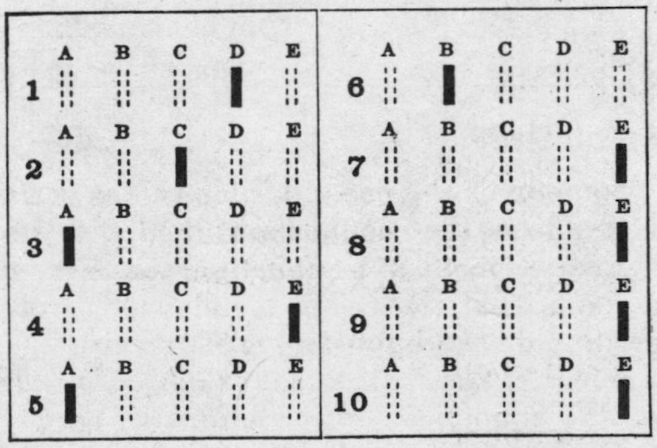

**MECHANICAL
AND NONVERBAL**

Sometimes questions testing knowledge of mechanical facts are included in tests for mechanical positions. Often, however, such positions, particularly those at the apprentice level, require aptitude rather than knowledge. Many types of questions, some measuring aptitude, others measuring knowledge and ability, are likely to be found in mechanical tests. Illustrations are given on this page and on pages 89 through 98.

Tools and Mechanical Principles

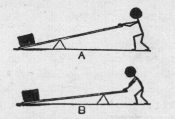

1. In which, if either, of the figures shown above can the man lift more weight?
   A) A
   B) B
   C) The men in figures A and B can lift equal weights
   D) The man who can lift more weight cannot be determined.

   The position of the fulcrum gives the man in figure A a greater mechanical advantage so space A is blackened for question 1.

2. In the gears shown above, as gear X turns in a counterclockwise direction, gear Y turns
   A) clockwise at the same speed
   B) clockwise at a faster speed
   C) counterclockwise at a slower speed
   D) counterclockwise at the same speed

3. In order to smooth and standardize a straight or tapered hole, the best of the following tools to use is a
   A) reamer
   B) drill
   C) tap
   D) cold chisel
   E) compass saw

4. The tool illustrated above is a
   A) counterbore
   B) tap
   C) center punch
   D) rose countersink
   E) pin punch

Information and Judgment

5. Which one of the following frequencies is most commonly used in the United States in alternating-current lighting circuits?
   A) 10 cycles
   B) 25 cycles
   C) 40 cycles
   D) 60 cycles
   E) 110 cycles

6. The device used to mix the air and the fuel in a gasoline engine is called the
   A) carburetor
   B) cylinder
   C) distributor
   D) manifold
   E) valve

7. Which one of the following would cause excessive backlash in the rear axle assembly?
   A) bent rear axle shaft
   B) chipped differential gears
   C) improper lubrication
   D) worn differential gears and thrust washers
   E) ring gear adjusted too close to pinion

8. As a driver brought his truck into a long curve to the left at 40 miles per hour, he made a moderate application of his air brakes, and at that point he felt a pull to the right on the steering wheel. Which one of the following could *not* have caused that pull?
   A) sudden loss of air from right front tire
   B) lack of superelevation on curve
   C) lack of adequate tread on front tires
   D) unbalanced adjustment of brakes

	A	B	C	D	E			A	B	C	D	E
1	█						5				█	
2		█					6	█				
3	█						7				█	
4				█			8				█	

MECHANICAL AND NONVERBAL TESTS

Messenger and Guard

For some positions in the lower pay grades of messenger and guard, no experience is necessary; but for the higher pay grades, experience either in one of the armed services or in a position whose duties were similar to those which a messenger or guard must fulfill is required.

A test of word meaning is given in addition to the test described below.

Each box below contains several names. You will be given a few minutes to memorize the arrangement, and then you will be given a list of names. For each name, you will mark on the answer sheet the letter of the box in which the name appears. For example, question 1 is Gaynor. Gaynor is in box c, so the answer sheet is marked to show that c is the answer to question 1.

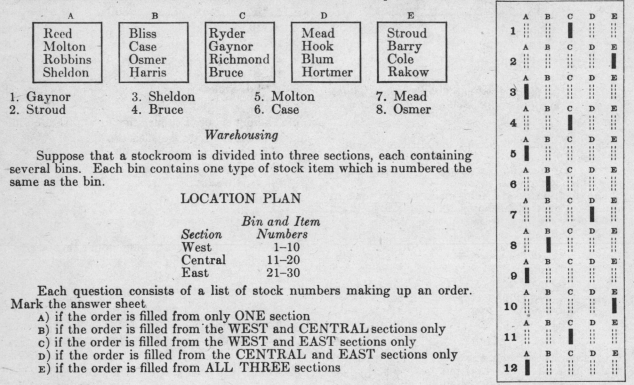

A	B	C	D	E
Reed	Bliss	Ryder	Mead	Stroud
Molton	Case	Gaynor	Hook	Barry
Robbins	Osmer	Richmond	Blum	Cole
Sheldon	Harris	Bruce	Hortmer	Rakow

1. Gaynor   3. Sheldon   5. Molton   7. Mead
2. Stroud   4. Bruce   6. Case   8. Osmer

Warehousing

Suppose that a stockroom is divided into three sections, each containing several bins. Each bin contains one type of stock item which is numbered the same as the bin.

LOCATION PLAN

Section	Bin and Item Numbers
West	1–10
Central	11–20
East	21–30

Each question consists of a list of stock numbers making up an order. Mark the answer sheet

A) if the order is filled from only ONE section
B) if the order is filled from the WEST and CENTRAL sections only
c) if the order is filled from the WEST and EAST sections only
D) if the order is filled from the CENTRAL and EAST sections only
E) if the order is filled from ALL THREE sections

9. 26, 28, 29.
    The answer to question 9 is A, because all three items in this order are found in only ONE section.

10. 2, 12, 25, 29.
    The answer is E, because items must be taken from ALL THREE sections to fill this order.
    From time to time, bins and the items they hold will be moved from one section to another. Also, items may become unavailable and other items will be substituted for them. Write the location plan out and make the changes in the plan.

Change 1. Bins 11 and 12 are moved from Central to West.
    Bin 21 is moved from East to Central.
    Item 15 is discontinued and is replaced by item 25.
    Item 27 is discontinued and is replaced by item 3.

Your location plan should now look like this:

11. 2, 11, 22, 23.
    After the changes this order is filled from the WEST and EAST sections, so the answer is c.

12. 15, 24, 29.
    Item 25 is now used for 15, and the order is filled from only ONE section; the answer is A.

(handwritten location plan:)

Section	Bin and Item Numbers		
West	1–10	1–12	
Central	11–20	13–21	For 15 use 25
East	21–30	22–30	For 27 use 3

Identical Forms

In each question there are five drawings lettered A, B, C, D, and E. Four of the drawings are alike in every way. Find the one that differs from the rest, and mark the answer sheet under the letter of that drawing.

1.

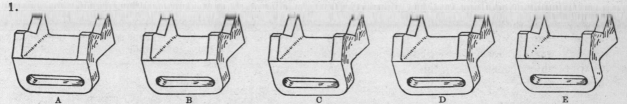

In question 1 the object in drawing E has a wall across the back of the shelf-like space. All the other objects are open at the back. The answer sheet is marked E for question 1.

2.

3.

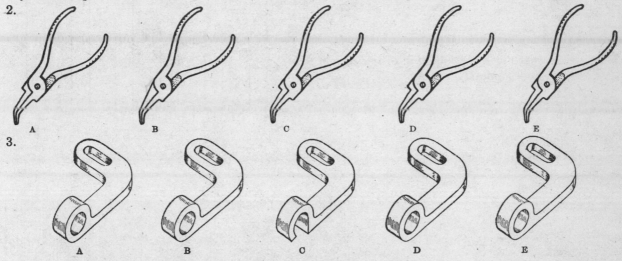

Touching Cubes

Questions 4 and 5 are based on one group of touching cubes, and questions 6 and 7 on another group. All the cubes are exactly the same size, and there are only enough hidden cubes to support the ones you can see. The question number is on a cube in the group. You are to find how many cubes in that group touch the numbered cube. A cube is considered to touch the numbered cube if any part, even an edge or a corner, touches. Then mark the Sample Answer Sheet to show how many cubes touch the numbered cube by blackening space—

A if the answer is 1 or 6 or 11 cubes
B if the answer is 2 or 7 or 12 cubes
C if the answer is 3 or 8 or 13 cubes
D if the answer is 4 or 9 or 14 cubes
E if the answer is 5 or 10 or 15 cubes

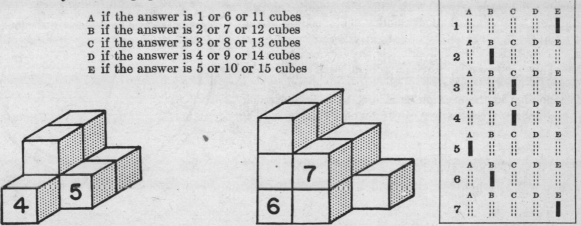

In question 4, there are three cubes that touch the cube marked 4—the one right behind it which you cannot see, the one on top of that, and the one marked 5. Because the answer is three cubes, the space marked C should be blackened.

**MECHANICAL
AND NONVERBAL**

Graph Reading

Many jobs require ability to read graphs and charts, or to make graphs and charts from collected information so that others can find the information there.

The following questions can be answered by reading the bar graph at the right.

1. In the year in which the total output of the factory was the least, the percentage of that output which consisted of television sets was approximately

   A) 10%
   B) 20%
   c) 25%
   D) 30%
   E) 40%

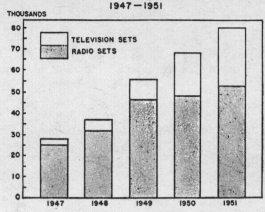

OUTPUT OF RADIO SETS AND TELEVISION SETS BY FACTORY "K" 1947—1951

2. In which year did the production of television sets total approximately 20,000?

   A) 1947
   B) 1948
   c) 1949
   D) 1950
   E) 1951

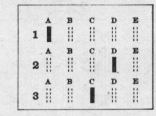

Meter Reading

3. The position of the pointer on the meter scale is nearest to
   (A)2.6   (B)3.1   (C)3.2   (D)3.3

An examination of the meter scale shows, first, that only the even numbers are given on the dial. Between each pair of numbers are 10 small subdivisions. The position of the odd numbers is indicated by the slightly longer subdivision mark. Since there are five subdivisions between the positions of two successive whole numbers, each subdivision indicates ⅕ or .2.

The pointer in the example is closest to one subdivision beyond 3; the correct reading of the meter would be 3 + ⅕, or 3.2.

For a reading of 3.1, the pointer would be midway between the mark corresponding to 3 and the mark corresponding to 3.2.

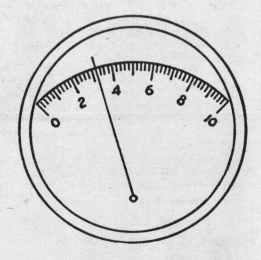

Matching Parts and Figures

These questions test understanding of spatial relations. They also present problems found in making templates and patterns. The first two questions show, at the left side, two or more flat pieces. In each question select the arrangement lettered A, B, C, or D that shows how these pieces can be fitted together without gaps or overlapping. The pieces may be *turned around* or *turned over* in any way to make them fit together. On the answer sheet you should blacken the space lettered the same as the figure that you have selected.

From these pieces   *which one of these arrangements can you make?*

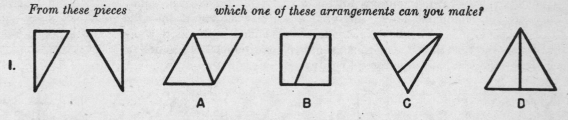

In sample question 1, for instance, only the arrangement lettered D could be formed by fitting together the pieces on the left. Note that the pieces are turned around to make D. None of the other arrangements shows pieces of the given size and shape.

From these pieces   *which one of these arrangements can you make?*

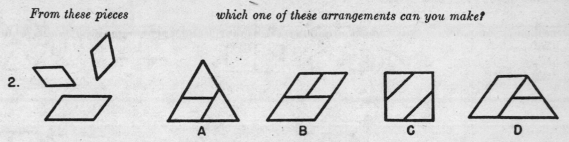

The next questions are based on the four solid patterns shown below.

Each of the questions shows *one* of these four patterns cut up into pieces. For each question, decide which one of the four patterns could be made by fitting *all of the pieces* together without having any edges overlap and without leaving any space between pieces. Some of the pieces may need to be *turned around* or *turned over* to make them fit. The pattern must be made in its exact size and shape.

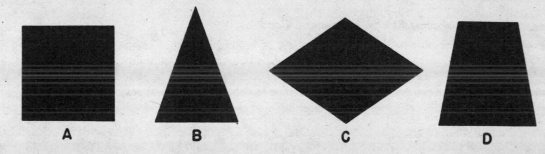

Look at sample question 3. If the two pieces were fitted together they would make pattern D. The piece on the left fits at the bottom of pattern D, and the piece at the right is turned around and over to make the top of the pattern.

**MECHANICAL
AND NONVERBAL**

Perception of Form

Look at the rows of drawings below. In each row, the design at the left is contained in *one or more* of the more complex drawings. A drawing is to be marked as an answer if it contains the exact design in the same position. The designs in the drawings need not be alined with the original design, but they are not to be *turned*. The designs and drawings are two-dimensional. In some rows more than one drawing contains the exact design in the correct position. In these cases, you should mark more than one answer on your answer sheet.

Look at question 1. The design at the left is contained in the more complex drawings B and C, so these are marked as answers for question 1. The design is also in drawing D, but not in the correct position, so this is not an answer.

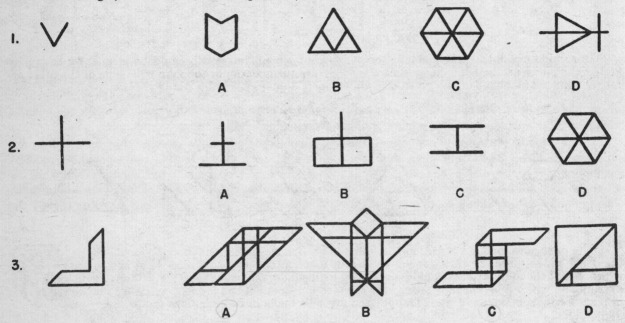

Matching Solid Figures and Parts

In each question the object pictured at the left is a combination of two pieces. One *set* of the five sets of pieces at the right can be combined to make the object at the left. Watch both the sizes and shapes of the pieces. The section of answer sheet at the right is blackened under the letter for the correct set of pieces in each question.

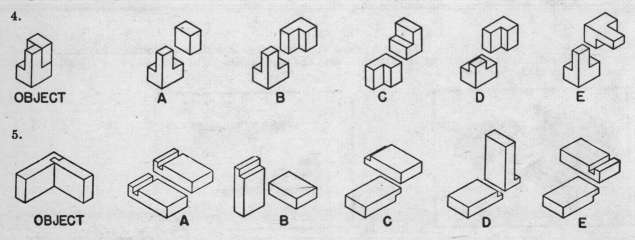

Cube Turning

The drawing at the left in each of the two following sample questions represents a cube. There is a different design on each of the six faces of the cube. Four other drawings of cubes are lettered A, B, C, and D.

You are asked to show, by marking the correct space on your Answer Sheet, which one of the four could possibly be the cube on the left turned to a different position. (The cube at the left may have been turned *over*, it may have been turned *around*, or it may have been turned *both* over and around, and faces not seen in the drawing on the left may become visible.)

1.

In sample question 1 you will notice that only B could be the same cube as that shown on the left. Study the sample carefully and be sure you understand why B is the cube on the left turned to a different position. Also, be sure you understand why A, C, and D could *not* be the same cube. For instance, A is wrong because when the block is turned with the square on the right and the cross in front, the triangle would be on top, but it would point toward the cross instead of away from it.

If the cube were turned upside down, the cross and triangle would appear as they do in C, but the square would be on the bottom and would not show; the former bottom, now the top, would have a different design, since no two faces are alike. Or if the original cube were given a quarter-turn clockwise, the square would still be on top and the cross would be in front as in C—but again a new face would show, which could not be a triangle. D is not the answer either, since the triangle ought to point toward the cross, and in D it points toward a circle.

2.

Pattern Folding

In questions like No. 3, you are to select the *one* object, A, B, C, or D, that could be made from the flat piece shown at the left, if this flat piece were folded on the dotted lines shown in the drawing, or rolled so that the edges meet.

3.

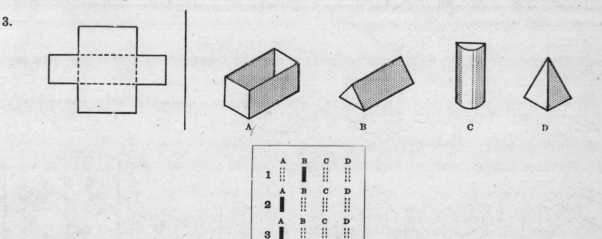

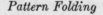

**MECHANICAL
AND NONVERBAL**

Elevations and Perspective

An elevation is a drawing of one side of an object. Think of an object inside a glass box. The tracing of the object's shape on the top of the box would be a "top elevation" or "top view." Tracings can be made from any side. In mechanical drawing, usually three views are given.

Directions: In the following questions you are given a top view, a front view, and a view of the right side of a solid object. The problem is to find the *one* of the four objects lettered A, B, C, and D that would look like these views; then mark the letter of that object on the answer sheet.

1. TOP

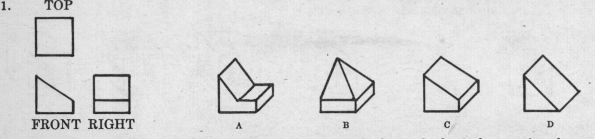

In question 1, both A and c have the correct right view; both c and D have the top view shown; but only c looks like the view marked "FRONT." c is therefore the answer to the question.

2. TOP

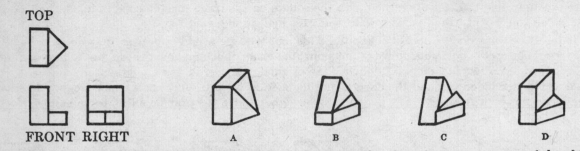

When you work these problems, you may check any one of the views first; one or more of the objects may show up as being clearly different from this view. Then compare the other views with the remaining objects. You will find that only one object finally remains which looks like all three of the given views.

In question 2, for example, beginning with the front view: A is ruled out at first glance, B has one line in the wrong place, but c and D are left. Now a check of the top view shows that c should have a line which is not in the given top view, and a final check of the right side view against D shows that D is the answer.

If you had started with the top view in question 2, you would have had A and D remaining as possibilities. Then a check of either the front or right view would have eliminated A, and D would be the correct letter to mark on the answer sheet. If you had started with the right view, you could have found the answer on the first try. There is no way to tell which order will prove to be the quickest for any given question—as you see in question 1, the front view would have given the answer at once. It is best, if you have the time, to check all views of each object so that you are sure you have found the *one* answer.

3. TOP

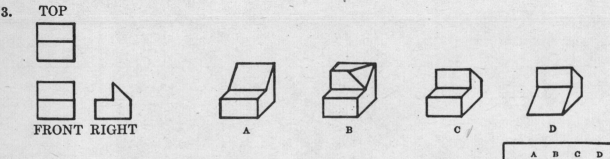

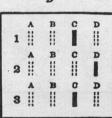

Question 3 is harder. A, c, and D all look alike from both top and front. B is evidently incorrect, since it does not check with any of the views shown. To find the correct answer among A, c, and D, however, it is necessary to check all views, and it can then be seen that only c has the correct side view.

Observation and Memory

This kind of test is used in examinations for various kinds of investigators, for example, Treasury Enforcement Agent. Read the directions under the picture.

Study the picture for 5 minutes. Observe all the details of the scene—what the people are wearing, what kinds of furniture and equipment are in the room, and where each object is. Do not make any written notes.

After 5 minutes, turn the page and see if you can answer the questions at the top of the next page without looking back at the picture.

**MECHANICAL
AND NONVERBAL**

Observation and Memory—Continued

Do not read these questions until you have studied the picture on the other side of this sheet. After you have studied the picture for 5 minutes, you must not look back at it for the answers to the questions. *After* you have answered the questions, look at the bottom line on this page.

1. Which one of these things can be seen in the picture?
   A) a telephone
   B) an initialed belt buckle
   C) a list of names on the blackboard
   D) a brief case
   E) a calendar with one date circled

2. The man in the light suit is
   A) holding a pencil in his left hand
   B) smoking a pipe
   C) holding a slide rule in his right hand
   D) pointing to the blackboard
   E) opening a loose-leaf notebook

3. The secretary in this picture
   A) wears no jewelry
   B) has a light-colored dress
   C) is writing in a loose-leaf binder
   D) wears a short-sleeved dress
   E) is looking at the blackboard

4. The man who is smoking a pipe is also
   A) pointing to a statistical chart
   B) leaning on the table
   C) wearing a bow tie
   D) writing on the map
   E) wearing rimless glasses

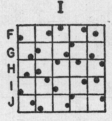

Test of Fine Dexterity

This test is used to examine competitors for a position that requires carefulness, patience, and accuracy of sight and movement. Competitors who have excessive trouble with this test would probably not qualify for work that involves the assembly of delicate timing devices (to give one example), and almost certainly would not like such work if they did manage to qualify.

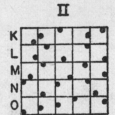

Each competitor receives a diagram resembling the one on the right, a small card with a diagram like that at the left below, and a fine pin. The first part of the test is to make pin-holes in the card in the exact pattern of the dots on the printed diagram. Note that there is only one dot to each square, and that it could be in the center, at one corner, at the middle of one side, or at one side halfway between the middle and the corner.

After the competitors have punched all the squares in the small diagram, the large diagram is taken away. Then for the second part of the test the competitors mark the answer sheet to show where each dot was made, according to a code that describes each possible position. This code is a large square with all possible positions of the pin-prick shown, and differently lettered. If the competitor has placed his pin-pricks in exactly the right place, he will be able to read the right letters from the code square. If he has made a pin-prick in the wrong position, he will read the wrong letter from the code and mark the wrong answer.

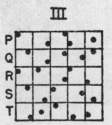

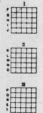

If you wish to practice this test, use a fine pin or a needle to punch the very small squares, and try to copy the position of each dot in the larger squares. Then, reading from the small squares, describe the location of each pin prick and check it with the large diagram.

For a test of dexterity that is not so hard as this, see page 97.

Answers to Memory Test: 1. e; 2. c; 3. d; 4. b

MECHANICAL AND NONVERBAL

Dexterity Tests

Many kinds of work require some degree of accuracy and skill with your hands. If you have the right amount of this aptitude, you can be successful on the job; if you do not, you would probably not enjoy the work, since you would find it difficult to do.

The test on this page is one of a variety of tests that measure hand skill. Cut out the gage at the right on the dotted lines, and trim it off carefully on the left-hand edge. (Save it for the questions on page 50 also.) Each question in the test has 5 rectangles lettered the same as those on the gage. Measure each one, laying the gage down so that the rectangles overlap a little and all the thin lines run the same way. Use A on the gage to measure A in the question; B to measure B, and so on. One of the five is just a little too large or too small; the letter of that rectangle is the answer to the question. These drawings show how the gage is used.

MEASURING GAGE

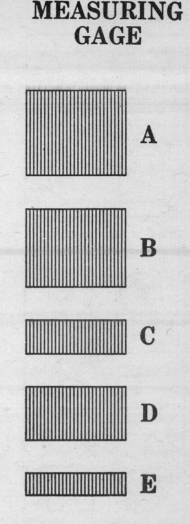

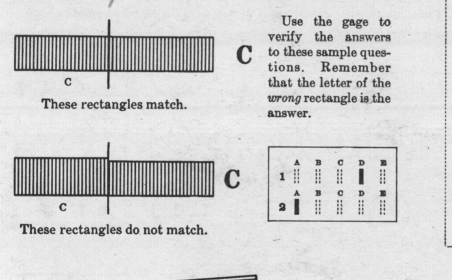

C

These rectangles match.

C

These rectangles do not match.

Use the gage to verify the answers to these sample questions. Remember that the letter of the *wrong* rectangle is the answer.

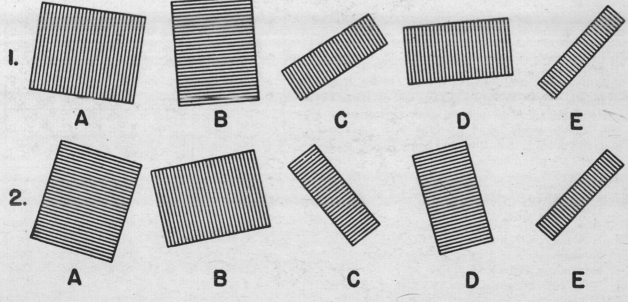

1.

A   B   C   D   E

2.

A   B   C   D   E

CODE FOR INSPECTION TEST

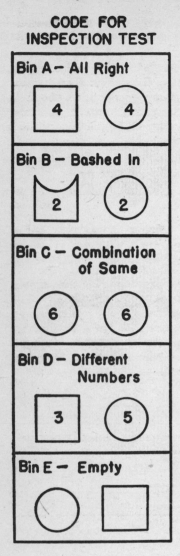

Bin A – All Right

Bin B – Bashed In

Bin C – Combination of Same

Bin D – Different Numbers

Bin E – Empty

MECHANICAL AND NONVERBAL

Inspection Tests

The ability to inspect, sort, and examine objects of many kinds can be tested by some pencil and paper tests. Two of these are described here.

The diagram at the left shows five bins into which pairs of parts are to be sorted. In each pair of parts, one part should be round and the other square; both should have the same number.

Bin A is for pairs that are ALL RIGHT.

Bin B is for pairs that have a part which is BASHED IN.

Bin C is for a COMBINATION of two round or two square parts.

Bin D is for pairs in which the parts have DIFFERENT numbers.

Bin E is for pairs in which the number spaces are EMPTY.

Look at each pair of parts below, and decide which bin they go into. The letter of that bin should be recorded on the answer sheet. (To save space, the answer sheet is not reproduced here, but the correct answers are indicated.)

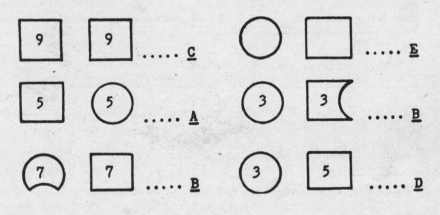

For another type of inspection test the competitor counts small objects. Each question asks for the number of x's or o's, or both, in a certain area of the diagram shown. Count the objects as directed. If an x or o falls across a line dividing one area from another, count it as being in the area in which most of it falls. Look for your answer among those suggested, and mark the answer sheet accordingly. If your answer is not listed, mark E. (To save space, the answer sheet is not printed here, but the correct answers are given below.)

1. How many x's are there in Row 1, Col. 2? A)12 B)13 c)14 D)15 E)none of these
2. How many o's in Row 1, Columns 1 and 2? A)13 B)14 c)15 D)17 E)none of these
3. How many x's in Row 2, Col. 1? A)11 B)13 c)14 D)16 E)none of these
4. How many o's in Row 3, Col. 3? A)11 B)13 c)15 D)16 E)none of these
5. How many x's and o's in Row 3, Col. 2? A)22 B)23 c)24 D)25 E)none of these
6. How many o's in Row 2, Col. 3? A) 9 B)10 c)11 D)12 E)none of these

The correct answers are: 1.B; 2.D; 3.C; 4.E; 5.A; 6.B.

Gross Dexterity Test

This is a timed test that shows how quickly and accurately you can work, by finding and filling in the spaces on the answer sheet. Look at the picture on page 41 and notice that the answer sheet has an upper and a lower section. Since there are 25 numbers in each column, the upper section has the first 10 of each group of 25—that is, numbers 1 to 10, 26 to 35, 51 to 60, 76 to 85, and 101 to 110. On this page, only the upper section is reproduced, and all the questions given here are to be marked in that section. In a real examination the questions would be scattered all over the page.

To work this test, simply go down the list and mark each space as you are directed. The first question is 26. B; blacken space B after number 26 on the answer sheet. Work as fast as you can.

26. B	77. E	8. B	7. D	60. D	55. B
57. C	81. A	104. D	106. A	4. B	107. E
31. D	105. A	6. C	108. E	83. A	79. B
9. E	53. B	80. C	51. E	102. A	35. A
110. D	106. C	34. E	78. A	29. D	27. D

Following Oral Directions

This is another test which uses only the answer sheet. In this test the examiner reads directions aloud, and the competitors mark their answer sheets as directed. You can use this material for practice by reading each sentence aloud and covering the directions while you follow them, or by copying the directions and having someone else read them to you. Try to work quickly. In the examination room the reading of each paragraph is timed carefully, so that all competitors have the same time to work. (Note: If you have worked the Gross Dexterity Test above on the answer sheet below, you do not have to erase your answers—the samples for Following Oral Directions will not interfere with them.)

"Mark E for 7, 8, 10, (slight pause) 3, and 52. (Pause.)

"Mark C for 32, 35, and 78. (Pause.)

"Mark D as in dog for 26, 35, (slight pause) 76, and 10. (Pause.)

"For the next set of questions, mark space E and also mark the letter I call, unless E is already marked. If E is already marked for that number, do not make any mark for that number.

"Mark B as in boy for 56, 3, (slight pause) 80, and 84. (Pause.)

"Mark A for 33, 29, (slight pause) 8, and 58. (Pause.)

"Mark C for 79, 52, (slight pause) and 28."

NOTE: This answer sheet provides spaces for both types of questions on this page. You do not have to erase your answers to one practice test before you work the other.

	A B C D E		A B C D E		A B C D E		A B C D E		A B C D E
1		26		51		76		101	
2		27		52		77		102	
3		28		53		78		103	
4		29		54		79		104	
5		30		55		80		105	
6		31		56		81		106	
7		32		57		82		107	
8		33		58		83		108	
9		34		59		84		109	
10		35		60		85		110	

TECHNIQUES OF STUDY AND TEST-TAKING

Although a thorough knowledge of the subject matter is the most important factor in succeeding on your exam, the following suggestions could raise your score substantially. These few pointers will give you the strategy employed on tests by those who are most successful in this not-so-mysterious art. It's really quite simple. Do things right . . . right from the beginning. Make successful methods a habit. Then you'll get the greatest dividends from the time you invest in this book.

You're going to pass this examination because you have received the best possible preparation for it. But, unlike many others, you're going to give the best possible account of yourself by acquiring the rare skill of effectively using your knowledge to answer the examination questions.

First off, get rid of any negative attitudes toward the test. You have a negative attitude when you view the test as a device to "trip you up" rather than an opportunity to show how effectively you have learned.

APPROACH THE TEST WITH SELF-CONFIDENCE.
Plugging through this book was no mean job, and now that you've done it you're probably better prepared than 90% of the others. Self-confidence is one of the biggest strategic assets you can bring to the testing room.

Nobody likes tests, but some poor souls permit themselves to get upset or angry when they see what they think is an unfair test. The expert doesn't. He keeps calm and moves right ahead, knowing that everyone is taking the same test. Anger, resentment, fear . . . they all slow you down. "Grin and bear it!"

Besides, every test you take, including this one, is a valuable experience which improves your skill. Since you will undoubtedly be taking other tests in the years to come, it may help you to regard this one as training to perfect your skill.

Keep calm; there's no point in panic. If you've done your work there's no need for it; and if you haven't, a cool head is your very first requirement.

Why be the frightened kind of student who enters the examination chamber in a mental coma? A test taken under mental stress does not provide a fair measure of your ability. At the very least, this book has removed for you some of the fear and mystery that surrounds examinations. A certain amount of concern is normal and good, but excessive worry saps your strength and keenness. In other words, be prepared EMOTIONALLY.

Pre-Test Review

If you know any others who are taking this test, you'll probably find it helpful to review the book and your notes with them. The group should be small, certainly not more than four. Team study at this stage should seek to review the material in a different way than you learned it originally; should strive for an exchange of ideas between you and the other members of the group; should be selective in sticking to important ideas; should stress the vague and the unfamiliar rather than that which you all know well; should be businesslike and devoid of any nonsense; should end as soon as you get tired.

One of the *worst* strategies in test taking is to do *all* your preparation the night before the exam. As a reader of this book, you have scheduled and spaced your study properly so as not to suffer from the fatigue and emotional disturbance that comes from cramming the night before.

Cramming is a very good way to *guarantee poor test results*.

However, you would be wise to prepare yourself factually by *reviewing your notes* in the 48 hours preceding the exam. You shouldn't have to spend more than two or three hours in this way. Stick to salient points. The others will fall into place quickly.

Don't confuse cramming with a final, calm **review** which helps you focus on the significant areas of this **book** and further strengthens your confidence in your **ability** to handle the test questions. In other words, **prepare** yourself FACTUALLY.

Keep Fit

Mind and body work together. Poor physical condition will lower your mental efficiency. In preparing for an examination, observe the common-sense rules of health. Get sufficient sleep and rest, eat proper foods, plan recreation and exercise. In relation to health and examinations, two cautions are in order. Don't miss your meals prior to an examination in order to get extra time for study. Likewise, don't miss your regular sleep by sitting up late to "cram" for the examination. Cramming is an attempt to learn in a very short period of time what should have been learned through regular and consistent study. Not only are these two habits detrimental to health, but seldom do they pay off in terms of effective learning. It is likely that you will be *more confused* than better prepared on the day of the examination if you have broken into your daily routine by missing your meals or sleep.

On the night before the examination go to bed at your regular time and try to get a good night's sleep. Don't go to the movies. Don't date. In other words, prepare yourself PHYSICALLY.

T-HOUR MINUS ONE

After a very light, leisurely meal, get to the examination room ahead of time, perhaps ten minutes early . . . but not so early that you have time to get into an argument with others about what's going to be asked on the exam, etc. The reason for coming early is to help you get accustomed to the room. It will help you to a better start.

Bring all necessary equipment . . .

. . . pen, two sharpened pencils, watch, paper, eraser, ruler, and any other things you're instructed to bring.

Get settled . . .

. . . by finding your seat and staying in it. If no special seats have been assigned, take one in the front to facilitate the seating of others coming in after you.

The test will be given by a test supervisor who reads the directions and otherwise tells you what to do. The people who walk about passing out the test papers and assisting with the examination are test proctors. If you're not able to see or hear properly notify the supervisor or a proctor. If you have any other difficulties during the examination, like a defective test booklet, scoring pencil, answer sheet; or if it's too hot or cold or dark or drafty, let them know. You're entitled to favorable test conditions, and if you don't have them you won't be able to do your best. Don't be a crank, but don't be shy either. An important function of the proctor is to see to it that you have favorable test conditions.

Relax . . .

. . . and don't bring on unnecessary tenseness by worrying about the difficulty of the examination. If necessary wait a minute before beginning to write. If you're still tense, take a couple of deep breaths, look over your test equipment, or do something which will take your mind away from the examination for a moment.

If your collar or shoes are tight, loosen them.

Put away unnecessary materials so that you have a good, clear space on your desk to write freely.

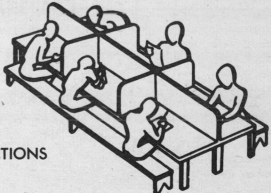

You Must Have
TO GIVE YOUR
Best Test
PERFORMANCE

(1) A GOOD TEST ENVIRONMENT

(2) A COMPLETE UNDERSTANDING OF DIRECTIONS

(3) A DESIRE TO DO YOUR BEST

WHEN THEY SAY "GO" — TAKE YOUR TIME!

Listen very carefully to the test supervisor. If you fail to hear something important that he says, you may not be able to read it in the written directions and may suffer accordingly.

If you don't understand the directions you have heard or read, raise your hand and inform the proctor. Read carefully the directions for *each* part of the test before beginning to work on that part. If you skip over such directions too hastily, you may miss a main idea and thus lose credit for an entire section.

Get an Overview of the Examination

After reading the directions carefully, look over the entire examination to get an over-view of the nature and scope of the test. The purpose of this over-view is to give you some idea of the nature, scope, and difficulty of the examination.

It has another advantage. An item might be so phrased that it sets in motion a chain of thought that might be helpful in answering other items on the examination.

Still another benefit to be derived from reading all the items before you answer any is that the few minutes involved in reading the items gives you an opportunity to relax before beginning the examination. This will make for better concentration. As you read over these items the first time, check those whose answers immediately come to you. These will be the ones you will answer first. Read each item carefully before answering. It is a good practice to read each item at least twice to be sure that you understand it.

Plan Ahead

In other words, you should know precisely where you are going before you start. You should know:
1. whether you have to answer all the questions or whether you can choose those that are easiest for you;
2. whether all the questions are easy; (there may be a pattern of difficult, easy, etc.)
3. The length of the test; the number of questions;
4. The kind of scoring method used;
5. Which questions, if any, carry extra weight;
6. What types of questions are on the test;
7. What directions apply to each part of the test;
8. Whether you must answer the questions consecutively.

Budget Your Time Strategically!

Quickly figure out how much of the allotted time you can give to each section and still finish ahead of time. Don't forget to figure on the time you're investing in the overview. Then alter your schedule so that you can spend more time on those parts that count most. Then, if you can, plan to spend less time on the easier questions, so that you can devote the time saved to the harder questions. Figuring roughly, you should finish half the questions when half the allotted time has gone by. If there are 100 questions and you have three hours, you should have finished 50 questions after one and one half hours. So bring along a watch whether the instructions call for one or not. Jot down your "exam budget" and stick to it INTELLIGENTLY.

EXAMINATION STRATEGY

Probably the most important single strategy you can learn is to do the easy questions first. The very hard questions should be read and temporarily postponed. Identify them with a dot and return to them later.

This strategy has several advantages for you:
1. You're sure to get credit for all the questions you're sure of. If time runs out, you'll have all the sure shots, losing out only on those which you might have missed anyway.

2. By reading and laying away the tough ones you give your subconscious a chance to work on them. You may be pleasantly surprised to find the answers to the puzzlers popping up for you as you deal with related questions.

3. You won't risk getting caught by the time limit just as you reach a question you know really well.

A Tested Tactic

It's inadvisable on some examinations to answer each question in the order presented. The reason for this is that some examiners design tests so as to extract as much mental energy from you as possible. They put the most difficult questions at the beginning, the easier questions last. Or they may vary difficult with easy questions in a fairly regular pattern right through the test. Your survey of the test should reveal the pattern and your strategy for dealing with it.

If difficult questions appear at the beginning, answer them until you feel yourself slowing down or getting tired. Then switch to an easier part of the examination. You will return to the difficult portion after you have rebuilt your confidence by answering a batch of easy questions. Knowing that you have a certain number of points "under your belt" will help you when you return to the more difficult questions. You'll answer them with a much clearer mind; and you'll be refreshed by the change of pace.

Time

Use your time wisely. It's an important element in your test and you must use every minute effectively, working as rapidly as you can without sacrificing accuracy. Your exam survey and budget will guide you in dispensing your time. Wherever you can, pick up seconds on the easy ones. Devote your savings to the hard ones. If possible, pick up time on the lower value questions and devote it to those which give you the most points.

Relax Occasionally and Avoid Fatigue

If the exam is long (two or more hours) give yourself short rest periods as you feel you need them. If you're not permitted to leave the room, relax in your seat, look up from your paper, rest your eyes, stretch your legs, shift your body. Break physical and mental tension. Take several deep breaths and get back to the job, refreshed. If you

don't do this you run the risk of getting nervous and tightening up. Your thinking may be hampered and you may make a few unnecessary mistakes.

Do not become worried or discouraged if the examination seems difficult to you. The questions in the various fields are purposely made difficult and searching so that the examination will discriminate effectively even among superior students. No one is expected to get a perfect or near-perfect score.

Remember that if the examination seems difficult to you, it may be even more difficult for your neighbor.

Think!

This is not a joke because you're not an IBM machine. Nobody is able to write all the time and also to read and think through each question. You must plan each answer. Don't give hurried answers in an atmosphere of panic. Even though you see a lot of questions, remember that they are objective and not very time-consuming. Don't rush headlong through questions that must be thought through.

Edit, Check, Proofread . . .

. . . after completing all the questions. Invariably, you will find some foolish errors which you needn't have made, and which you can easily correct. Don't just sit back or leave the room ahead of time. Read over your answers and make sure you wrote exactly what you meant to write. And that you wrote the answers in the right place. You might even find that you have omitted some answers inadvertently. You have budgeted time for this job of proofreading. PROOFREAD and pick up points.

One caution, though. Don't count on making major changes. And don't go in for wholesale changing of answers. To arrive at your answers in the first place you have read carefully and thought correctly. Second-guessing at this stage is more likely to result in wrong answers. So don't make changes unless you are quite certain you were wrong in the first place.

FOLLOW DIRECTIONS CAREFULLY

In answering questions on the objective or short-form examination, it is most important to follow all instructions carefully. Unless you have marked the answers properly, you will not receive credit for them. In addition, even in the same examination, the instructions will not be consistent. In one section you may be urged to guess if you are not certain;

in another you may be cautioned against guessing. Some questions will call for the best choice among four or five alternatives; others may ask you to select the one incorrect or the least probable answer.

On some tests you will be provided with worked out fore-exercises, complete with correct answers. However, avoid the temptation to skip the directions and begin working just from reading the model questions and answers. Even though you may be familiar with that particular type of question, the directions may be different from those which you had followed previously. If the type of question should be new to you, work through the model until you understand it perfectly. This may save you time, and earn you a higher rating on the examination.

If the directions for the examination are written, read them carefully, at least twice. If the directions are given orally, listen attentively and then follow them precisely. For example, if you are directed to use plus (+) and minus (−) to mark true—false items, then don't use "T" and "F". If you are instructed to "blacken" a space on machine-scored tests, do not use a check (✔) or an "X". Make all symbols legible, and be sure that they have been placed in the proper answer space. It is easy, for example, to place the answer for item 5 in the space reserved for item 6. If this is done, then all of your following answers may be wrong. It is also very important that you understand the method they will use in scoring the examination. Sometimes they tell you in the directions. The method of scoring may affect the amount of time you spend on an item, especially if some items count more than others. Likewise, the directions may indicate whether or not you should guess in case you are not sure of the answer. Some methods of scoring penalize you for guessing.

Cue Words. Pay special attention to qualifying words or phrases in the directions. Such words as *one, best reason, surest, means most nearly the same as, preferable, least correct,* etc., all indicate that *one* response is called for, and that you must select the response which best fits the qualifications in the question.

Time. Sometimes a time limit is set for each section of the examination. If that is the case, follow the time instructions carefully. Your *exam budget* and your watch can help you here. Even if you haven't finished a section when the time limit is up, pass on to the next section. The examination has been planned according to the time schedule.

If the examination paper bears the instruction "Do not turn over page until signal is given," or "Do not start until signal is given," follow the instruction. Otherwise, you may be disqualified.

Pay Close Attention. Be sure you understand what you're doing at all times. Especially in dealing with true-false or multiple-choice questions it's vital that you understand the meaning of every question. It is normal to be working under stress when taking an examination, and it is easy to skip a word or jump to a false conclusion, which may cost you points on the examination. In many multiple-choice and matching questions, the examiners deliberately insert plausible-appearing false answers in order to catch the candidate who is not alert.

Answer clearly. If the examiner who marks your paper cannot understand what you mean, you will not receive credit for your correct answer. On a True-False examination you will not receive any credit for a question which is marked both true and false. If you are asked to underline, be certain that your lines are under and not through the words and that they do not extend beyond them. When using the separate answer sheet it is important *when you decide to change an answer,* you erase the first answer completely. If you leave any graphite from the pencil on the wrong space it will cause the scoring machine to cancel the right answer for that question.

Watch Your "Weights." If the examination is "weighted" it means that some parts of the examination are considered more important than others and rated more highly. For instance, you may find that the instructions will indicate "Part I, Weight 50; Part II, Weight 25, Part III, Weight 25." In such a case, you would devote half of your time to the first part, and divide the second half of your time among Parts II and III.

A Funny Thing . . .

. . . happened to you on your way to the bottom of the totem pole. You *thought* the right answer but you marked the *wrong* one.

1. You *mixed answer symbols!* You decided (rightly) that Baltimore (Choice D) was correct. Then you marked *B* (for Baltimore) instead of *D.*

2. You *misread* a simple instruction! Asked to give the *latest* word in a scrambled sentence, you correctly arranged the sentence, and then marked the letter corresponding to the *earliest* word in that miserable sentence.

3. You *inverted digits!* Instead of the correct number, 96, you wrote (or read) 69.
Funny? Tragic! Stay away from accidents.

Record your answers on the answer sheet one by one as you answer the questions. Care should be taken that these answers are recorded next to the appropriate numbers on your answer sheet. It is poor practice to write your answers first on the test booklet and then to transfer them all at one time to the answer sheet. This procedure causes many errors. And then, how would you feel if you ran out of time before you had a chance to transfer all the answers.

When and How To Guess

Read the directions carefully to determine the scoring method that will be used. In some tests, the directions will indicate that guessing is advisable if you do not know the answer to a question. In such tests, only the right answers are counted in determining your score. If such is the case, don't omit any items. If you do not know the answer, or if you are not sure of your answer, then *guess.*

On the other hand, if the directions state that a scoring formula *will* be used in determining your score or that you are *not to guess,* then *omit* the question if you do not know the answer, or if you are not sure of the answer. When the scoring formula is used, a percentage of the *wrong* answers will be subtracted from the number of *right* answers as a correction for haphazard guessing. It is improbable, therefore, that mere guessing will improve your score significantly. It may even lower your score. Another disadvantage in guessing under such circumstances is that it consumes valuable time that you might profitably use in answering the questions you know.

If, however, you are uncertain of the correct answer but have *some* knowledge of the question and are able to eliminate one or more of the answer choices as wrong, your chance of getting the right answer is improved, and it will be to your advantage to *answer* such a question rather than *omit* it.

BEAT THE ANSWER SHEET

Even though you've had plenty of practice with the answer sheet used on machine-scored examinations, we must give you a few more, last-minute pointers.

The present popularity of tests requires the use of electrical test scoring machines. With these machines, scoring which would require the labor of several men for hours can be handled by one man in a fraction of the time.

The scoring machine is an amazingly intricate and helpful device, but the machine is not human. The machine cannot, for example, tell the difference between an intended answer and a stray pencil mark, and will count both indiscriminately. The machine cannot count a pencil mark, if the pencil mark is not brought in contact with the electrodes. For these reasons, specially printed answer sheets with response spaces properly located and properly filled in must be employed. Since not all pencil leads contain the necessary ingredients, a special pencil must be used and a heavy solid mark must be made to indicate answers.

(a) Each pencil mark must be heavy and black. Light marks should be retraced with the special pencil.

(b) Each mark must be in the space between the pair of dotted lines and entirely fill this space.

(c) All stray pencil marks on the paper, clearly not intended as answers, must be completely erased.

(d) Each question must have only one answer indicated. If multiple answers occur, all extraneous marks should be thoroughly erased. Otherwise, the machine will give you *no* credit for your correct answer.

Be sure to use the special electrographic pencil!

HERE'S HOW TO MARK YOUR ANSWERS ON MACHINE-SCORED ANSWER SHEETS:

Make only ONE mark for each answer. Additional and stray marks may be counted as mistakes. In making corrections, erase errors COMPLETELY. Make glossy black marks.

Your answer sheet is the only one that reaches the office where papers are scored. For this reason it is important that the blanks at the top be filled in completely and correctly. The proctors will check this, but just in case they slip up, make certain yourself that your paper is complete.

Many exams caution competitors against making any marks on the test booklet itself. Obey that caution even though it goes against your grain to work neatly. If you work neatly and obediently with the test booklet you'll probably do the same with the answer sheet. And that pays off in high scores.

3

PART THREE

The Jobs In Civil Service

JOBS IN CIVIL SERVICE

This section of the book contains actual job announcements for Federal positions which are classified by the nature of the work to be performed and the requirements necessary to qualify for each position. It is possible that the requirements for some of the positions have changed slightly since the publication of this book, and in addition some positions may have been slotted into slightly different pay grades. Therefore, it is suggested that if you are interested in a particular position and you seem to meet the requirements for it, that you request a current job announcement from the nearest U.S. Office of Personnel Management.

CLERICAL JOBS

NEARLY half the jobs in the federal civil service are clerical, and since World War II the government's demand for clerical workers has exceeded the supply. Agencies have not been able to fill all the competent stenographers, typists, tabulating-machine operators and file clerks they need.

In government the title "clerk" describes more positions than it does in private industry. An editor or a writer may be called a clerk (Editorial Clerk), a purchasing agent with fairly important responsibilities may be a clerk (Purchasing Clerk), or an accountant may be called a clerk (Cost Accounting Clerk).

These are the names of some of the government clerical jobs: Clerk-Stenographer, Clerk-Typist, Correspondence Clerk, Varitypist, Dictating Machine Operator, Shorthand Reporter, Mail Clerk, File Clerk, Record Clerk and Business Machine Operator.

Clerks do personnel work, auditing and statistical operations, property and supply work and proofreading. They make blueprints and photostats, prepare payrolls, supply information, work on traffic plans, operate switchboards, decipher codes, and work in engraving and printing plants.

Clerical salaries have risen sharply in recent years, probably exceeding average salaries for similar jobs in private industry. Entering pay varies from GS-1 to GS-6 a year and is sometimes higher. There are usually good opportunities for advancement, and clerk jobs can be the start of a real career in the government.

Here are some of the requirements for clerical positions.

CLERK, GS-2, GS-3

DESCRIPTION OF WORK: A wide variety of clerical positions will be filled from this examination. Among the basic duties to be performed are, for example: searching for and compiling information and data; indexing, filing, and maintaining records; receiving and routing mail; answering inquiries orally or by correspondence; coding information for mechanical tabulation; maintaining time, leave, payroll, personnel, retirement, or other records; and other similar duties.

BASIS OF RATING: Competitors will be rated on the basis of scores on the verbal abilities and clerical abilities tests. The ratings will be based on a scale of 100. Better performance in the test will be required to establish eligibility at grade GS-3 than at grade GS-2.

WORKING FOR THE U.S. POSTAL SERVICE

ONE of the most popular jobs in the government service is post office work. The working conditions and the rates of pay have not always been, in the opinion of many, good enough for the importance of the work, but these defects have been at least partially remedied during the past ten years; more attention has been paid to employee grievances and pay has increased.

The U.S. Postal Service has been delegated the authority to conduct their own competitive examinations for entrance into the Postal Service. Applications for these positions are therefore issued and received by the Post Office where the appointments are to be made.

Examinations are given for Postmaster, Substitute Clerk-Substitute Carrier, Substitute Mail Handler, Rural Carrier, some positions in the Motor Vehicle Service (for example, Garageman and Motor Vehicle Operator), and certain custodial positions.

The jobs of Assistant Postmaster, Superintendent of Mails, Foreman, Postal Inspector, and Inspector in Charge are filled by promotion from the ranks. Most promotions are made by the local postmaster and no examinations are given for them. The postmaster promotes by whatever standards he chooses, or by no standards at all. Promotion to one position, however—that of Postal Inspector—is made through examinations held by the Postal Service.

Here are the salaries, duties, and requirements for postal positions.

POSTMASTER

Postmasterships fall into four groupings, depending upon the size of the community and the volume of mail. Rates of pay and requirements vary sharply for each of the four classes and even within them.

Vacancies in postmaster positions at offices of the first, second and third class may be filled through open competitive examinations or through persons already in the Service. But appointments must be made by the President with the confirmation of the Senate: hence the entry of political considerations. Vacancies in fourth class post offices are filled through open competitive examinations or appointments by the Postmaster General upon recommendations of post office inspectors who have visited and secured applications in localities where vacancies exist.

REQUIREMENTS:

To be eligible for the first three classes the applicant must have lived in the community served by the post office for at least one year. For the fourth class the applicant must be living in the community at the time he submits his application.

Applicants for the larger first class postmasterships will have to show by their experience that they have the ability to "organize, plan and schedule the work of a large business organization in order to operate efficiently within a fixed budget." They also must show that they can deal with the public agreeably and effectively and negotiate with all users of the mail, large or small.

Applicants must be over eighteen. There is no maximum age limit.

BASIS OF RATING: Applicants for the highest first class postmasterships which are graded as levels ten through nineteen are not required to take a written examination, but are rated on a scale of one hundred on the basis of their fitness and experience. All applicants for first, second and third class postmastership under level 10 are examined on the basis of a written test and experience. They must attain a rating of, at least, seventy on both the written test and experience, respectively. Larger fourth class post offices are filled by open competitive examination. The smaller ones in rural communities are usually run together with some other business, and the postmastership goes to a person who can show that he has space and is acceptable to his neighbors.

Applicants taking a written test are questioned on verbal abilities, such as reading comprehension and vocabulary, as well as post office business management and arithmetic. No experience in managing a post office is actually required, however, to pass the test.

S1904

POST OFFICE CLERK AND LETTER CARRIER

The postal clerk and letter carrier enter the service as substitutes, and they usually take an examination called Substitute Clerk and Substitute Carrier.

DUTIES: Substitute Clerks handle heavy sacks of letter mail, paper mail, and parcel post weighing 80 pounds or more; and distribute mail to post offices and to carrier routes in accordance with established schemes. They may also perform a variety of services at public windows of the main post office, post office branches or stations; and perform related duties as assigned. The work involves continuous standing, throwing of mail, stretching, and reaching. Substitute Clerks are normally assigned to relieve regular employees, to serve during peak workload hours, and such other tours as needed, and usually involve evening or night duty.

Substitute Carriers are responsible for the prompt and efficient delivery and collection of mail on foot or by vehicle under varying conditions in a prescribed area or on various routes. They must serve in all kinds of weather and may be required to drive motor vehicles in all kinds of traffic and road conditions to deliver parcel post from trucks and make collections of mail from various boxes in the city. They may be required to carry on their shoulders loads weighing as much as 35 pounds and to load and unload full sacks of mail from trucks.

The duties of some Substitute Carrier positions include driving motor vehicles and appointees will not be assigned to such positions unless they possess a valid and appropriate Motor Vehicle Operators Permit, or succeed in obtaining such a permit within 30 days.

The duties of newly appointed substitute clerks, carriers and special delivery messengers are at times interchangeable.

REQUIREMENTS: Applicants must not have any physical defect which would prevent them from performing work which requires arduous physical exertion. Eyesight must be at least 20/30 in one eye. Applicants must be over eighteen years, but there is no maximum age limit.

BASIS OF RATING. A two hour written examination is given. Test subjects are of the following types: 1) following instructions or 2) address checking

RURAL CARRIER

REQUIREMENTS: Applicants must live in the delivery zone of the post office for at least a year, and be at least eighteen years of age. They must be physically able to do the work.

BASIS OF RATING: A written test, covering general subjects and arithmetic.

MAIL HANDLER

DUTIES: The handler loads and unloads trucks, sets up and takes down bag racks, makes simple distribution of parcel post, and cares for canceling machines.

REQUIREMENTS: Applicants must be physically able to do the work, have good vision and normal hearing. Only those who live in the area served by the post office issuing the exam are eligible.

BASIS OF RATING: An elementary written test is given, designed to determine ability to read and write and perform simple tasks. Applicants must also pass a strength test, by shouldering and carrying a mail sack weighing 100 pounds.

LABOR AND MECHANICAL

MOST citizens do not realize that the Government of the United States is the largest employer of mechanical, manual, and laboring workers in the country.

The government is more than offices: it is factories, shipyards, shops, docks, and power plants. The government makes gimmicks and battleships, runs irrigation systems and a printing office in Washington, mints and powerhouses. In time of war there were more than a million mechanical and manual workers in the government. In peacetime there are nearly as many.

APPRENTICES

The government hires mechanics, craftsmen, and laborers, of course; but several of the agencies conduct their own apprentice training programs. A young man who wants to learn a trade may come in under this program and earn his way from the very beginning. There are apprenticeship training programs in many occupations, among them: carpenter, coppersmith, electrician, electronics mechanic, electroplater, glass apparatus maker, instrument maker, joiner, letterer and grainer, machinist, modelmaker, painter, patternmaker, pipefitter, plumber, refrigeration and air conditioning mechanic, sheetmetal worker, toolmaker, and welder.

Apprentices are employed in navy yards, arsenals, other Army and Navy Department establishments, and the Government Printing Office. Four classes of apprentices have been established in some of the Navy Yard trades. There is, usually, no hard and fast pay scale for all apprentices. The apprentice pay rate is usually set in ratio to the journeyman pay in the trade.

Apprentices must often buy textbooks and certain other equipment.

The age limit for apprentices is usually eighteen. There is no maximum age limit.

As a beginner in a skilled trade the apprentice receives instruction through an apprentice school and shop assignments in the rudiments of his trade, in technical subjects such as mechanical drawing, mathematics, blueprint interpretation. He learns to work with the machinery and materials of his trade and does elementary tasks under the supervision of a shop instructor.

Apprenticeship usually lasts four years, or eight six-month periods, made up of approximately 1,025 shop and school hours. The first year's shop and school work is considered a trial period. Apprenticeships in the Government Printing Office are of longer duration.

There are no educational requirements, but the applicant for an apprenticeship must take a written test.

Advancement comes regularly to the apprentice who completes his service satisfactorily; and when he has finished his prescribed period of training, he is promoted to the status of artisan in his trade, no matter what his age.

SKILLED AND SEMI-SKILLED POSITIONS

We must preface our survey of the skilled and semi-skilled jobs in the government by reminding the reader that this is only a selection. The full list of such positions includes probably every kind of job in this class. Most, but not all, such positions are paid at hourly rates, which may vary somewhat for different sections of the country. The government usually follows the custom of the trade, paying, in some cases, on a piecework basis. Overtime is on a time-and-a-half basis, rather than, as in jobs of other types, at straight time. The rate of pay in many cases is determined by skill. Some positions are available on both hourly and annual salary. The age limit is usually eighteen, the applicant must be physically able to do the work.

Here are some of the positions found in federal establishments:

Steamfitter, Stationary Boiler Fireman, Auto Equipment Repair Assistant Foreman, Engineer Equipment Repair Foreman, Auto Equipment Repairer, Shoe Repair Foreman, Sheet-Metal Worker, Sheet-Metal and Welding Foreman, Carpenter, Packer and Crater, Engineering Equipment Operator, Plumber, Woodworker, Aircraft Mechanic, Metalsmith (Aviation), Radio Mechanic, Electrician, Upholsterer, Electrotyper (Molder), Electrotyper (Finisher), Stereotyper, Printer (Monotype Keyboard Operator), Printer (Slug Machine Operator), Printer Proofreader, Photoengraver, Carpenter (Junior), Carpenter (Superintendent), Refrigeration and Air-Conditioning Mechanic, Mason (Brick and Stone), Painter, General Helper, Toolmaker, Model Maker, Machinist Helper, Machinist, Aircraft Painter and Doper, Aircraft Parachute and Clothing Repairer, Radio and Electrical Instrument Repairer, Radio and Electronics Mechanic.

Radar Mechanic, Typewriter Cleaner and Case Repairer, Typewriter Repairman, Duplicating Machine Mechanic, Computing Machine Mechanic, Water Plant Operator, Wire Worker (Aviation), Office Appliance Repairer, Aircraft Jet Engine Mechanic, Automotive Mechanic, Aircraft Service Mechanic, Preflight Mechanic, Flight Test Mechanic, Assistant Engineer (Pipeline Dredge-Class), Fireman (Marine), Leverman, Mate (Pipeline Dredge-Class), Mate (Pipeline Dredge-Class), Operator (Pushboat).

Cook, Locksmith, Gardener, Laborer, Operator (Road-Building Equipment), Butcher, Blacksmith, Laborer, Box Shop Helper, Laborer (Warehouse), Auto Trade Laborer, Utilities Trades Laborer, Carpenter Shop Laborer, Munitions Handler, Freight Handler, Handyman, Trackman, Junior Reclamation Worker, Mail Handler (this is an Army, not a Post Office position), Lineman, Groundman, Line Truck Operator, Laundry Helper.

Skilled and semi-skilled craft positions are also open on a full-time, annual-salary basis. Here are some typical positions of this kind:

ELECTRICIAN — PLUMBER — CARPENTER — PAINTER: Applicants must have completed a four-year apprenticeship or have been in trade at least four years to qualify. Another year's journeyman experience is required for a higher-paid post; and two years' journeyman experience for the top-rated post.

OPERATING ENGINEER: Applicants for the job must show two years' experience or three years' experience in operating or installing such equipment as boilers in buildings. And experience is required in steam generation, air conditioning, or refrigeration.

OFFICE APPLIANCE REPAIRMAN: Three years of experience are required.

PHOTOGRAPHER: One to four years of experience in photography work required. A resident course in photography may be substituted for part of the experience. There is also a photographer position which requires 6 months experience. The job includes routine photo lab work and aid to photographers. It is a good spot for young people to learn the field.

UNSKILLED POSITIONS

Thousands of positions in the government service are open to persons with no skills or with only a small amount of training. Here are some of them:

HOUSEKEEPING AID: Performs routine manual domestic work such as making beds, quarters, hallways, bathrooms, etc. Restricted to veterans.

KITCHEN HELPER: Assists in the preparation of foods for cooking and service. Sets dining room tables, washes dishes, scrubs kitchen. Restricted to veterans.

JANITOR: Three months' experience in manual work using physical effort.

MESSENGER: No experience; restricted to veterans; written examination tests ability to learn.

ELEVATOR OPERATOR: Three months' experience.

LABORER (GENERAL): Three months' experience.

LABORER (CUSTODIAL): Male, female. These jobs are restricted to veterans and require at least three months of exprience in manual work requiring strength and physical effort.

LAUNDRY WORKER: From three to six months experience in laundry operations such as checking, sorting, washing and ironing.

MESS ATTENDANT: No specific experience of any particular kind is required. This position is open to veterans only.

STOREKEEPING CLERK: No experience needed for the lowest grade.

PROFESSIONAL

Since so many jobs must be filled, the Government cannot accept applications for all kinds of jobs all the time. Opportunities to apply for specific types of positions are announced when there is a need to fill such positions. The "announcement" tells about the jobs — what experience or education you must have before your application will be accepted, whether a written test is required, where the jobs are located, what the pay is, and so on. The "announcement" foreshadows your test. You have to know something about it in order to read and understand it.

PROFESSIONAL AND ADMINISTRATIVE CAREER EXAMINATION

THIS examination is designed primarily to provide an avenue through which young people of professional caliber may begin a career in the Federal Government. An applicant must have a college degree, be a junior or senior college student studying for a degree, or have comparable qualifying experience. The qualifying examination is used by the departments and agencies of the Government to fill a wide variety of positions at the entrance or trainee level. Those who measure up to the high standards required and who demonstrate their ability to grow and develop on the job may aspire to the highest career assignments and work on programs of national and international importance. Positions are filled in various agencies in Washington, D.C. and throughout the U.S. and its territories. A few overseas positions may also be filled. Appointments are made primarily to positions at GS-5 and GS-7. While most appointments are made at GS-5, many applicants are appointed at GS-7 because they have either superior academic achievement or additional, graduate-level education.

Successful candidates will be assigned for training in such fields as:

Personnel management, general administration, economics and other social sciences, social security administration, management analysis, tax collection, electronic data processing, budget management, park ranger activities, statistics, investigation (including wage and hour), procurement and supply, housing management, archival science, adjudication and other quasi-legal work, food and drug inspection, and others.

Some agencies offer a limited number of what are, perhaps, the most coveted assignments. These are known as management internships. Specially planned programs are designed to develop persons with unusual promise as future administrators. Persons considered for these internships will be required to pass additional tests of greater difficulty. Those selected for one of these programs receive specialized instruction, varied work assignments and understudy or other types of training designed to develop managerial skills and knowledges.

The *Professional-Administrative Career Exam* is open from the fall of one year into the spring of the following year, and written tests are scheduled several times during this period.

LEGAL POSITIONS

When a position is open and a civil service examination is to be given for it, a job announcement is drawn up. This is generally from two to six printed pages in length and contains just about everything an applicant should know. The announcement begins with the job title and salary. A typical announcement then describes the work, the location of the position, the education and experience requirements, the kind of examination to be given, the system of rating. It may also have something to say about veteran preference and the age limit. It tells which application form is to be filled out, where to get the form, and where and when to file it. Study the job announcement carefully. It will answer many of your questions and help you decide whether you like the position and are qualified for it.

Application for Attorney positions should be made direct to the particular Government agency in which employment is desired. The Commission is ordinarily not informed of openings and does not, therefore, maintain or publish lists of Federal agencies which may desire to employ Attorneys. Each Federal agency is responsible for determining in accordance with appropriate standards the qualifications of Attorneys who apply to it for employment as well as for making the appointments.

Attorney positions are thus, to an extent, in the category of patronage jobs. The lawyer who wants a federal job should use whatever contacts he has, besides getting in touch with the agencies in which he is interested. He would be wise, too, to keep up with news of new agencies and bureaus as they are formed, and pull whatever strings he can to get in at the start. Recommendations from politicians, college professors, and other influential persons really count.

Federal judges are appointed by the President, as are federal district attorneys and assistant district attorneys. Patronage is an important factor in these positions; the advice of senators and representatives and the local party political leaders pretty much decides who gets the job. The political services of the prospective judge or district attorney are likely to be a telling consideration.

Judges employ legal secretaries. Those who work for the Supreme Court Justices are usually topflight graduates recommended by deans of the best law schools. Those who work for circuit or district judges are more likely to be appointed through recommendation, personal acquaintance, or patronage.

Congressional committees also use lawyers to investigate, question witnesses, gather evidence, and write reports. The lawyer who wants that kind of job should make the acquaintance of political leaders and cultivate the party leaders who are in a position to hand out such posts. Keeping posted on congressional events and following up on the creation of special committees is important, of course.

These positions, varying in grade and salary with the duties involved, range from higher-grade legal positions that require full professional legal training, but do not require admission to the bar, to those in the lower grades, requiring legal training but little or no experience.

For example, the previously described *Professional-Administrative Career Exam* is used to fill a variety of entrance level positions for which legal training is either required or highly desirable.

INVESTIGATION AND LAW ENFORCEMENT

THE highly publicized Federal Bureau of Investigation is only one of the federal agencies which enforces the law. A dozen government agencies employ "cops" or detectives for jobs from guarding property and patrolling borders to the most highly technical intelligence operations. Agencies which employ investigators or law-enforcement personnel include: Department of Justice, State Department, Treasury, Post Office, Army Department, Navy Department, Civil Service Commission, Atomic Energy Commission, Food and Drug Administration, Securities and Exchange Commission, and Customs Bureau. Most Federal agencies also employ inspectors in various capacities.

The work of law-enforcement officers and investigators is often dramatic, but as often arduous, too, and dangerous. In one of the security positions the training is as tough as that given commando units in the armed forces. The work may be dull for days and weeks, but it may become intense and exciting.

It frequently requires long absence from home and family and operations under trying physical conditions.

Most of the posts naturally have stiff physical requirements, calling for well-proportioned, healthy, agile men. Eyesight and hearing requirements are higher than on most other federal jobs, and full use of arms and legs is a must. Speech defects, scars, blemishes, or other defects which might interfere with the appointee's duties will cause rejection.

The positions mentioned below are representative of the law-enforcement, investigating, and inspection positions in the federal service.

SPECIAL AGENT, FBI

The Civil Service Commission does not hire Federal Bureau of Investigation personnel for either clerical or the more specialized posts. Applications may be filed at any time, and they will be sent if you write the Director, Federal Bureau of Investigation, Washington, D.C., or any of the Bureau's offices, which are located in most of the larger cities.

DUTIES: The special agent is engaged in enforcing federal law, investigating its violations, gathering evidence for prosecution, checking the background of individuals, and tracing criminals. The work extends from enforcing antitrust laws to tracing bribes or uncovering evidence of espionage.

REQUIREMENTS: The applicant must be a male citizen between the ages of twenty-three and forty-one and meet high educational requirements. He must be at least 5 feet 7 inches tall. His vision must be not less than 20/40 in one eye and 20/50 in the weaker eye without glasses, 20/20 vision is required in each eye corrected, and color blindness will cause rejection. He must be able to hear ordinary conversation at least fifteen feet away with each ear. The applicant must be able to perform strenuous physical exertion and have no defects which would interfere with the use of firearms or participation in raids, dangerous assignments, or defensive tactics. He must be willing to serve in any part of the United States or its possessions, and must know how to drive a car. The applicant must be either (a) a law school graduate with at least two years of resident, undergraduate college work or (b) a college graduate majoring in accounting with at least three years of practical accounting experience.

BASIS OF RATING: Applicants who meet the basic requirements are afforded a detailed interview as well as written examinations. The latter are of a practical nature designed to test knowledge of law or accountancy. Any necessary travel expense incident to these tests must be borne by the applicant, and at no time should it be assumed that an appointment will be made because the opportunity for examination is offered. Prior to any appointment being made, applicants possessing the basic qualifications and who have successfully passed the necessary examinations are thoroughly investigated for the purpose of securing additional evidence of their qualifications and fitness for the position.

SECURITIES INVESTIGATOR

SALARY: GS-9 to GS-11 at entrance.

DUTIES: Securities Investigators work under the supervision of a Regional Administrator. They examine the books, records, and financial statements of national securities exchanges, members of national securities exchanges, brokers and dealers in the over-the-counter market, and investment advisers, in order to determine their financial condition and compliance with the acts administered by this Commission, its rules and regulations, and the rules and regulations of securities exchanges and national securities associations. They also conduct investigations involving the fraud and other provisions of the acts requiring the examination of books and records of individuals and various business organizations, and prepare reports of such examinations in accordance with accepted accounting principles.

REQUIREMENTS: Except for the substitution of education for general experience, applicants must have had, as a minimum, experience of the length specified in the table below and of the types described in the paragraphs following. The grade level and rating assigned to the applicant will depend primarily on the quality, scope, and responsibility of experience rather than the length.

Grade of		Experience Required	
Position	General	Special	Total
GS-9	3 years	2 years	5 years
GS-11	3 years	3 years	6 years

The general experience must have been progressively responsible accounting or accounting-investigative experience of a scope and quality sufficient to demonstrate conclusively the ability to handle complex technical accounting assignments commensurate with the duties of the position.

In addition to the required general experience, applicants must have acquired responsible accounting, auditing, investigative, or administrative experience in the securities field which has provided a broad knowledge of stock exchange procedure and stock brokerage accounting in what is generally known in the trade as "back office" experience.

BASIS OF RATING: Competitors will not be required to report for a written test but will be rated on a scale of 100, on the extent and quality of their experience and training relevant to the duties of the position. Such ratings will be based upon competitors' statements in their applications and upon any corroborative evidence obtained.

INTERNAL REVENUE AGENT

SALARY: GS-5 and GS-7 at entrance.

DESCRIPTION OF WORK: Internal Revenue Agents examine and audit the accounting books and records of individuals, partnerships, fiduciaries, and corporations to determine their correct Federal tax liabilities.

REQUIREMENTS: Applicants must have a minimum of 4 years of college with concentration in accounting, 3 years of experience comparable to a full 4-year professional accounting curriculum, any time-equivalent combination of education and experience, or possession of a Certified Public Accountant certificate.

BASIS OF RATING: Applicants qualifying on a basis of education will be rated on their academic achievement. Those qualifying on a basis of experience or possession of a CPA certificate will be rated on the quality, diversity, and extent of their experience. Applicants qualifying on a basis of experience will be required to take a written test on accounting principles not required of those qualifying on a basis of education or possession of a CPA certificate.

TREASURY ENFORCEMENT AGENT

SALARY: GS-5 and GS-7 at entrance.

DUTIES: Treasury Enforcement Agents enforce the laws coming under the jurisdiction of the Treasury Department. Positions are located in the seven enforcement arms of the Treasury: The Customs Agency Service; the Coast Guard's Intelligence Division; the U.S. Secret Service; the Bureau of Narcotics; and the Internal Revenue Service's Intelligence, Alcohol and Tobacco Tax, and Inspection Divisions. The techniques employed range from surveillance and undercover work to presenting evidence to Government prosecutors and testifying in court.

REQUIREMENTS: Experience in dealing with groups and in criminal investigation, 4 years of college study, membership in the Bar, or possession of a CPA certificate. Only men over the age of 21 are eligible because of the hazardous nature of these positions.

BASIS OF RATING: Applicants are rated on the basis of their performance on the Treasury Enforcement Agent examination.

SPECIAL AGENT, INTERNAL REVENUE SERVICE

SALARY: GS-5 and GS-7 at entrance.

DUTIES: Special Agents conduct investigations of alleged criminal violations of Federal tax laws, make recommendations with respect to criminal prosecution, prepare technical reports, and assist the United States Attorney in the preparation of the case and during the trial.

REQUIREMENTS: 3 years of responsible experience which required the knowledge and application of commercial accounting and auditing principles and practices sufficient to demonstrate the ability to analyze accounting and audit records and reports or a 6-year LL.B. degree or 4 years of college level study that included 12 semester hours in accounting. A written test is required.

BASIS OF RATING: Applicants are rated on the basis of their performance on the Treasury Enforcement Agent examination.

CORRECTIONAL OFFICER

SALARY: GS-6 a year at entrance.

DUTIES: The work involves supervising, safeguarding, and training inmates of federal institutions.

REQUIREMENTS: These applicants must have excellent character backgrounds, be cool in emergencies, and have good morals, patience, and capacity for leadership. Applicants must be physically able to do the work. There are no height or weight limits, but weight must be in proportion to height. Vision may not be less than 20/100 in each eye, corrected to 20/30 with glasses, and hearing in both ears must be normal. Applicants with hernia, organic heart disease, severe varicose veins, serious deformities of extremities (including weak feet), mental or nervous disorder, chronic constitutional disease, marked abnormality of speech, or facial disfigurement will be rejected. The age limits are twenty-five to forty-five. Applicant must also have had at least three and a half years of progressively responsible experience which required dealing effectively with individuals or groups of persons. Some substitution of higher or specialized education is permitted.

BASIS OF RATING: A written test is given to measure verbal abilities, judgment, and ability to make decisions on the basis of information given orally.

OPPORTUNITIES FOR ADVANCEMENT: The federal prison system offers a career; persons who start as correctional officers can advance to several kinds of higher positions. Opportunities are available not only in the institution where the officer happens to be stationed, but throughout the prison system. Supervisory and administrative positions which may be reached by promotion and transfer include work in such fields as custody, education, vocational training, skilled trades, social services, parole, recreation, culinary service, accounting, and farm activities.

GUARD

DUTIES: Guards patrol buildings or other premises to prevent trespass, fire, theft, damage or defacement of premises or their content; prevent unlawful removal of property; protect the occupants of the buildings from outside annoyances and interferences; control traffic; etc.

REQUIREMENTS: No experience is required for GS-2. One year active service in the armed forces, Coast Guard, Merchant Marine, or in any position whose duties were those described above is required for GS-3. Applicants' vision must be correctible to 20/30; color blindness disqualifies; hearing must be normal. Physical defects which would interfere with the work cause rejection. The minimum age limit for these positions is twenty-one; this age limit, however, does not apply to persons entitled to Veterans' Preference.

BASIS OF RATING: All competitors will be required to take a written test of reading comprehension and ability to follow oral directions. Competitors for these positions will be rated on the written test on a scale of 100. Competitors must attain a rating of at least seventy on the written test as a whole and will be required to attain a rating of seventy on each of the two parts of the test. Applicants will be notified when and where to report for the written test.

Inspector

Inspection work is related to investigating jobs. Inspectors see that building construction, elevators, fire escapes, plumbing, and other projects comply with regulations. They test weights and measures and act to enforce sanitary, food and drug, and public health laws. Among the various kinds of inspection are electrical, elevator, materials (seeing that supplies such as cement, asphalt, tile, coal meet specifications of quality and weight), motor-vehicle inspection, playground inspection, industrial-safety inspection, waterpipe inspection, lock and vault inspection, boiler inspection, wage-hour-law inspection, mattress inspection and food-law inspection.

A government inspector may check public works, street lighting and overhead lines, transportation, or public-safety devices. Certain of these positions are filled through the *Professional-Administrative Career Exam* such as that for Food and Drug Inspector; others, by special examination.

Now, a resume of the salaries, requirements, and tests prescribed for typical government inspectors.

SAFETY INSPECTOR

SALARY: GS-5 at entrance.
DUTIES: The Safety Inspector enforces the Interstate Commerce Commission's motor carrier safety regulations. Safety inspectors advise bus companies and others in the development of safety activities, accident prevention plans, and driver education; inspect motor vehicles for the condition of equipment; investigate causes of accidents; and work with state agencies.

REQUIREMENTS: Two years' experience investigating highway accidents, inspecting motor vehicles, conducting hearings on traffic violations, maintaining of motor carrier fleets, or important work on highway safety programs. Work as a traffic officer, motor vehicle dispatcher, or insurance claims adjuster does not qualify. The applicant must never have been held criminally responsible for any motor vehicle accident involving loss of life. For up to two years of experience, one year of appropriate education in transportation or mechanical engineering may be substituted for each six months of experience.
BASIS OF RATING: Applicants for GS-5 positions are rated entirely on the basis of a written test.

PATENT EXAMINER

SALARY: GS-5 through GS-13 at entrance.

DESCRIPTION OF WORK: The Patent Examiner performs professional scientific and technical work in the examination of applications for United States Patents. He evaluates the invention, determines if it will perform as claimed, uncovers any previous teachings or knowledge comparable to the invention claimed in the application, and determines if the application and its claimed invention meet all legal requirements for the granting of patents.

REQUIREMENTS: All applicants must have completed the requirements for a bachelor's or higher degree in professional engineering or in a scientific option at an accredited college. Experience may be combined with education if the combination is equivalent to the standard 4-year college course. Applicants for the higher grades must have had additional experience, or education, or both. Superior college students or those with trainee experience may qualify for higher grades than those to which their experience and education would otherwise entitle them.

BASIS OF RATING: Competitors will not be required to report for a written test but will be rated on a scale of 100, on the extent and quality of their experience and training relevant to the duties of the position. Such ratings will be based upon the competitors' statements in their applications and upon any additional evidence which may be secured.

MEDICINE, DENTISTRY, NURSING

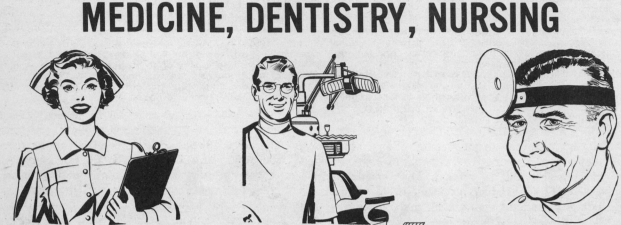

WITH the growth of social services in the past fifty years the government has developed a need for physicians, medical researchers, nurses, and similar workers in more and more fields. Wars have led to the establishment of a permanent corps of medical specialists and their assistants. The growth of psychiatric concepts, the development of occupational therapy, the public demand that veterans who need medical care should have it—all these factors demand a force of practitioners working for the government.

Research activities include the study of bacteriological warfare, the hunt for protection against the effects of radioactivity, the preparation of new vaccines, serums and other biological products. Medical jobs involve inspection of laboratories and testing of pharmaceuticals, running such public-relations campaigns as the one against syphilis, examining those entering the public service, the medical care of Indians on reservations, and straight medical work from the care of colds to the most complex plastic surgery.

Medical and related work in the federal service includes these jobs: Medical Officer, Hospital Administrator, Medical Technician, Dental Officer, Pharmacist, Physical Therapist, Public Health Nurse, Hospital Nurse, Dietitian, First-aid Attendant, Hospital Attendant, Dental Hygienist, Dental Mechanic, Occupational Therapist, Physiotherapist, Psychiatrist, Psychiatric Nurse, Coroner, and Embalmer. To this group might be added the Veterinary and the Veterinary Inspector.

The department which employs most medical workers in peacetime is the Veterans' Administration. The Army and Navy have medical and dental corps, which, of course, grow enormously during war. Other agencies which need doctors and their aides are the Public Health Service, a department which does notable work in improving public health and guarding against dangerous mass diseases, the Atomic Energy Commission, the Food and Drug Administration, the Children's Bureau of the Department of Health, Education, and Welfare—where extensive research is conducted in maternal and child health, and services are provided crippled children—the Bureau of Indian Affairs of the Interior Department, where, besides serving in hospitals, doctors make home calls and field trips, conduct school examinations and administer general public-health measures among the Indians, and in the Canal Zone, where they do dispensary and quarantine work. American physicians also accompany our missions in the Foreign Service. Incidentally, the Public Health Service supervises hospitals serving the Coast Guard, Merchant Marine, Army Engineer Corps, Army Transport Service and federal employees injured in the line of duty. Many federal agencies employ nurses in the emergency rooms which they maintain for their employees. Nurses also serve in U.S. hospitals and in a consultant capacity to state health departments on programs to control tuberculosis and venereal disease.

The government maintains an extensive nurse-training program, paying student nurses while teaching them.

Now let us have a look at some of the medical positions with their qualifications and requirements.

MEDICAL OFFICER

Medical officers occupy positions in the Public Health Service; in the Food and Drug Administration, in the Children's Bureau, in the Department of

Health, Education and Welfare; in the Office of Indian Affairs, Department of the Interior; in The Panama Canal Company; in the Veterans' Administration; and in many other Federal agencies.

They are on duty in marine hospitals, where they care for members of the Merchant Marine and Coast Guard, and for civilian employees of the Government who are injured in line of duty; they are also assigned to duty in marine quarantine stations and air ports, where they inspect vessels and airplanes entering the ports, harbors, and airfields of the United States, and where they examine aliens entering the United States.

Medical officers determine that medicines are labeled according to their composition and content; they conduct extensive research in maternal and child health and in services to crippled children. They serve in Indian hospitals, make calls to the homes of Indians who are ill, make field trips, and administer special health measures among the Indians. They serve as district physicians in small Government dispensaries in the Panama Canal Zone. They have the opportunity of working in teaching hospitals in the Federal service which are approved by the American Medical Association; here they may obtain a wide variety of medical experience, particularly in the field of tropical diseases.

PROFESSIONAL NURSE

Professional nurses serve in hospitals on Indian reservations, in Alaska, and in the Panama Canal Zone. Civilian nurses are employed at times in hospitals of the Department of the Army when there are not sufficient nurses from the Army Nurse Corps to meet hospital needs. The Department of the Navy employs some civilian nurses for duty in Navy hospitals, to care for dependents of Regular Navy personnel.

There are two personnel systems through which nurses in the Public Health Service may seek employment—the Commissioned Corps and the Federal Civil Service. There are approximately 2,200 Civil Service positions for nurses and 300 positions in the Commissioned Corps. The majority of available positions are in the U.S. Public Health Service hospitals located in the major port cities in the United States, the Clinical Center at the National Institutes of Health, and hospitals and clinics of the Indian Health Service. The level of nursing positions ranges from staff nurse through nurse consultant and chief of a Division.

Public-health nursing consultants are employed in the Children's Bureau, where they work with State agencies in connection with maternal and child-health programs, crippled children's programs, and programs concerned with the care of children with rheumatic heart disease.

Applicants for all positions of professional nurse must have completed a full 3-year course in residence in an approved school of nursing, or a full 2-year course plus additional appropriate nursing experience or pertinent education. Applicants must also be currently registered as professional nurses in a State or territory of the United States or the District of Columbia, or expect to apply for registration at the first opportunity.

In addition, for positions in grades GS-6 and above, they must have had progressively responsible specialized professional experience appropriate to the position for which they apply. For Nurse Anesthetist positions, additional courses of study in an approved school of anesthesia or certain prescribed experience will be necessary to meet the requirements. For some positions, part of the experience or training must have been gained within the past 2 to 5 years, depending on the position for which applying.

The degree of responsibility involved and the scope of the experience required must have been proportionately greater for each successive higher grade.

For Public Health Nurse and Nursing Consultant positions, training must have included or been supplemented by at least 30 semester hours in a program of study in public health nursing.

Male nurses who have not had clinical practice in obstetric and pediatric nursing may substitute the same number of hours of organized instruction and months of successful clinical practice in psychiatric and/or genito-urinary nursing.

The entrance salary for a professional nurse in the position of staff nurse is GS-5 to GS-7 a year, and in the position of head nurse, GS-7 to GS-9 a year.

Nurse consultant positions pay GS-11 to GS-13. The education and experience requirements vary with the grade of the position.

The pay of public-health nurse positions is from GS-7 to GS-9 at entrance.

DENTAL ASSISTANT

SALARY: GS-4 at entrance.
DESCRIPTION OF WORK: The Dental Assistant performs duties of either a specialized or a general nature. He receives and prepares patients, assists the dentist in both non-surgical and surgical dentistry, and may perform dental X-ray or prosthetic work. He keeps records of appointments, examinations, treatments, and supplies.
REQUIREMENTS: Applicants must have had 2 years of dental assistant experience including or supplemented by 1 year of specialization in restoration, dental X-raying, dental surgery, dental prosthetics, or a combination of these appropriate to the position being filled. Applicants may substitute successful completion of dental assistant courses approved by the American Dental Assistants Association

on a month-for-month basis for experience. The successful completion of dental assistant courses in the Armed Forces, in government or private hospitals, or in schools other than those mentioned above will receive credit appropriate to their length and content. Only training clearly dealing with a specialization may be substituted for experience in specialization.

BASIS OF RATING: No written test is required. Applicants' qualifications will be rated on a scale of 100, and will be judged from a review of the information furnished concerning their education and training, and on corroborative evidence.

DENTAL HYGIENIST

SALARY: GS-4 to GS-5 at entrance.

DESCRIPTION OF WORK: Dental Hygienists give oral prophylaxis to patients in hospitals and clinics. They conduct programs of oral hygiene education and instruct hospital and clinic personnel in the techniques of the maintenance of oral hygiene.

REQUIREMENTS: Applicants for all grades must be currently licensed to practice as dental hygienists in the United States. Applicants for GS-4 must have successfully completed a full course of 2 years in Dental Hygiene accredited by the Council on Dental Education of the American Dental Association. Applicants with 1 year of experience and 1 year of education and those with 2 years of experience will also qualify.

Applicants for GS-5 must have completed successfully a full course of 2 academic years in Dental Hygiene accredited by the Council on Dental Education of the American Dental Association and have 1 year of experience; or they may have 1 year of education and 2 years of experience; or they may have 3 years of experience.

Each academic year of education leading toward a bachelor's degree in Dental or Oral Hygiene or in closely related fields will count as six months of experience for those positions involving instruction and demonstration of oral hygiene for groups.

BASIS OF RATING: No written test is required. Applicants will be rated on a scale of 100 on the extent and quality of their education, experience, and personal qualities required in these positions. Such ratings will be based on information in the applications and upon any corroborative evidence secured by the Board of Civil Service Examiners.

OTHER POSITIONS

Other positions in the medical and nursing field include medical technician, laboratory helper, X-ray technician, photofluorographic operator, occupational therapist, orthopedic technician, dental technician, and veterinarian. Entrance salaries for these positions range from GS-2 to GS-14 a year.

ECONOMICS AND STATISTICS

THE complexities of modern government require the services everywhere of people who "understand figures." Hardly an activity exists in any department which does not demand the work of an accountant, statistician, economist, or mathematician. Every citizen knows of the work done by the men in the Internal Revenue Service. Statisticians in the Census Bureau prepare all kinds of data for businessmen and keep facts on the ups and downs of business. Other statisticians work with scientists, collecting and analyzing statistical reports on agriculture, for instance, reports which are frequently the basis of long-range national policy. They work on problems dealing with production, marketing, distribution, taxation, and other economic questions.

Accountants and budget examiners go over the dollars and cents spent by various departments, submit estimates, and sometimes cut spending programs. They make up payrolls, work on retirement mathematics, examine the books of stock exchange firms. They study the backgrounds of bankruptcies, audit the books of public utility companies, check into the financial conditions of banks. In another sphere they may analyze the fiscal policy of the United States and determine methods of adapting that policy to the economic needs of the country. They make up the nation's budget and suggest appropriations for all government activities.

Mathematicians work with scientists in all their activities, from plotting the course of planets to devising formulas in atomic physics. They work with engineers building bridges, they solve equations about heat conduction or electrical circuits, make computations to predict weather, determine the path of missiles and the intensity of earthquakes.

The "figure" men are so important that it is no overstatement to say modern government could not function without them. The Department of Agriculture, the Tennessee Valley Authority, the Department of Labor and its Bureau of Labor Statistics, the National Labor Relations Board, the Census Bureau, the Treasury Department and the Securities and Exchange Commission, the Atomic Energy Commission, are only some of the agencies which need workers with mathematics or economics backgrounds.

As the government grows more complex the need for men who can work with the intangibles of statistics and economics, as well as those who can examine a set of figures in books, will grow. Salaries range from GS-5 to GS-15.

Some typical government positions in these fields are examined below.

ACCOUNTANT AND AUDITOR

SALARY: GS-5 and GS-7 at entrance.
DUTIES: The duties of this position vary, depending upon the agencies. They are all alike, however, in that they all give an opportunity for a diversity of experience in a program emphasizing the systematic development of full professional skill.
REQUIREMENTS: For GS-5, applicants must meet one of the following: four years of study in accounting above the high-school level; three years of progressive experience; an equivalent combination of both; a C.P.A. certificate.

For GS-7, applicants must meet the requirements for GS-5 plus completion of one year of graduate study in accounting or one year of experience in professional accounting.

BASIS OF RATING: Applicants qualifying on a basis of education only or a C.P.A. certificate do not take an examination. Those who offer some qualifications of experience must take an examination.

ACCOUNTANT AND AUDITOR

SALARY: GS-9 through GS-15.
DESCRIPTION OF WORK: Accountants and Auditors collect and evaluate data, maintain and examine accounting records, plan new accounting systems and revise old ones, prepare accounting statements, examine transactions to determine their accuracy and legality, and analyze financial reports.

REQUIREMENTS: Applicants must have experience of a length and quality like that shown in the following table:

Grade of Position	General	Professional Type A	Type B	Total
GS-9	3 years	1 year	1 year	5 years
GS-11 through GS-15	3 years	1 year	2 years	6 years

BASIS OF RATING: Applicants for Grades GS-9, 11, and 12 who have completed 4 years of college with concentration in accounting or who possess a CPA certificate and applicants eligible for Grade GS-13 and above are the only applicants exempt from the written accounting test. All competitors who meet the experience requirements and pass the written test will be rated on a score of 100 on the quality, diversity, and extent of their experience. Such ratings will be based on information in the application forms and on additional evidence obtained.

REVENUE OFFICER

SALARY: GS-5 and GS-7 at entrance.
DUTIES: Revenue Officers perform personal contact work involved in the collection of delinquent taxes and the securing of delinquent tax returns. They deal with corporate executives, attorneys, accountants, and individual taxpayers in all walks of life. They investigate and analyze business situations, negotiate agreements to satisfy tax obligations, enforce tax law by seizure and sale, and perform other related work to safeguard the Government's interests.

REQUIREMENT AND BASIS OF RATING: The PACE examination is used to fill this position.

TAX TECHNICIAN

SALARY: GS-5 and GS-7 at entrance.
DUTIES: Tax Technicians represent the Internal Revenue Service in consultations with taxpayers of all kinds—individual wage earners, small businessmen, professional men, corporate executives, and others. They talk with taxpayers in the office and correspond with them to identify and explain tax issues and to determine correct tax liability.

REQUIREMENTS AND BASIS OF RATING: The Federal Service Entrance Examination (see page 82) is used to fill this position. Preferably, graduates should have 24 semester hours in subjects such as accounting, business administration, business economics, finance, and law.

STATISTICIAN

SALARY: GS-9 through GS-15 a year.
DESCRIPTION OF WORK: Statisticians do professional work or provide professional consultation requiring the application of statistical theory and techniques in a variety of subject-matter fields including the social, natural, and physical sciences and administration.

REQUIREMENTS: Applicants must have completed a full 4-year course leading to a bachelor's degree in an accredited college with specialization in mathematics and statistics. They must also have had from 2 to 3 years of experience in statistics. Substitutions of experience for education may be made.

BASIS OF RATING: No written test will be given. Applicants will be rated on a scale of 100 based upon statements in applications and any additional information acquired. As vacancies occur, the qualifications of those who meet the basic requirements will be reviewed. Competitors may be asked to supply additional information at this time.

ECONOMIST

SALARY: GS-9 and GS-11 through GS-15.
DESCRIPTION OF WORK: Economists research economic phenomena and interpret economic data, prepare reports on economic facts and activities, investigate and evaluate reports for their economic implications, write economic reports for official publication, and provide consultant services for Government policy makers.

BASIS OF RATING: Applicants will be rated on a scale of 100 on the amount and quality of their experience, education, and training in relation to the requirements of the position for which they apply.

MANAGEMENT ANALYST

SALARY: GS-9 to GS-12 a year at entrance.
DUTIES: The management analyst's work includes the evaluating of administrative systems and facilities for the management and control of government operations and developing new or improved procedures, systems, and organization structures.

REQUIREMENTS: Applicants must have had five or six years of experience (depending on the grade applied for) that has included two or three years in the development, evaluation, or revision of: programs, organization, methods, or procedures; specialty systems in such fields as tabulation and machine accounting, forms control, records management; or budgetary preparation and presentation. Graduate study in appropriate subjects may be substituted for this experience.

BASIS OF RATING: Applicants must pass a written examination.

BUDGET EXAMINER

SALARY: GS-9 to GS-12 at entrance.
DUTIES: The budget examiner surveys government programs, reviews budgets, and presents budgets to the proper authorities. He is often responsible for the development and operation of systems for reporting work performed and funds expended.

REQUIREMENTS: The requirements for this position are the same as for management analyst (see above).

BASIS OF RATING: Applicants must pass a written examination.

TEACHING AND LIBRARY POSITIONS

ALTHOUGH teaching is primarily a function of state and local governments, the federal government employs teachers and educators for a number of services. With the new emphasis on vocational guidance the opportunities for qualified teachers in the federal service have increased. Rates of pay compare favorably with those of the larger cities.

Among the agencies which employ teachers and educators are the Bureau of Indian Affairs of the Department of the Interior, the Veterans' Administration, the Department of Agriculture, and the Office of Education. The Indian Affairs Bureau alone employs more than 1200 teachers. In the Veterans' Administration teachers work at informal class teaching or individual bedside instruction, and assist in arranging for correspondence courses. The requirements for the job include college or teacher-training education and some teaching experience. Those who teach commercial subjects do not need a college degree. A number of teaching positions are available abroad. The Department of Health, Education and Welfare uses highly trained educational experts to work with colleges, universities, and state educational systems in setting up large educational programs. Qualified persons are comparatively well paid.

Among the other teaching jobs in the federal service are: educational research; in-service training work in all agencies of the government, training of federal employees for greater efficiency on their jobs; playground and recreation directing.

Almost every federal agency has a librarian who takes care of the agency's reading and reference material. Agencies which usually service the public with such information use many librarians; such agencies are the Departments of Agriculture and Commerce. In Washington librarians assist federal employees in their work by giving them reference material and by doing research for them. Branches of the Veterans' Administration have libraries which offer limited opportunities for trained librarians in the areas where they are located.

The largest number of librarians is employed in the Library of Congress; the jobs there are of great diversity and complexity—locating books and documents, hunting up facts for congressmen, working at major research projects, and writing reports which sometimes influence American policy. Employees of the Library of Congress are not under the civil service; applicants should write directly to the Director of the Library, in Washington, D.C.

Librarians are employed in two categories, subprofessional and professional. At the lowest levels no actual library experience is required. The higher levels require extensive educational qualifications. Salaries have risen in recent years, and go as high as GS-15 a year.

Here are some of the teaching and library posts available in the federal service.

BUREAU OF INDIAN AFFAIRS
Department of Interior

The Bureau of Indians Affairs, Department of Interior, is responsible for the education of Indian children who are not educated by public schools in the States where they live, and for a program of adult education which can bridge the gap between life on the reservation and the mainstream of contemporary America. When you work in an Indian school, you act as cross-cultural interpreter as well as a classroom teacher.

BIA operates 254 schools and 18 dormitories for children who attend public schools, serving over 50,000 students. The adult education aids over 31,000 Indians in 303 communities. Arizona, New Mexico, Alaska, North Dakota and South Dakota have the largest concentration of Indian population and schools, although some educators are needed each year in California, Oklahoma, Oregon, Utah, Kansas, Florida, Mississippi, Montana, North Carolina and Louisiana.

Classroom teachers and guidance counselors are especially needed. Most Bureau Indian schools are located in isolated rural locations more than 30 miles from the nearest urban community. The work involved in combating physical isolation as well as physical and emotional poverty demands dedication, imagination, and strength, but, as one young teacher put it, ". . . here I work, among a culturally rich, but culturally different people. The environment just has to be stimulating, and it is. I work twice as hard as I did in public school teaching and my rewards are multiplied many, many times."

For more information on working in Indian schools, write to the Federal Job Information Center, Albuquerque, New Mexico.

AGENCY FOR INTERNATIONAL DEVELOPMENT
Department of State

AID administers America's foreign aid program in the developing countries of Asia, Africa, and Latin America. Since the progress of an emerging country hinges critically on the ability of its people to read and comprehend, to learn the skills by which they can support and govern themselves, education plays an important part in that program.

As an AID educator, you would work with local officials on projects that vary from selecting textbooks to setting up educational TV. Your job would be to help plan educational programs that meet needs for particular areas and train the people of each area to run the programs themselves.

AID hires advisors in the field of elementary education, higher education, human resources development, teacher education, trade-industrial education, and vocational education. Classroom teaching alone does not provide the experience needed, and positions usually require advanced degrees and several years of administrative and program responsibility.

If you meet rigid professional standards, work with AID offers you the stimulation of working with other American and foreign professionals, and the opportunity to make unique, long-range contributions in your field. At a time when unrest is aggravated by the disparity between have and have-not nations, your work with AID can help close the gap.

For Jobs with AID:

Chief, Talent Search
Office of Personnel and Manpower
Agency for International Development
Washington, D.C. 20523

DEPARTMENT OF DEFENSE
OVERSEAS DEPENDENT SCHOOLS

Did you know the ninth largest American school system lies entirely outside the continental United States? Schools in 27 foreign countries are set up by the Department of Defense to provide education for children of overseas military and civilian personnel. In 1966, more than 167,000 dependents attended 292 such schools around the world.*

The largest single group of educators working for the Government work in this system, 7,100 of them in 1967. Jobs in the DOD schools correspond to those in any large American school system, including positions as administrators, counselors, classroom teachers, teachers of the physically and mentally handicapped, teachers of special subjects, and librarians. Two years of teaching experience are required.

Working with the DOD school system offers you the chance to live and travel in a foreign country and pursue your career at the same time. Vacations may be spent touring neighboring countries as well. Many dependent school teachers enroll in foreign institutes, language schools and universities, or work on advanced degrees through attendance at or correspondence with American universities and foundations overseas. So, in both the teaching and learning sense, the world is your classroom.

For jobs with Department of Defense Overseas Dependents Schools, contact your local United States Employment Service office.

---

*Positions filled from PACE examination.

FEDERAL CORRECTIONAL INSTITUTIONS

Far from the hardened master criminal stereotype, the average inmate in a Federal correctional institution is under 30 years old, has an educational level of fifth grade and is serving time for auto theft. He is, as one prison official put it, a "double dropout," having dropped out of school and out of life outside the institution. Educational programs within the system are aimed at helping him make a success of his second chance at useful citizenship.

21,000 offenders are assigned on the basis of social history, age, nature of offense, and rehabilitative potential to 36 institutions, from pre-release guidance centers to penitentiaries of 2,000 inmates. Academic programs range from remedial reading for functional illiterates to instruction at the high school level. Vocational training is aimed at providing marketable skills, including work as dental technicians, computer training, welding, masonry, small engine repair, and auto repair for the inmate who has loved cars "not wisely, but too well."

The Bureau of Prisons employs people in the field of remedial reading, library work, academic and vocational subjects, arts and crafts, recreation, guidance, supervisory and administrative work, occupational therapy, and research and development.

Since the educational program in Federal prisons is geared to reaching people who haven't succeeded in conventional educational systems, teachers are allowed both freedom to try experimental methods in getting their ideas across and the time to do so.

For the prisoner, a high school degree or a union card may make the difference between success or failure on his reentering society. As his teacher, you can help make that difference.

DEPARTMENT OF *
HEALTH, EDUCATION, AND WELFARE

Office of Education

The Office of Education links Federal education programs with State and local agencies, colleges and universities, international education organizations, and professional associations. Its role has many facets, ranging from school desegregation under the Civil Rights Act to administering funds for library construction; from research in educating handicapped children to compiling statistics; from consulting services to programs of adult and vocational education.

Surprisingly, while OE is involved in so many phases of education, it has virtually no opportunities for classroom teachers as such. The need is for experienced professionals, including college and university presidents and deans, department heads, administrators, research scholars, staff assistants, vocational and technical specialists, counseling and testing experts, and curriculum specialists. If you meet these qualifications, you will find being involved in the broad scale of OE programs interesting and stimulating work.

NOTE: Each year the Office of Education hires young men and women with bachelor's and master's degrees who are not educators as such. As a recent college graduate, you can put your general educational background to work in an administrative capacity in many of the programs at OE.

Public Health Education

The Public Health Educator specializes in getting health facts accepted and used. The work requires a rare blend of specific training and the ingenuity needed to communicate and work with widely-varying groups of people. For those few who meet the professional standards, it's a challenging, relatively new field for educators in Government.

EDUCATION RESEARCH AND PROGRAM SPECIALIST

SALARY: GS-9 to GS-15

DUTIES: An appointee may perform any of the following: make appraisals of educational practices both here and abroad; plan conduct and evaluate surveys and research; publish or promote publication of educational articles and bulletins; act as educational consultant to local, state, national or international bodies; plan and administer grants in aid. He may be assigned to any of these functions in one or more fields of specialization such as, elementary education, vocational, school administration, guidance, or international education.

REQUIREMENTS: Specialists must have finished a four-year college course including or supplemented by major study in education, and have had extensive experience in educational administration, educational research, or other activities in the field of education. The experience must demonstrate ability to plan and supervise, to recommend improvements in curricula, school service, or school finance, and to write or edit manuals. For the jobs paying GS-14 and higher the applicant must have made significant contributions to education and earned outstanding recognition in his special field. Credit is given for appropriate part-time and unpaid experience.

BASIS OF RATING: No written examination is required; candidates are judged on their background and experience. These factors are considered in assigning ratings: knowledge of current developments in the field of specialization; ability to plan and conduct scholarly research, organize an educational program, speak and write effectively, co-operate with colleagues, direct professional employees, work harmoniously with staff. Evidence of leadership in the specialty is demanded.

LIBRARY ASSISTANT

SALARY: GS-3 to GS-5 at entrance

DUTIES: Persons appointed to these positions will perform such duties as stack maintenance; book and bindery preparation; circulation work; making additions to serial, shelf-list, and catalog records; arranging inter-library loans; compiling lists of books; answering simple reference questions; checking in and routing periodicals; and other work of a comparable nature. GS-5 involves the supervising of library assistants in lower grades who are engaged in the activities listed above.

REQUIREMENTS: Depending upon the grade applied for, from one to three years of experience. Two thirds of this experience must have been specialized, including such duties as circulation work, answering simple reference questions, making additions to library records, book and bindery preparation and stack maintenance. Undergraduate study may be substituted on the basis of one year of education for nine months of experience. Also, each three semester hours of library science is equal to three months of experience.

BASIS OF RATING: As described above for archives assistant.

LIBRARIAN

SALARY: Grades GS-5 through GS-15 a year.

DESCRIPTION OF WORK: Librarians perform or direct the performance of work in Federal libraries involving acquisitions, cataloging and classification, or reference and bibliography. As many of the libraries are highly specialized, the work often lies in one field. Because many publications are in foreign languages, librarians in many positions must have a knowledge of one or more foreign languages.

At the higher levels, librarians may (1) assume complete charge of a large library containing both general and specific collections; (2) organize and direct the activities of a division in a large library; or (3) serve as consulting specialists to research personnel.

REQUIREMENTS: Applicants must have successfully completed a 4-year course of study in an accredited college including or supplemented by at least 24 semester-hours in library science; or they may have four years of progressive experience equivalent in quality to the course of study described above; and six months of which was at a level of difficulty comparable to the next lower grade, or 1 year of which was comparable in difficulty to the second lowest grade, in the Federal service; or they may combine experience and education to equal four years.

For positions at GS-7 and above, the following experience requirements must be met in addition to those already specified:

Grade of Position	Additional Experience Required
GS-7	1 year
GS-9	2 years

The quality of the experience rather than the length of time employed will be given primary consideration.

Applicants for GS-7 who have completed all the work for a master's degree or 1 full year of graduate study leading to a higher degree in addition to all work required for a bachelor's degree may qualify in full. Education may be substituted for experience only when it may be substituted in full, i.e., in grades GS-5 and GS-7. Applications will be accepted from students who are otherwise qualified and expect to complete all scholastic requirements within 9 months of filing the application.

BASIS OF RATING: Applicants for GS-5 and GS-7 who qualify on experience alone or on a combination of education and experience and who do not meet the experience requirements for grades GS-9 and above will be required to take a written test. All competitors who meet the experience requirements and who pass the written test when required will be rated on a basis of 100 upon an evaluation of their experience and training in library work. Consideration will be given for specialized experience in the field for which the examination is being given.

ARCHIVES ASSISTANT

SALARY: GS-3 to GS-5 at entrance.

DUTIES: Persons appointed perform work in receiving, sorting, filing, classifying and indexing non-current records and documents; searching for, charging out and providing information as requested; packing, sorting and preserving non-current records. At GS-5 many of the positions involve supervisory duties.

REQUIREMENTS: Depending upon the grade applied for, from one to three years of experience in the organization, maintenance or servicing of the records of a public or private institution; or from twelve to eighteen semester hours of college courses in either, history, government, political science, sociology, economics or public administration.

BASIS OF RATING: A written examination is given consisting of alphabetizing, arithmetic, and verbal abilities (including word meaning, spelling, and the meaning of written paragraphs). Competitors for grade GS-5 positions will also be required to take a test of supervisory judgment.

SOCIAL WORK

TWENTIETH century concepts of government include the notion that the ruling power must exercise some responsibility for the welfare of citizens. Thus there has grown up, in comparatively recent times, a new grouping of government activities built around certain basic needs of the people—social security, old age and unemployment insurance, and various welfare projects. The federal government interests itself in the blind, the poor, and the handicapped. It takes a hand in the dissemination of nutrition and health education, publishes cookbooks, even advises upon the proper care of babies. It grants aid to states for dealing with people suffering from emotional and psychological problems, and to some extent aids these people directly. Much of this humanitarian work is performed by trained social workers.

Let us look into the duties and the qualifications needed for this post.

SOCIAL WORKER

SALARY: GS-7 and GS-9 a year.
DESCRIPTION OF WORK: Social Workers work in correctional institutions to develop personal histories of new inmates, prepare progress reports on their adjustment both within the institution and in the outside environment, explain rules, policies, and decisions to prisoners, plan with them regarding parole and release, and advise them about personal and family problems. They make recommendations to the prison administration regarding the prisoners' special needs and requests and are responsible for the detention of prisoners assigned to them. Social Workers at grade GS-7 work as trainees; those at grade GS-9 work with a large degree of independence.

REQUIREMENTS: Applicants for GS-7 positions must have had 5 years of experience in social case work 1 year of which involved work in a correctional institution or in a crime or delinquency prevention program. A course of study leading to a bachelor's degree from an accredited college may be substituted for 4 of the 5 years of experience, but not for the year of correctional work. Completion of all the requirements for a master's degree in social work may be substituted for all 5 years; 1 year of graduate work in sociology in an accredited college may be substituted for the 1 year of correctional experience; and any combination of education and experience which is the equivalent of the three educational options listed above is acceptable. Those applicants who have fulfilled all the requirements for a master's degree in social work are eligible for GS-9. Other applicants must have, in addition to the requirements for GS-7, 1 additional year of correctional work or one year of graduate study in social work at an accredited college or university. Applications will be accepted from students who expect to fulfill all requirements within 6 months of filing the application. The quality of an applicant's experience will be evaluated to see if it is comparable with the position for which he is applying.

BASIS OF RATING: No written test is required. Applicants will be rated on a scale of 100 on the extent and quality of their experience. Such ratings will be based upon competitors' statements in their applications and upon any additional information secured by the Civil Service Commission.

SCIENCE AND ENGINEERING

The U.S. Civil Service Commission has been abolished since January 1, 1979 and its functions have been divided between two new agencies, the Office of Personnel Management (OPM) and the Merit Systems Protection Board (MSPB). The Office of Personnel Management has taken over many of the important responsibilities of the Civil Service Commission, including examinations and other employment matters, personnel investigations, personnel program evaluation, and training. The Merit Systems Protection Board is a separate and independent agency responsible for safeguarding both the merit system and the rights of individual employees in personnel matters. The addresses and telephone numbers for the new agencies remain the same as they had been under the Civil Service Commission.

SCIENTIFIC research and development are carried out in 25 federal departments and agencies, principally in the laboratories of the Departments of the Army, Navy, and Air Force, the National Aeronautics and Space Administration, the Atomic Energy Commission, the Department of Agriculture, the National Institutes of Health, the National Bureau of Standards, the Department of the Interior, the Federal Aviation Agency, and the Veterans Administration.

Within the last 10 years employment conditions for the scientist in the federal service have been radically improved. In 1955 there were 56,700 federal employees in the physical and biological sciences and 60,500 in engineering, altogether making up 9 percent of the federal white-collar work force. Now there are more than 71,000 in science and 116,000 in engineering, constituting 11½ percent of the white-collar work force.

In August of 1964 the Civil Service Commission issued new salary schedules for scientists and engineers in the federal service, setting pay rates for many professional engineering, scientific, and medical positions even above the newly enacted rates of the general salary schedule. The Commission took this action under the authority of the Federal Salary Reform Act of 1962, on the basis of a decision that the higher salaries were necessary to meet nongovernmental pay standards in occupations in which there is a shortage of manpower.

The 1962 Salary Act included several special features that help the federal service attract and retain high-quality personnel and stimulate excellent per-

formance. One of these was the special salary-rate authority mentioned in the opening paragraph of this article. Pay differentials between grades were increased for the middle and higher grades, and pay steps within the grade were also increased. (The classified salary structure consists of 15 regular grades and three "supergrades." There are several levels or steps within each grade, except for grade 18, the highest.) In addition to the regular periodic within-grade step increase, an additional step increase can be granted for high-quality performance; also, the regular within-grade increase can be withheld if work is not of an acceptable level of competence.

Professional positions in the physical and natural sciences, medicine, and research engineering were removed from the restrictions limiting the number of positions in grades 16, 17, and 18 (the "supergrades"). Federal agencies may now recommend to the Civil Service Commission, for its approval, inclusion of as many such positions in those grades as duties and responsibilities warrant. This change goes far toward eliminating a potent barrier to the proper matching of pay and responsibility at the highest levels.

A second highly significant legislative step was passage of the Government Employees Training Act of 1958. The Training Act authorizes employee training at full pay within the federal agency or at colleges, universities, professional institutes, industrial laboratories, or research foundations; full or partial payment of tuition and related costs; payment of travel expenses and registration fees for attendance at professional meetings; and cooperation among agencies in opening up training courses across agency lines.

Also, in shortage occupations, officials of federal agencies can now make immediate offers to well qualified candidates on the assumption that their names will be high enough on the appropriate register of eligibles when the grading of the civil service examination they have taken is completed.

Position classification in the federal civil service— the process by which the grade and salary level of a job are determined—is a flexible procedure in scientific fields. Traditionally, "the position, not the person, is classified," but in determining the grade level of research positions the qualifications, professional stature, and scientific contributions of the scientist are primary considerations. Also, the job can be tailored to fit the qualifications of an outstanding scientist.

Within the framework of government-wide personnel laws and policies, agency and laboratory directors can maintain a creative environment by providing privileges and recognition for their scientific personnel. This is done in ways such as the following: by (i) encouraging staff members to attend meetings of professional societies and to publish in professional journals; (ii) giving them credit lines on official publications of the laboratory; (iii) giving them freedom to teach and serve as consultants on the outside and to write books; (iv) maintaining a liberal patent policy; (v) providing reasonable flexibility of working hours; (vi) establishing meaningful professional titles; and (vii) encouraging co-workers of different grades to consider themselves colleagues, not boss and subordinate.

In the federal service there are some restrictions regarding conflict of interest and disclosure of classified material, but otherwise laboratory directors are given considerable discretion in using the measures listed above to build the type of environment they seek.

The jobs considered below are only a small portion of those that exist. They illustrate requirements, bases of rating, and salary levels for typical federal scientific and engineering positions.

CHEMIST

ENTRANCE SALARY: GS-5 to GS-15 a year, depending on past experience.

REQUIREMENTS: For the post paying GS-5, a four-year college or university course leading to a bachelor's degree in chemistry or four years of experience in the field of chemical engineering.

BASIS OF RATING: For Grades GS-5 through GS-12, no written test is required. Applicants' qualifications will be rated on a scale of 100, by subject specialists and will be determined by an evaluation of the experience, education and training.

For Grades GS-13 through GS-15, no written test is required. A preliminary review will be made of the training and experience of each applicant as described in his applica-

tion form. As vacancies occur, the qualifications of the applicants who meet the basic requirements will be evaluated in relation to the specific positions to be filled.

PHYSICIST

SALARY: GS-5 to GS-15 a year at entrance.

DUTIES: Appointees will perform professional work in one or more of the branches of physical science, conducting or assisting in technical projects and applying scientific knowledge to the solution of scientific problems.

REQUIREMENTS: For the post paying GS-5, a four-year college course leading to a bachelor's degree. This study must include courses in physics totaling at least 24 semester hours.

Requirements for GS-7 through GS-15: In addition to meeting the appropriate requirements shown in the first part of this section for the GS-5 grade of the position for which application is made, applicants must meet the experience requirements listed below:

Grade	Total Professional Experience	Specialized Experience in Physics
GS-7	1 year	1 year
GS-9	2 years	1 year
GS-11, 12, 13 14, 15	3 years	2 years

BASIS OF RATING: Applicants' qualifications will be rated on a scale of 100 and will be judged from a review of their experience, education and training and on corroborative evidence secured by the Commission.

ENGINEER

SALARY: GS-5 through GS-15 at entrance.

FIELDS OF ENGINEERING: Agricultural, Civil (Bridge, Highway, Sanitary, Surveying-Topographic, and Hydraulic), Electrical, Electronic, Mining, and others.

REQUIREMENTS: All applicants must have successfully completed a full 4 year course in engineering leading to a bachelor's degree. They may also have a combination of engineering education and experience equivalent in quality and quantity to a 4 year college course. They must also have passed the Engineer-in-Training Examination, participated in certain specialized courses, or have demonstrable professional stature. Applicants for grades higher than GS-5 must have, in addition, either education or experience of the following amounts and types:

Grade of Position	General	Specialized	Total
GS-7	1 year	none	1 year
GS-9	1 year	1 year	2 years
GS-11 through GS-15	2 years	1 year	3 years

Superior academic achievement, creative research or development contribution, or extensive graduate work may qualify applicants in all grades for higher positions.

BASIS OF RATING: All applicants except those for GS-13 and GS-15 will be rated on a basis of 100 on experience, education, and training. Ratings will be made for grade levels and for specialties. Applicants for GS-13 and GS-15 will be notified upon review of their applications of the engineering specialities for which they are qualified. As vacancies occur, the qualifications of the applicants who meet the requirements of the specialization will be reviewed. For all grades, applicants' qualifications will be judged from a review of their experience.

ENGINEERING DRAFTSMAN

SALARY: GS-2 through GS-7 at entrance.

DESCRIPTION OF WORK: Engineering Draftsmen perform drafting work which is directly related to highly technical engineering activities of a professional and scientific nature. Draftsmen use arithmetical calculations and drafting instruments in making working drawings, assemblies, and layouts of various types of equipment. They exercise care in maintaining uniformity in line weights and widths for similar features, details, and symbols.

REQUIREMENTS: For all grades, applicants must meet the specified experience requirements as modified by the indicated substitutions for education.

Grade	General Experience	Specialized experience	Total
GS-2	6 months	None	6 months
GS-3	1 year	None	1 year
GS-4	1 year 6 months	6 months	2 years
GS-5	2 years, 3 months	9 months	3 years
GS-7	3 years	1 year	4 years

General experience must be in performing the work of a cartographic, engineering, or statistical draftsman; experience in skilled and mechanical trades and related scientific and engineering technician occupations in which the interpretation of blue-prints or schematic diagrams was required may be substituted for up to half of the required general experience.

Education at the high-school level and above may be substituted, with special provisions, for both general and specialized experience in specified amounts. Education may not be substituted for the specialized experience required for GS-7.

BASIS OF RATING: Competitors for GS-3 and GS-2 will be rated on a written test on a scale of 100 and must achieve a rating of at least 70 to be eligible.

Competitors for GS-4, GS-5, and GS-7 will be rated on a scale of 100 on the extent and quality of their experience, education, and training relevant to the position. The rating will be based on the statements in the application, on the sample (consisting of three drawings) of engineering drafting work submitted, and on any additional information secured by the Board.

ENGINEERING AID
(Highway)

SALARY: GS-3 a year.

DESCRIPTION OF WORK: Engineering Aids will be assigned to sub-professional engineering tasks in the highway construction field. They assist on highway location surveys, highway construction, minor inspection of highway and/or bridge construction, and make minor mathematical calculations. Assignments involve acting as chainman and/or rodman, marking and driving stakes, recording survey notes, reducing simple cross section notes, and plotting cross sections and profiles. Work is performed under supervision of higher grade employees.

REQUIREMENTS: Applicants must have had 1½ years total experience. The experience must have been in engineering, but experience in mathematics or in the physical sciences may be substituted up to the extent of 1 year. The successful completion of a full four-year or senior high-school curriculum may be substituted for 1 year of the required experience, and, depending on quality and quantity, education at a higher level that included courses in drafting, mathematics, applied engineering sciences, or engineering may be substituted.

BASIS OF RATING: Competitors will be rated on a basis of 100 on the extent and quality of their education, experience, and training. Such ratings will be based upon competitors' statements in their applications and upon any additional information and evidence secured by the U.S. Civil Service Commission.

GEOLOGIST

SALARY: GS-9 to GS-15 a year.

DESCRIPTION OF WORK: Persons appointed to these positions will perform professional geological work in one or more of the major occupational fields or specialties within these fields. Typical duties involve geological mapping, making and recording geological field observations and collecting samples for laboratory analysis, identifying and studying samples, compiling and interpreting field, laboratory, and published data, making special studies, and preparing professional scientific and economic reports for publication.

REQUIREMENTS: Applicants must show successful completion of a 4-year course leading to a bachelor's degree with concentration in geology and related sciences or a combination of education and professional experience equivalent in quality and quantity to the 4-year course.

Grade	Education Requirement	Experience Requirement General	Specialized	Total
GS-9	2 years graduate study	1 year	1 year	2 years
GS-11	All requirements for Ph. D	1 year	2 years	3 years
GS-12 to GS-15	No substitution	1 year	2 years	3 years

Superior academic achievement, professional work experience combined with this experience, and creative investigation or research contribution may qualify applicants for higher grades. Students who expect to complete all education requirements within 9 months of filing application may apply for positions at GS-9 and GS-11.

BASIS OF RATING: No written test is required. All ratings will be based on an evaluation of experience, education, and training which may be obtained. Each applicant will be rated in the option for which he is best qualified.

Applicants for grades GS-9 through GS-13 will be assigned numerical ratings on a basis of 100. Applicants for grades GS-14 and GS-15 will be notified as to whether they meet the basic requirements for these positions. As vacancies occur, the qualifications of candidates who meet the basic requirements will be evaluated in relation to the specific position to be filled, and candidates will be rated accordingly.

METALLURGIST

SALARY: GS-5 and GS-7 at entrance.

REQUIREMENTS: For Grade GS-5, a four-year college course including at least 20 semester hours in metallurgy. For GS-7, an additional requirement is one year of professional experience in metallurgy or one year of graduate study in metallurgy.

BASIS OF RATING: Applicants are assigned numerical ratings on a scale of 100 based on an evaluation of their education and experience.

RESEARCH PSYCHOLOGIST

SALARY: GS-9 to GS-15 at entrance.

TYPES OF WORK: Experimental and Physiological Psychology; Personnel Measurement and Evaluation; Social Psychology, Engineering Psychology.

REQUIREMENTS: Depending upon the grade applied for, applicants must have had from two to four years of progressively responsible professional experience which must have included the administration or conduct of significant research or applied studies in the specific field of psychology for which the applicant is being rated. Up to two years of graduate study may be substituted for experience.

BASIS OF RATING: No written examination is required. Applicants will be rated on an evaluation of their personal and professional qualifications.

FORESTRY, AGRICULTURE, AND CONSERVATION

TWO departments of the government—Agriculture and Interior—employ men who know soil, forestry, and water resources. Although the work they do is often difficult and sometimes dangerous, those who hold these positions express a real love for the tasks they perform. The pay is not always high, but it has been increasing in recent years. As the nation learns how vital it is to conserve and improve its natural resources the jobs should grow in importance. Occupational experts believe that jobs in forestry, agriculture, and conservation are "good bets" in coming years.

Among the tasks performed by government men in agriculture, horticulture, soil science, conservation, and farming are: the development, standardization and use of agricultural techniques and products; inspecting and grading samples of farm products; care of trees; experimental landscape gardening; research on soils to see what they can grow; testing fruits, vegetables, trees, shrubs; dairy sanitation and efficiency studies; determining the mineral, water and agricultural resources of public lands; control and prevention of soil erosion; moisture conservation; research to bring about rapid reforestation; experimental farming; grazing research; the care, breeding, and feeding of farm and dairy animals; research to conserve forests and to use their products; and the economics of all these subjects.

AGRICULTURAL MANAGEMENT, performing a broad range of functions in carrying out supervised credit and technical assistance programs for people in rural communities. The work involves such activities as crop and livestock production, preparation and marketing of products, and supporting financial, management, rural housing and community resource development activities.

Course Requirements—Major in farm, livestock, or ranch management, agricultural economics, agricultural education, agronomy, husbandry, agricultural engineering, general agriculture, horticulture, etc. *Those qualifying on the basis of combined education and experience* must have 30 semester hours in such courses.

AGRONOMY, performing research, administering or advising on scientific work in the fundamental principles of plant, soil, and related sciences as they apply to crop breeding and production, conservation, propagation and seed production, ground maintenance, and plant adaptation and varietal testing.

Course Requirements—30 semester hours, or equivalent, in the basic plant sciences (e.g. botany, plant taxonomy, plant ecology, plant breeding or genetics, microbiology, soil science), with a minimum of 15 semester hours in agronomic subjects such as those dealing with plant breeding, crop production, and soil and crop management.

FORESTRY, working in the development, production, conservation, utilization, and protection of natural forest resources; management of these resources, including timber, forage, watersheds, wildlife, and land, to meet present and future public needs. Research work involves development of new, improved or more economic scientific instruments and techniques necessary to perform such work.

Course Requirements—24 semester hours in forestry, sufficiently diversified to fall into at least 4 of the following areas: 1) silviculture, i.e. such subjects as forest soils, forest ecology, dendrology, silvics, and silviculture; 2) forest management; 3) forest protection; 4) forest economics, i.e. such subjects as forest finance and forest valuation; 5) forest utilization, i.e. such subjects as logging and milling; product preparation and use of wood, etc.; 6) related studies, i.e. such subjects as forest engineering, forest recreation, watershed management, wildlife management. To assure proper diversification of course work, no more than 6 semester hours credit will be given for courses in any one of the specializations listed. *Those qualifying on the basis of combined education and experience* must have 30 semester hours in any combination of the biological, physical or mathematical sciences or engineering, including 24 hours in forestry subjects as described above. *For administrative positions,* applicants must meet the requirements above or have college education in range conservation, soil science, wildlife, biology, geology, or engineering, provided that the training has been supplemented by a sufficient amount of professional experience, gained in a work situation which required the joint application of full professional knowledges of forestry and related fields in solving highly technical and complex problems concerned with the planning, developmental, and administrative phases of multiple-use forest land management.

HUSBANDRY, developing new and improved methods of breeding, feeding, and nutrition of poultry and livestock; improving the management and utilization of poultry and livestock and the quality of meat, poultry, and dairy products.

*Course Requirements—*30 semester hours, or equivalent, in basic biological and agricultural sciences with a minimum of 20 hours in animal sciences. Of these 10 semester hours must be in the appropriate field of husbandry.

PLANT QUARANTINE AND PEST CONTROL, applying knowledge of the biological and plant sciences and of the transportation and shipping industries and quarantine techniques to the establishment and enforcement of plant quarantines governing movement of injurious plant pests of economic significance, or to the survey, detection, identification, control, or eradication of plant pests.

Course Requirement 20 semester hours, or equivalent,

of course work in any combination of one or more of the following: entomology, botany, plant pathology, nematology, horticulture, mycology, invertebrate zoology, or closely related fields. *Those qualifying on the basis of combined education and experience* must have 30 semester hours in such fields.

RANGE CONSERVATION, inventorying, analyzing improving, protecting, utilizing, and managing the natural resources of rangelands and related grazing lands; regulating grazing on public rangelands; developing cooperative relationships with range users; assisting landowners to plan and apply range conservation programs; developing technical standards and specifications; conducting research on the principles underlying rangeland management; and developing new and improved instruments and techniques.

*Course Requirements—*30 semester hours, or equivalent, in any combination of the plant, animal, and soil sciences and natural resources management,

SOIL CONSERVATION, advising on, administering, coordinating, performing, or supervising scientific work in a coordinated program of soil, water, and resource conservation which requires the application of a combination of agricultural sciences in order to bring about sound land use and to improve the quality of the environment.

*Course Requirements—*A major in soil conservation, or closely related agricultural or natural resource sciences, such as agronomy, forestry, wildlife biology, regional planning, agricultural education, or agricultural engineering. The study must have included 30 semester hours, or equivalent in natural resources or agricultural fields including the equivalent of 3 semester hours in soils.

SOIL SCIENCE, studying and investigating soils from the standpoint of their morphology, genesis, and distribution; their interrelated physical, chemical, and biological properties and processes; their relationships to climatic, physiographic, and vegetative influences; and their adaptation to use and management in agriculture.

WILDLIFE BIOLOGY, working in the conservation and management of wildlife, or in the determination, establishment, and application of the biological facts, principles, methods, techniques, and procedures necessary for the conservation and management of wildlife.

WILDLIFE REFUGE MANAGEMENT, developing management and operational plans for bird and game refuges; seeing that the wildlife is properly protected; and working with individuals, organizations, and the general public on matters pertaining to refuge and related wildlife management programs.

Course Requirements— 9 semester hours, or equivalent, in zoology; 6 semester hours in such wildlife courses as mammalogy, ornithology, animal ecology, or wildlife management, or equivalent studies in the subject matter field; 9 semester hours in botany.

ZOOLOGY, administering or performing research in the occurrence, structure, identification, and life histories of parasitic and nonparasitic organisms affecting plants and domestic and wild animals; pathology, epidemiology, immunology, physiology, and host relationships; and biological physical, and chemical control.

*Course Requirements—*30 semester hours, or equivalent, in biological science, including at least 20 hours in zoology and related animal sciences

PART FOUR

After You Pass The Test

4

YOU BECOME AN "ELIGIBLE"

Note: The Civil Service Commission is now called the Office Of Personnel Management.

People who are found to meet the requirements in the announcement are called "eligibles." Their names are put on a "list of eligibles." An eligible's chances of getting a job depend on how high he stands on this list and how fast agencies are filling jobs from the list.

Federal agencies can fill jobs in several ways—for instance, by promoting an employee already within the agency or by hiring an employee from another Federal agency who wants to change jobs. But when a job is to be filled from a list of eligibles, the agency asks the Civil Service examiners for the names of people on the list of eligibles for that job.

When the examiners receive this request, they send to the agency the names of the three people highest on the list. Or, if the job to be filled has specialized requirements, the examiners send the agency, from the general list, the names of the top three persons who meet those requirements. An applicant who has said he would not accept appointment in the place where the job is located is, of course, not considered.

The appointing officer makes a choice from among the three people whose names were sent to him. If that person accepts the appointment, the names of the other persons are put back on the list so that they may be considered for future openings.

That is the rule in hiring from all kinds of eligible lists, whether they are for typist, carpenter, chemist, or something else. For every vacancy, the appointing officer has his choice of any one of the top three eligibles on the list. This explains why the person whose name is on top of the list sometimes does not get an appointment when some of the persons lower on the list do. If the appointing officer chooses the No. 2 or No. 3 eligible, the No. 1 eligible doesn't get a job at once, but stays on the list until he is appointed or the list is terminated.

VETERANS GET PREFERENCE

If you are a veteran, you may be eligible for additional benefits in getting a Government job and also in keeping it after you are hired. For example, "veteran preference" will add extra points to your passing score.

Disabled veterans or their wives, widows of certain veterans, and widowed or divorced mothers of some veterans who died in service or who were totally and permanently disabled get 10 extra points. Most other honorably discharged veterans get 5 points, depending upon length or dates of service.

KINDS OF APPOINTMENTS

If you are offered a job, the letter or telegram will show what kind of appointment is involved. Most appointments are either temporary, term, career-conditional, or career. You should know what these mean.

A *temporary* appointment does not ordinarily last more than 1 year. A temporary worker can't be promoted and can't transfer to another job. He is not under the retirement system. Persons over 70 can be given only temporary appointments, but they can be renewed.

A *term* appointment is made for work on a specific project that will last more than 1 year but less than 4 years. A term employee can be promoted or reassigned to other positions within the project for which he was hired. He is not under the retirement system.

If you accept a temporary or term appointment,

your name will stay on the list of eligibles from which you were appointed. This means that you will remain eligible for permanent jobs that are normally filled by career-conditional or career appointments.

A *career-conditional* appointment leads after 3 years' service to a career appointment. For the first year, the employee serves a probationary period. During this time, he must demonstrate that he can do a satisfactory job and may be dismissed if he fails to do so. A career-conditional employee has promotion and transfer privileges. After a career-conditional employee completes his probation, he cannot be removed except for cause. However, in reduction-in-force (layoff) actions, career-conditional employees are dismissed ahead of career employees.

A *career* employee also serves a probationary period, as described above, and has promotion and transfer privileges. After he completes his probation, however, he is in the last group to be affected in layoffs.

WHY YOU MAY BE BARRED

Applicants may be denied examinations and eligibles may be denied appointments for any of the following reasons:

1. Dismissal from employment for delinquency or misconduct.

2. Physical or mental unfitness for the position.

3. Criminal, infamous, dishonest, immoral, or notoriously disgraceful conduct.

4. Intentional false statements, deception, or fraud.

5. Refusal to furnish testimony which the Commission may require.

6. Drunkenness.

7. Reasonable doubt as to loyalty to the Government of the United States.

8. Any legal or other disqualification.

An old conviction for civil or criminal offense will not of itself bar an applicant from U. S. government employment. Ordinarily a person who has been convicted of a felony must wait two years after release before his application will be considered. Exceptions can be made by the Civil Service Commission, which also decides whether or not to accept applications from persons who have been convicted of misdemeanors or who are under suspended sentence or on probation.

OTHER REQUIREMENTS

When you are being considered for a job, and again when you are appointed, you will learn about certain requirements you must meet — over and above the requirement that you be able to do the work. You will be informed of certain rules which, as a Federal employee, you will be expected to observe.

RESIDENCE REQUIREMENTS

Appointments to some positions in Washington, D.C., are apportioned by law among the States and territories. Persons being considered for these positions may be required to send in proof that they meet a 1-year residence requirement. This proof will be requested, when necessary, by the agency that is considering you for appointment.

MEMBERS OF FAMILY

Unless you are entitled to veteran preference, you may not be appointed (except temporarily) if two or more members of your family who live under the same roof have permanent Federal jobs. The agency that is considering you for appointment will ask you for this information.

AFFIDAVITS

You will be asked to swear (or affirm) to certain statements. If you swear to or affirm statements that are not true, you may be dismissed as a result. You must swear (or affirm):
— that you will support and defend the Constitution of the United States;
— that you are not a Communist or a Fascist, and that you do not advocate, or belong to any organization that advocates the overthrow of the Government of the United States by force or violence;
— that you will not strike against the Government or join any organization that claims the right to strike against the Government.

You may also be asked to swear (or affirm) that you did not pay, or offer to pay, any money or anything of value to get your appointment.

FINGERPRINTS

Your fingerprints will be taken, either when you report for duty or when the investigation is begun. The fingerprints will be sent to the Federal Bureau of Investigation for checking against their records. If you were ever convicted (for anything other than a minor traffic violation), and you did not admit the conviction on your qualifications statement, you may be dismissed, or if you are an applicant you may be denied appointment.

INVESTIGATION

In connection with your appointment, an investigation will be made to determine whether you are reliable, trustworthy, of good conduct and character, and of complete and unswerving loyalty to the United States. If your appointment is to a sensitive position (a position of trust in which you may have access to classified information), a determination will also be made as to whether your employment in the Government service would be clearly consistent with the interests of the national security.

REPORTING FOR DUTY

If you must travel in order to report for duty, you ordinarily pay your own way. The Government pays these travel expenses for only a few hard-to-fill positions.

PHYSICAL EXAMINATION

If necessary, you will be given a physical examination by a medical officer before appointment. If he finds that you are not physically qualified for the position, you cannot be appointed.

HOLDING OUTSIDE EMPLOYMENT

You will not be allowed to hold outside employment or to engage in other activities not compatible with the full and proper discharge of the duties and responsibilities of your Government employment. Your employing agency will judge whether outside activities are proper in any case.

POLITICAL ACTIVITY

You will not be allowed to take an active part in partisan politics while you are a Federal employee. You may, of course, vote as you please and express your opinions as a private citizen. Federal Employee Facts Leaflet No. 2 tells what kinds of political activity are permitted and what kinds are prohibited.

WORKING FOR THE U.S.

Note: The Civil Service Commission is now called the Office Of Personnel Management.

Working for the government is different from working in private industry. You can't always give orders and expect them to be carried out pronto; you're likely to bump into a regulation. You can't be too active politically; if you are, you'll be slapped down. There is a complicated system of judging and reporting on your work—a system that may affect your earning power. It's pretty easy to get fired. And with what seems sickening frequency, some Congressman sounds off against "inefficient bureaucrats"—meaning you. On the other hand, if you work authorized overtime, you get paid for it, your vacation and sick-leave time is generous, chances for promotions and pay increases are frequent, and the government often gives valuable training on the job. If you make government service a career, you'll retire with a substantial annuity.

SALARY AND WORKING CONDITIONS

After selecting its employees on the basis of merit, the Government pays them, and promotes them, on the same basis.

Employees are paid according to the principle of "equal pay for equal work." When jobs in the higher grades become vacant, or new ones are set up, the general practice is to fill them by promoting employees in lower grades who are qualified to perform the more difficult duties.

You will want to know more about these matters, and about other features of Federal employment. As you learn about them, you will find that the Government, the largest employer in the United States, is also a progressive employer.

PAY

In general, the Government pays good salaries. Its policy is that salaries of Government employees should be comparable to those paid by private employers for work of the same level of difficulty and responsibility.

Government salaries are reviewed frequently and changes made, or recommended to Congress, as needed. This means that persons choosing careers in Government may expect, over the years, pay realistically geared to the economy.

The Government has several pay plans. For most trades positions, wages are set from time to time to bring them into line with prevailing wages paid in the same locality by private industry.

A few Federal agencies and a few classes of employees have still other pay plans. The Tennessee Valley Authority, the Postal Service, the Foreign Service (Department of State), and physicians, dentists, and nurses in the Department of Medicine and Surgery of the Veterans Administration are examples.

Other employees (45 percent) are paid under the General Schedule (GS), which applies to most white-collar employees and to protective and custodial employees such as guards and messengers. Positions are graded by number according to how difficult the work is, starting with grade GS–1 and going up to grade GS–18.

Each grade has a set salary range; thus the grade of a position sets the pay. Hard-to-fill positions frequently have a higher salary range than other positions in the same grade. In all cases, salaries are listed in the announcement or in a separate supplement.

S118

Hiring usually is done at the first rate of a grade. Employees who perform their work at an acceptable level of competence receive within-grade increases at intervals. They may qualify for these increases every year for 3 years; then the increases occur less frequently until the top rate of the grade is reached. Employees may be awarded additional within-grade increases for exceptionally meritorious work, but not above the top of the grade.

You will be interested in knowing how jobs get to be in one grade or another. Position classifiers study the duties of the jobs. They find out how difficult the duties are, how much responsibility the person holding the job has, and what knowledge or experience or skill goes into performing the duties. Then they put the jobs in appropriate grades under standards set by the Civil Service Commission.

HOURS OF WORK

The usual Government workweek is 40 hours. Most Government employees work 8 hours, 5 days a week, Monday through Friday, but in some cases the nature of the work may call for a different workweek.

As in any other business, employees sometimes have to work overtime. If you are required to work overtime while a Government employee, you will either be paid for overtime or given time off to make up for the extra time you worked.

ADVANCEMENT

Many of the men and women in top jobs in the Government began their careers "at the bottom of the ladder." They did their jobs well, and prepared for the job ahead. They learned more and more about the work of their agencies. As they became more useful on the job, they were promoted to one more important position after another.

Most agencies fill vacancies, whenever possible, by promoting their own employees. Promotion programs in every agency are designed to make sure that promotions go to the employees who are among the best qualified to fill higher positions. How fast employees are promoted depends upon openings in the higher grades, and upon their ability and industry.

Federal employees receive on-the-job training. They may also participate in individualized career development programs and receive job-related training in their own agency, in other agencies, or outside the Government (for example, in industrial plants and universities).

It is not always necessary to move to a new job in order to advance in grade. Sometimes an employee's work assignments change a great deal in the ordinary course of business. His job "grows." When that happens it is time for a position classifier to study the job again. If he finds that the job should be put in a higher grade because of the increased difficulty or responsibility of the duties, the change is made.

TRANSFERS

Transferring to other civil service jobs for which an employee is qualified is another way of getting a better job.

Agencies consider the qualifications of an employee for promotion as higher grade positions become vacant. However, for transfer to positions in other agencies, an employee would have to "find his own job," by such means as interviews with officials in those agencies. If he can find a vacant position in another agency, and if the hiring officer is impressed with his qualifications, arrangements may be made to transfer him.

Occasionally, the Job Information Center may be able to assist Federal employees in locating vacancies.

EFFICIENCY COUNTS

At intervals, employees are rated on their job performance. In most agencies, the ratings are "Outstanding," "Satisfactory," and "Unsatisfactory."

Employees with "Outstanding" ratings receive extra credit for retention in layoffs.

An employee whose rating is "Unsatisfactory" must be dismissed or assigned to another position with duties which he can be expected to learn to do satisfactorily.

INCENTIVE AWARDS

Government agencies encourage their employees to suggest better ways, or simpler ways, or more economical ways, of doing their jobs. They may give a cash award to an employee for a suggestion or invention that results in money savings or improved service. They may also reward outstanding job performance or other acts that are particularly meritorious and deserving of recognition.

VACATION AND SICK LEAVE

Most Federal employees earn annual leave, for vacation and other purposes, according to the number of years (civilian plus creditable military service) they have been in the Federal service. They earn it at the rate of 13 days a year for the first 3 years and 20 days a year for the next 12 years. After 15 years, they earn 26 days of annual leave each year.

Sick leave is earned at the rate of 13 days a year. You can use this leave for illnesses serious enough to keep you away from your work, and for appointments with a doctor, dentists, or optician. Sick leave that is not used can be saved for future use. It is one of the best forms of insurance an employee and his family can have in case of extended periods of illness.

New Year's Day, Washington's Birthday, Memorial Day, Independence Day, Columbus Day, Veterans' Day, Thanksgiving and Christmas are some of the holidays granted Federal employees. Most are celebrated on Mondays, in accordance with the new Monday Holiday Law.

INJURY COMPENSATION

The Government provides liberal compensation benefits, including medical care, for employees who suffer injuries in the performance of official duty. Death benefits are also provided if an employee dies as a result of such injuries.

GROUP LIFE INSURANCE

As a Federal employee, you may have low-cost term life insurance without taking a physical examination. Two kinds of insurance are provided — life insurance and accidental death and dismemberment insurance.

This low cost insurance is available to employees in amounts that usually exceed one's annual base pay by $2,000. The Government pays one-third of the premium cost and the employee, through payroll deductions, pays the remainder. The minimum amount of each kind of protection is $10,000. In addition, an employee may purchase an extra $10,000 of optional insurance; for this he pays full premium, also through payroll deductions.

HEALTH BENEFITS

The Government sponsors a voluntary health insurance program for Federal employees. The program offers a variety of plans to meet individual needs, including basic coverage and major medical protection against costly illnesses. The Government contributes part of the cost of premiums and the employee pays the balance through payroll deductions.

RETIREMENT

Seven percent of a career or career-conditional employee's salary goes into a retirement fund. This seven percent comes out of every paycheck. This money is withheld as the employee's share of the cost of providing him or his survivors with an income after he has completed his working career.

If you leave the Government before you complete 5 years of service, the money you put into the retirement fund can be returned to you. If you leave after completing 5 years of service, you have a choice of having your money returned or leaving it in the fund. If you leave it in the fund, you will get an annuity starting when you are age 62.

The Government has a liberal retirement system. For example, after working for 30 years, you may retire at age 55 and get a life-time annual income equal to 56¼% of the highest average salary you earned during any three consecutive years of your working career. Also, an employee who becomes disabled after at least five years of Government service may retire on an annuity at any age.

LAYOFFS

In Government, layoffs are called *reductions in force*, and may be caused by a cut in appropriations, a decrease in work, or some similar reason.

In a reduction in force, the four things which determine whether an employee goes or stays are: Type of appointment (career, career-conditional, temporary); whether he has veteran preference for this purpose (20-year retired veterans generally do not); seniority (how long an employee has worked for the Government); and job performance.

UNEMPLOYMENT COMPENSATION

Federal employees who are separated in layoffs or whose appointments are terminated are entitled to unemployment compensation similar to that provided for employees in private industry. They are covered by the unemployment insurance system under conditions set by the State in which they worked.

SEVERANCE PAY

Federal employees who are involuntarily separated without cause, and who are not entitled to an immediate retirement annuity, may be eligible for severance pay. This pay is based on years of service and years of age over 40, and may not exceed 1 year's basic compensation.

EMPLOYEE ORGANIZATIONS

There are a number of unions and other employee organizations in the Federal Government. Some of them are for special groups, such as postal employees. Others have general membership among Government employees. Their main objective is to improve the working conditions of Federal employees.

Federal employees are free to join or to refrain from joining such organizations. But, as mentioned before, they may not join an organization which asserts the right to strike against the Government of the United States.

GETTING ADDITIONAL INFORMATION

Information about Federal civil service job announcements can be obtained from any Federal Job Information Center and at many post offices.

CIVIL SERVICE REFORM ACT

For the first time in law, nine basic merit principles are to govern all personnel practices in the Federal Government. The law also defines prohibited practices, and requires disciplinary action to be taken against offenders.

Personnel Practices and Actions in the Federal Government Require:

- Recruitment from all segments of society, and selection and advancement on the basis of ability, knowledge, and skills, under fair and open competition.
- Fair and equitable treatment in all personnel management matters, without regard to politics, race, color, religion, national origin, sex, marital status, age, or handicapping condition, and with proper regard for individual privacy and constitutional rights.
- Equal pay for work of equal value, considering both national and local rates paid by private employers, with incentives and recognition for excellent performance.
- High standards of integrity, conduct, and concern for the public interest.
- Efficient and effective use of the Federal work force.
- Retention of employees who perform well, correcting the performance of those whose work is inadequate, and separation of those who cannot or will not meet required standards.
- Improved performance through effective education and training.
- Protection of employees from arbitrary action, personal favoritism, or political coercion.
- Protection of employees against reprisal for lawful disclosures of information.

Officials and Employees Who Are Authorized to Take Personnel Actions Are Prohibited From:

- Discriminating against any employee or applicant.
- Soliciting or considering any recommendation on a person who requests or is being considered for a personnel action unless the material is an evaluation of the person's work performance, ability, aptitude, or general qualifications, or character, loyalty, and suitability.
- Using official authority to coerce political actions, to require political contributions, or to retaliate for refusal to do these things.
- Willfully deceiving or obstructing an individual as to his or her right to compete for Federal employment.
- Influencing anyone to withdraw from competition, whether to improve or worsen the prospects of any applicant.
- Granting any special preferential treatment or advantage not authorized by law to a job applicant or employee.
- Appointing, employing, promoting, or advancing relatives in their agencies.
- Taking or failing to take a personnel action as a reprisal against employees who exercise their appeal rights; refuse to engage in political activity; or lawfully disclose violations of law, rule, or regulation, or mismanagement, gross waste of funds, abuse of authority, or a substantial and specific danger to public health or safety.
- Taking or failing to take any other personnel action violating a law, rule, or regulation directly related to merit system principles.

The New Organization for Personnel Management

As a result of Reorganization Plan No. 2, the U.S. Civil Service Commission is abolished January 1979, and its functions divided between two new agencies. An Office of Personnel Management (OPM) is to provide leadership in managing the Federal work force. An independent Merit Systems Protection Board (MSPB) is to resolve employee complaints and appeals. A third new agency, the Federal Labor Relations Authority (FLRA), is to administer the Federal labor relations program and investigate unfair labor practices.

The functions of the agencies are described below:

Office of Personnel Management

The Office of Personnel Management helps the President carry out his responsibilities for management of the Federal work force. The Office is headed by a director and deputy director appointed by the President and confirmed by the Senate.

OPM takes over many of the responsibilities of the Civil Service Commission. These include central examining and employment operations, personnel investigations, personnel program evaluation, executive development, and training. OPM also administers the retirement and insurance programs for Federal employees and exercises management leadership in labor relations and affirmative action.

As the central personnel agency, OPM develops policies governing civilian employment in Executive branch agencies and in certain agencies of the Legislative and Judicial branches, and helps agencies carry out these policies. Subject to its standards and review, OPM also delegates certain personnel powers to agency heads.

Merit Systems Protection Board

The Merit Systems Protection Board is the independent agency to safeguard both the merit system and individual employees against abuses and unfair personnel actions. The MSPB is headed by three board members, appointed on a bipartisan basis to 7-year nonrenewable terms. The Board hears and decides employee appeals and orders corrective and disciplinary actions against an employee or agency when appropriate. It also oversees the merit system and reports annually to Congress on how the system is functioning.

The Federal Employee Appeals Authority and Appeals Review Board is abolished when MSPB is created.

Within the MSPB is an independent Special Counsel, appointed by the President for a 5-year term. The Special Counsel has the power to investigate charges of prohibited personnel practices, including reprisals against whistleblowers; to ask MSPB to stop personnel actions in cases involving prohibited personnel practices; and to bring disciplinary charges before the MSPB against those who violate merit system law.

Federal Labor Relations Authority

The Federal Labor Relations Authority oversees the creation of bargaining units, supervises elections, and deals with labor-management issues in Federal agencies. The FLRA is headed by a chairman and two members, who are appointed on a bipartisan basis to staggered 5-year terms. (This agency will replace the Federal Labor Relations Council.)

Within the FLRA, a General Counsel, appointed to a 5-year term, investigates alleged unfair labor practices and prosecutes them before the FLRA. Also within the FLRA and acting as a separate body, the Federal Service Impasses Panel resolves negotiation impasses.

Performance Appraisal Systems

Each agency is to develop and phase-in its own appraisal system(s). Performance appraisals are to be a basis for decisions to train, reward, assign, promote, demote, retain, or remove employees (for reasons other than misconduct). Agencies are encouraged to have employees participate in establishing performance objectives for their jobs.

Specifically, the appraisal systems must make it possible for agencies to:
- advise employees on what the critical elements of their jobs are;
- establish performance standards that will permit accurate evaluation of job performance on the basis of objective, job-related criteria;
- assist employees to improve unacceptable performance; and
- reassign, demote, or remove those employees whose performance continues to be unacceptable, but only after they have been given an opportunity to show that they can perform acceptably and have failed to improve.

Agencies are required to inform employees of the critical elements and performance standards of their jobs.

If any agency proposes to remove or demote an employee because of poor performance, and if that employee's performance becomes acceptable and remains acceptable for one year, the record of the poor performance will be removed from agency files.

Procedures for Adverse Actions and Appeals

Adverse actions, such as removals, suspensions for over 14 days, and reductions in grade or pay, may be appealed to the Merit Systems Protection Board. Employees in organized bargaining units may be able under their negotiated agreements to ask their union to seek arbitration instead of appealing to MSPB.

If an agency proposes to demote or remove an employee because of unacceptable performance, that employee is entitled to:
- receive written notice from the agency 30 days before the proposed action;
- be represented by an attorney or other representative;
- answer orally and in writing within a reasonable time; and
- receive a written decision (agreed to by a higher level supervisor than the one who proposed the action) which states the reason for the action.

An agency's final decision will be provided in writing within 30 days after the end of the notice period.

If an agency decides to demote or remove an employee at the end of the notice period, the employee may appeal to the MSPB for a hearing, or, if within a bargaining unit, the employee may use the grievance arbitration procedure. The agency's decision will be upheld if it is shown by substantial evidence that the employee failed to meet performance standards for one or more critical elements of the job. For adverse actions based on grounds other than poor performance, an agency's decision to remove an employee must be supported by a preponderance of evidence.

An agency's decision will not be upheld if an employee shows that the decision:
- was based on harmful procedural errors on the part of the agency;
- was based on any prohibited personnel practice; or
- was unlawful.

The same standards will apply whether the adverse action is appealed to MSPB or resolved by an arbitrator.

Agencies whose decisions are reversed may be required in certain cases to pay employees for reasonable attorney fees. These payments might occur in cases where agencies engaged in prohibited personnel practices.

Decisions or orders of MPSB are appealable to the U.S. Court of Appeals, or, in matters of pay, the Court of Claims.

Complaints Involving Discrimination

Procedures to handle discrimination complaints in two situations are established.

The first situation includes agency actions which the employee claims were discriminatory and which are of a type that may be appealed to MSPB (e.g. removals and demotions). These are called "mixed cases." An agency has 120 days to try to resolve the discrimination issue by using counseling and investigation. If an employee is not satisfied with the final agency decision, or if time runs out, that employee may appeal to MSPB. Instead of going to MSPB with a "mixed case," the union may call for grievance arbitration.

An employee may not directly appeal a "mixed case" to the Equal Employment Opportunity Commission (EEOC). However, an employee may ask EEOC to review the MSPB decision. Other steps would be followed if EEOC and MSPB do not agree.

The second type of situation includes discrimination complaints about actions or failures to act which are not appealable to MSPB (e.g. promotions or working conditions). In this case, an employee may appeal the final agency action to EEOC, or a union may call for grievance arbitration procedures. Appeals to EEOC will follow the current procedures for processing discrimination complaints. MSPB plays no part in these decisions.

Regardless of whether the decision is made by MSPB,

EEOC, or an arbitrator, an employee will have the right to appeal that decision to a U.S. District Court.

EEOC is also responsible for approving agency goals and timetables in affirmative action plans.

Special Counsel Protections

The Special Counsel to the Merit Systems Protection Board is, in effect, an independent investigator and prosecutor. This individual is appointed by the President for a 5-year term.

Specifically, the Special Counsel investigates charges that agency officials:
- undertook prohibited personnel practices, including reprisals against whistleblowers;
- engaged in prohibited political activity;
- withheld information under the Freedom of Information Act without just reason;
- discriminated in violation of law; or
- carried out activities prohibited by any other civil service law, rule, or regulation.

After these investigations, the Special Counsel may bring disciplinary charges before the MSPB against officials if the evidence shows a probable violation. They may be reprimanded, removed, fined, or barred from Federal employment.

The Special Counsel has authority to protect *whistleblowers*. Whistleblowers are those employees or applicants who expose practices which they reasonably believe to be a violation of law, rule, or regulation, or which they believe constitute mismanagement, gross waste of funds, abuse of authority, or a danger to public health or safety. Employees or applicants who make disclosures specifically prohibited by law or Executive order will not be protected.

The Special Counsel investigates charges of reprisal without revealing the identity of the whistleblower, and may petition any member of the MSPB to stop any personnel action while the matter is under investigation. The results of the investigation will be reported to the whistleblower.

Agencies may be required to conduct investigations and prepare reports on the substance of complaints made by whistleblowers. In such cases, the Special Counsel will review the agency reports to determine whether they contain sufficient information and whether the findings appear reasonable. Copies of the agency reports will be sent to the President and to Congress, and to the persons who filed the complaints.

Grade and Pay Retention

Pay retention provisions will make it possible for employees to retain their grades for two years and to avoid taking considerable cuts in salary as the result of downgrading actions for which they were not responsible.

Employees to be placed in lower-graded positions as the result of reductions-in-force or reclassification actions may, (if they have held their current positions for one year), retain their current grades for two years from the date of demotion. Pay for these employees will not be reduced.

At the end of the two-year period, the grades of these employees will be lowered. Should their pay at that time exceed the maximum rate of their new grades, they will retain their current rate of pay but will receive only 50% of their annual comparability pay increases. If or when their pay is lower than or equal to the maximum rate of their new grades, they will then receive full comparability pay increases.

These special benefits will continue only as long as the employees remain in their same positions and will apply to all reductions-in-force or reclassification actions taken on or after January 1, 1977.

Veterans' Preference and Benefits

Veterans with service-connected disabilities of 30% or more are entitled to receive additional benefits, including:
- appointment without competitive examination, with a right to be converted to career appointments, and
- retention rights over other preference eligibles in reductions-in-force.

Veterans with disabilities of 30% or more also have the right to be notified in advance and respond to any decision in which:
- they are considered ineligible for a position due to physical requirements of the position;
- they would be passed over by an agency in the course of filling a position from a civil service

certificate; or
- they are deemed ineligible for retention in a position during a reduction-in-force due to the physical requirements of the position.

On October 1, 1980, veterans' preference is eliminated for non-disabled military retirees who retire from the service at or above the rank of major or its equivalent.

Changes in Federal Labor Relations

The Civil Service Reform Act contains a number of new provisions which clarifies the roles and responsibilities of labor organizations and which, to an extent, expands the rights of employees in collective bargaining units.

The Act affirms the basic rights of Federal employees to form, join, and assist labor organizations (or to refrain from doing so). It prohibits strikes and work slowdowns, as well as picketing that interferes with government operations.

For most matters, employees working in organized bargaining units must use the grievance arbitration procedures negotiated by the union. However, an exception is made for adverse actions and discrimination complaints. In such cases, employees may use either the negotiated procedures *or* the appeals procedure. The union is required to represent all employees in the bargaining unit who choose the negotiated procedures, whether or not they are members of the union.

The issues subject to collective bargaining are to generally continue. However, departments and agencies (such as OPM, OMB, and GSA) which issue government-wide regulations affecting Federal employees, are required to consult with labor organizations representing a substantial number of employees over any substantive changes. In addition, a union that represents, in one bargaining unit, a majority of affected employees is able to negotiate without regard to their own agency's regulations on matters otherwise within the scope of bargaining.

The Act makes all types of management actions subject to collective bargaining unless specific "management rights" exist. These reserve to agency officials the authority to make decisions and take actions which are not subject to the collective bargaining

process, and exclude bargaining on Federal pay and benefits or nonvoluntary payments to unions by employees. The changes in the management rights area will: (1) *prohibit* agencies from bargaining on mission, budget, organization, number of employees, or internal security; and (2) *permit,* but not require, them to negotiate over the methods, means, and technology of conducting agency operations. Management has the right to determine whether vacant positions may be filled only by persons within the agency *or* by persons within and outside the agency.

Other provisions in the Act include:
- A time limit of 45 days for agency heads to decide if a proposed action is negotiable. This decision will be appealable to the Federal Labor Relations Authority.
- Court enforcement of FLRA decisions and orders, including judicial review in unfair labor practice cases.
- Provisions for back pay and attorney fees for employees subject to unjustified or unwarranted personnel actions.
- Dues withholding—based on voluntary allotments by employees—at the exclusive union's request. (Allotments are irrevocable for one year, and the withholding service is at no charge to the employee or labor organization.)
- Official time during regular working hours for employees representing unions in negotiations.

Trial Period for New Managers and Supervisors

First-time supervisors and managers will be required to serve a trial period before their appointments become final. Those who do not satisfactorily complete the trial period will be returned to positions of no lower pay and grade than those they occupied before assuming their managerial or supervisory assignments.

Previously, ineffective first-time supervisors and managers could normally be removed only through the application of adverse action procedures. Those who do not perform well during the trial period are to be removed from managerial responsibilities forthwith.

Merit Pay for Managers and Supervisors

A merit pay system is implemented in which the pay increases of managers and supervisors in grades GS-

13 through GS-15 will be directly linked to their performance, rather than to their length of service. Employees covered will no longer receive automatic within-grade increases, but will be eligible each year for merit pay increases.

Managers covered under the merit pay system will receive a minimum of one-half of the annual comparability pay increases authorized for white collar employees, but this minimum can be increased by OPM. The funds for merit raises are to be derived from a combination of the remainder of the annual comparability increases and from funds formerly used for step increases and quality step increases for these employees.

The amounts agencies award in merit increases will vary to recognize distinctions in the performance of individual managers and supervisors and of the organizations they direct. Agencies must base their decisions on a formal appraisal system. Factors taken into account in awarding merit pay increases will include cost efficiency; timeliness of performance; and improvements in efficiency, productivity, and quality of work or service.

All managers and supervisors in grades GS-13 through GS-15 are to be brought into the merit pay system. No employee will suffer a salary loss in the conversion to the new system.

Senior Executive Service

The Senior Executive Service (SES) is to include managers at GS-16 through Executive Level IV or their equivalents in the Executive branch. The SES will make it easier for the Federal Government to attract and keep top managers, to use their abilities productively, and to pay them according to their performance.

The large majority of SES executives are to be career managers. There is a 10% government-wide ceiling on the number who may be noncareer. In addition, about 45% of SES positions will be career-reserved; that is, they can be filled only by career executives.

SES executives may be reassigned to other positions within their own agencies, but may not be involuntarily transferred to other agencies.

Entry Into SES

OPM will determine the number of SES positions in each agency. Individuals who presently occupy those positions which their agencies designate to become a part of the SES have 90 days in which to choose either to enter the Service or to remain under their present appointment authorities. Those who choose not to join the SES will keep their present pay and benefits, but will not be eligible for promotions. Those who enter the SES at a later date must have their managerial qualifications evaluated by qualification review boards within the Office of Personnel Management, and must serve a trial period of one year. Veterans' preference will not apply in the SES.

Compensation and Benefits

Base pay for SES executives will be set at one of five levels, with the minimum at the equivalent of GS-16, step 1, and the maximum at the salary for Executive Level IV. In addition, performance awards may be given to 50% of the career executives in amounts up to 20% of base salary. Each year, up to 5% of SES executives may receive the rank of "Meritorious Executive," with a special award of $10,000. Up to 1% may receive the rank of "Distinguished Executive," with a special award of $20,000. A ceiling will be set on total compensation for SES members equal to the pay of Executive Level I (now $66,000). Only career executives in the SES will be eligible for performance awards and ranks.

Retention and Removal

Retention in the SES will be based on good performance. Executives will be evaluated annually by their supervisors, who will measure their individual performance and that of the organizations they direct. Among the evaluation criteria are improvements in efficiency and productivity; work quality; timeliness of performance; and success in meeting affirmative action goals.

Ratings will range from "fully successful," a rating which makes one eligible for performance awards, to "marginal" or "unsatisfactory," ratings which indicate a need for corrective action and improvement. Failure to improve would cause removal from the SES.

Career executives who are removed from the SES for

poor performance cannot appeal but may state their case in a hearing before the Merit Systems Protection Board. They are entitled to placement in non-SES positions at GS-15 or above, at no loss in base pay. Executives with 25 years of government service or with 20 years of service at age 50 may choose retirement under such circumstances.

Other Features of the Civil Service Reform Act

Agencies are to conduct MINORITY RECRUITMENT PROGRAMS to help eliminate underrepresentation of minority groups in the Federal work force. The Office of Personnel Management and the Equal Employment Opportunity Commission will provide guidelines and assistance.

NONPAID WORK BY STUDENTS in connection with educational programs is permitted, provided they do not reduce opportunities for regular employees.

Employees who would otherwise be separated under reductions-in-force may be RETRAINED for jobs in other agencies.

Until January 1981, the TOTAL NUMBER OF CIVILIAN EMPLOYEES in the Executive branch is limited to the number of employees on board as of September 30, 1977. (Postal Service and Postal Rate Commission employees are excluded from this total.)

Employees who are age 50 with 20 years of service, or who, regardless of age, have 25 years of service, may choose EARLY RETIREMENT in major reorganizations, transfers of function, or reductions-in-force.

OPM must notify the U.S. Employment Service about competitive examinations it administers. Agencies must provide both OPM and the U.S. Employment Service EMPLOYMENT INFORMATION about positions for which they are seeking candidates outside of the civil service system.

THE MOBILITY PROGRAM authorized by the Intergovernmental Personnel Act has been extended to include additional types of organizations and individuals. Federal employees who accept these assignments must return to the Federal Government for a period equal to that of the assignments.

Subject to its standards and review, OPM may DELEGATE AUTHORITY FOR PERSONNEL MANAGEMENT FUNCTIONS, including certain competitive examinations, to the heads of agencies employing persons in the competitive service.

The COMBINED RETIREMENT PAY AND FEDERAL CIVILIAN SALARY received by future retirees of the uniformed services may not exceed the pay for Executive Level V.

Federal agencies are authorized to adopt OPM's MERIT SYSTEM STANDARDS as a personnel requirement for grants to state and local governments.

DIRECTORY

Below is a listing of addresses and telephone numbers (FTS and commercial) for the headquarters and regional offices of the Office of Personnel Management (OPM) and Merit Systems Protection Board (MSPB). Area Offices and Federal Job Information Centers of the U.S. Civil Service Commission will also become part of OPM.

The headquarters address and telephone numbers of the Federal Labor Relations Authority (FLRA) are listed below. The regional structure for FLRA has not yet been determined.

OFFICE OF PERSONNEL MANAGEMENT

Headquarters Offices	1900 E. Street, NW Washington, DC 20415	Com/202-632-6101
Regional Offices		
Atlanta	1340 Spring Street, NW Atlanta, GA 30309	Com/404-881-2436
Boston	Post Office and Courthouse Building Boston, MA 02109	Com/617-223-2538
Chicago	Federal Office Building 230 S. Dearborn Street Chicago, IL 60604	Com/312-353-2901
Dallas	1100 Commerce Street Dallas, TX 75242	Com/214-749-3352
Denver	Building 20 Denver Federal Center Denver, CO 80225	Com/303-234-2023
New York	New Federal Building 26 Federal Plaza New York, NY 10007	Com/212-264-0440
Philadelphia	Federal Building 600 Arch Street Philadelphia, PA 19106	Com/215-597-4543
St. Louis	1256 Federal Building 1520 Market Street St. Louis, MO 63103	Com/314-425-4262
San Francisco	Federal Building, Box 36010 450 Golden Gate Avenue San Francisco, CA 94102	Com/415-556-0581
Seattle	Federal Building, 26th Floor 915 Second Avenue Seattle, WA 98174	Com/206-442-7536

MERIT SYSTEMS PROTECTION BOARD

Headquarters

Offices	1717 H Street, NW Washington, DC 20415	Com/202-254-3063

Regional Offices

Atlanta	1340 Spring Street, NW Atlanta, GA 30309	Com/404-881-3631
Boston	100 Sumner Street, Rm. 1736 Boston, MA 02110	Com/617-223-2556
Chicago	Federal Office Building 230 S. Dearborn Street Chicago, IL 60604	Com/312-353-2923
Dallas	1100 Commerce Street Dallas, TX 75242	Com/214-749-3451
Denver	Building 46 Denver Federal Center Box 25025 Denver, CO 80225	Com/303-234-3725
New York	New Federal Building 26 Federal Plaza New York, NY 10007	Com/212-264-9372
Philadelphia	U.S. Customhouse, Rm. 501 Second and Chestnut Streets Philadelphia, PA 19106	Com/215-597-4446
St. Louis	1256 Federal Building 1520 Market Street St. Louis, MO 63103	Com/314-425-4295
San Francisco	Federal Building, Box 36010 450 Golden Gate Avenue San Francisco, CA 94102	Com/415-556-0316
Seattle	Federal Building, 26th Floor 915 Second Avenue Seattle, WA 98174	Com/206-442-0395

FEDERAL LABOR RELATIONS AUTHORITY

Headquarters

Offices	1900 E Street, NW Room 7469 Washington, DC 20415	Com/202-632-6878

VETERAN'S PREFERENCE

Note: The Civil Service Commission is now called the
Office Of Personnel Management.

A large system of special advantages is available to veterans who seek work with the government, and to those already in federal jobs. These advantages extend from preferential treatment in getting jobs to preferential treatment if layoffs should occur. Certain disabled veterans' wives, veterans' widows, and veterans' mothers are included in this system of advantages.

Here, in capsule form, are the major privileges which veterans enjoy.

Disabled veterans have 10 points added to the grade they earn on a civil service exam. Thus if a disabled vet gets a mark of 70, he is granted an additional 10 points—bringing him up to 80 and much closer to the job he wants. Non-disabled veterans are granted five additional points.

On any examination, the veteran must make 70 before 5- or 10-point preference is added.

A federal employee who left his position to enter the armed forces is entitled to his old job back (unless it was a temporary job) or a position of like status, pay, and seniority.

In all positions except scientific and professional positions in grade GS-9 or higher disabled veterans with a compensable service-connected disability of 10 per cent or more go to the top of the lists of those to be appointed.

No appointing officer may pass over a veteran on a Civil Service Commission certificate of eligibles to appoint a non-veteran without giving his reasons in writing to the Civil Service Commission.

In making temporary appointments for which no examination is needed agencies must give consideration first to disabled veterans, with a compensable service-connected disability of 10 per cent or more, second to other disabled veterans and then to non-disabled veterans before any consideration is given to non-veterans.

When layoffs take place the veteran must be retained longer than the non-veteran. Under the Veteran's Preference Act veterans who have satisfactory or better performance (efficiency) ratings are retained in preference to all non-veterans, irrespective of their efficiency ratings or length of service, who rate "in competition with them" for retention.

Other privileges are given the veteran. In most examinations, he is granted a waiver of height, weight, and age requirements. He gets credit for experience and training in the armed forces. Under certain conditions an examination already "closed" will be opened for him. His protections against dismissal extend to other disciplinary actions—suspension, furlough without pay, demotion, debarment from future employment. If a veteran, after getting his extra points on an exam, has the same grade as a non-veteran, he is entered ahead of the non-veteran as a job prospect. The veteran isn't required to need the "members-of-family" rule—the rule that not more than two members of the family living under one roof may hold permanent federal positions. Nor will he be denied employment in case his state is "over-quota" in the number of its residents in armed forces.

Effective in January 1979, veterans with service-connected disabilities of 30% or more will receive additional benefits, including:
- appointment without competitive examination, with a right to be converted to career appointments, and
- retention rights over other preference eligibles in reductions in-force.

Veterans with disabilities of 30% or more will also have the right to be notified in advance and respond to any decision in which:
- they are considered ineligible for a position due to physical requirements of the position;
- they would be passed over by an agency in the course of filling a position from a civil service certificate; or
- they are deemed ineligible for retention in a position during a reduction-in-force due to the physical requirements of the position.

On October 1, 1980, veterans' preference will be eliminated for non-disabled military retirees who retire from the service at or above the rank of major or its equivalent.

JOBS FOR VETERANS ONLY

Appointments to certain positions are restricted to veteran-preference eligibles. Persons not entitled to preference may file for and compete in examinations for those positions, but their applications will not be rated or referred to agencies for appointment as long as sufficient veterans are available.

Restricted positions include guard, elevator operator, messenger, and custodian.

Restricted positions in the "guard" category include: air corps patrolman; patrolman; building guard; mint guard; private and special officer (Secret Service); chief guard-fire marshall; guard chauffeur; guard-fire-fighter; guard-fireman; guard laborer; guard (U. S. Engineer Department); lieutenant of the guard (Post Office Custodial Service); housemaster (U. S. Naval Academy); parking lot attendant; customs enforcement officer, project police (Public Housing Administration); safety and security chief, Terre Haute Ordnance Depot, Indiana; shipkeeper; and security officer (Bureau of Immigration and Naturalization).

Restricted examinations for custodial positions include: janitor and assistant foreman of janitors; engineman-janitor; head charwoman, laborer, matron, and window cleaner, Post Office Custodial Service; caretaker of abandoned Federal reservation, Federal cemetery, or small military reservation; caretaker-mechanic at inactive military reservation; charman; charwoman; clean-up man, Ordnance Department of the Army; dam tender; fireman-laborer; foreman of laborers (when duties are custodial); headwaiter, kitchen helper, and waiter, Veterans Administration; hopsital attendant; hospital servitor; housekeeper (custodial); laborer (custodial); lockman; lockmaster; maid (custodial); matron (custodial); mess attendant; restroom matron; shipkeeper (custodial), U. S. Maritime Commission Reserve Fleets; supervisor of hospital attendants; ward attendant; ward orderly; bridge tender; and maintenance foreman (housing).

Those for elevator operator include elevator starter, Post Office Custodial Service.

Restricted messenger positions do not include special delivery messenger at first-class post offices.

BACKGROUND OF VETERANS' PREFERENCE

It is estimated that about 65 per cent of the total number of men working for the government as civilians were veterans of the wars in which the United States has engaged. Eight per cent of all women workers were either veterans themselves or the widows of veterans or the wives of disabled veterans, or the mothers of deceased or disabled veterans. This is the result of a conscious move on the part of the government to grant preference in federal employment to veterans. Serious concern has been voiced in many quarters concerning the effect of this policy upon the efficiency of the government. It is pointed out that the concept of veterans' preference runs contrary to the concept of merit and fitness in government service; that a veteran has only barely to pass an examination to go to the top of the list, if he has a compensable service-connected disability of 10 per cent or more (except for professional and scientific jobs in grade GS-9 or higher) even though others may be far better qualified; that the federal establishment is tending to become overloaded with veterans; that opportunities for younger people and women in the federal service are being reduced.

On the other hand it is argued that veterans have lost out in economic competition with those who stayed at home during the wars and that the government owes them an opportunity to make up for this loss; that the number of veterans, particularly those of World War II, is so great that the government can be assured of quality personnel; that the need to help the veteran is an overriding consideration; that to get a federal job the veteran must meet certain minimum standards—and that these standards should be sufficienty high so that those who meet them are qualified for the positions. Moreover it is argued that the nation overwhelmingly desires a system of veterans' preference, although this argument has never been proved.

The policy of granting preference is not a new one. Even before the first Civil Service Act was passed in 1883, when all public jobs were dispensed on a patronage basis, Congress granted job preference to war veterans. The first such statute came one month before the end of the Civil War, in March 1865, giving preference to qualified persons discharged from the armed forces because of disabilities incurred while in service.

During the next half century Congress increased this preference so that veterans, along with their widows and orphans, received preferential treatment in the matter of discharge when a cut in personnel became necessary. After World War I, Congress granted preference in appointment to jobs in Washington to veterans and veterans' widows and also extended this preference to cover the wives of disabled veterans who could not qualify for appointment because of their disability. Each war has meant increased preference for veterans.

The present system of preference applies not only to veterans of World War II but to veterans of all wars in which the United States has engaged and certain "peacetime" veterans.

WIVES, WIDOWS AND MOTHERS

The wife of a disabled veteran is entitled to ten-point preference on all examinations, and all other veterans' advantages. She must show these facts to obtain preference: (1) that she is presently married to the veteran; (2) that her husband served on full-time active duty in the armed forces of the United States and received a discharge under honorable conditions; (3) that her husband is disqualified by his existing service-connected disability for civil service appointment along the general lines of his usual occupation. Only a Federal medical officer acting for the Civil Service Commission may make the determination that the veteran on whose service the preference claim is based is disqualified by his service-connected disability for civil service appointment along the general lines of his usual occupation. This determination is required for wife preference and for certain claims for mother preference.

The widow of a veteran is entitled to ten-point preference if she meets the following requirements:

1. That she was married to the veteran and was not divorced from him.
2. That the veteran is actually and legally dead and the widow has not remarried since his death, or her remarriage has been annulled.
3. That the veteran had served on full-time active duty in any branch of the armed forces of the United States:
   a. During a war, or
   b. During the period April 28, 1952, through July 1, 1955, or
   c. In a campaign or expedition for which a campaign badge (service medal) has been authorized.
4. That the veteran had been separated from such active duty under honorable conditions.

The mother of a veteran who lost his life while serving on active duty during periods listed under 3 in the preceding paragraph may qualify for mother preference. if she meets these additional qualifications:

1. That she is, or was, married to the father of the ex-service child and is the natural mother of the ex-service child.
2. That if she is presently living with her husband:
   a. That the father of her ex-service child or the husband of her remarriage, as the case may be, is totally and permanently disabled.
   b. If she is widowed, divorced or separated:
      1. That she is widowed by the death of, or is divorced or separated from the father of her ex-service child and has not remarried, or
      2. That if she has remarried she has been widowed by the death of, or is divorced or legally separated from the husband of her remarriage.

The mother of a disabled ex-service son or daughter must meet the following conditions in addition to those listed under 1 and 2 of the preceding paragraph:

1. That the ex-service son or daughter was separated under honorable conditions from full-time active duty performed in any branch of the armed forces of the United States at any time.
2. That her son or daughter is living and has an existing service-connected disability which disqualifies for civil service appointment along the general lines of his or her usual occupation.

SOMETIMES PREFERENCE CAN BE LOST

Conditions arise under which a person entitled to veterans' preference can lose it. Examples:

DIVORCE FROM VETERAN: The wife of a veteran loses preferences based on his service when she is divorced from him.

REMARRIAGE OF VETERAN'S WIDOW: The widow of a veteran loses preference when she remarries.

RECOVERY FROM DISABILITY: A veteran loses disability preference when he recovers from his disability, or ceases to receive compensation, pension, or disability retirement benefits. The wife of a veteran loses preference when her husband recovers from a service-connected disability. A mother loses her preference when she reunites with the father of her ex-service child, unless said father is permanently and totally disabled, or when she remarries, unless the husband of her remarriage is permanently and totally disabled. The mother of disabled ex-service sons or daughters loses preference when the child dies or recovers from disability to such an extent that he or she is no longer disqualified for Federal employment.

HOW TO SECURE A TEMPORARY JOB

We have learned that veterans get "first crack" at the many temporary positions available in government service. Probably the simplest way to learn about such temporary positions is to write directly to the agency for which you wish to work. Some persons even write to all federal agencies, asking that they be put on the list for consideration for temporary work in their occupations.

HOW TO CLAIM VETERANS' PREFERENCE

In order to obtain preference the veteran must submit evidence that he is entitled to it. He must answer questions about military service when he first fills out his application and later, when he is being considered for appointment, he will be required to submit documents.

NON-DISABLED VETERAN WHO SERVED IN TIME OF WAR: Claim for five-point preference based on war service is filed by answering the questions on the application form.

Later you'll be asked to submit proof of honorable separation from the armed forces.

NON-DISABLED VETERAN WHO SERVED IN CAMPAIGN OR EXPEDITION FOR WHICH CAMPAIGN BADGE WAS AUTHORIZED. Preference goes also to persons who served in various campaigns, as distinguished from wars. If you're among the veterans who served in a campaign or expedition, you'll need to fill out Standard Form 15, which you can obtain at the same office which gives out application blanks. In addition you'll need to submit proof of honorable separation and official notice of the award of the campaign badge.

DISABLED VETERAN: If you are disabled, you file the following documents: Standard Form 15; proof of honorable separation from the armed forces; either an official statement from the Veterans' Administration, Army, Navy, Air Force, Coast Guard, or Public Health Service certifying the existence of a service-connected disability, or an official statement from the Veterans' Administration that you are receiving compensation or an official statement from the Veterans' Administration, Army, Navy, Air Force, Marine Corps, Coast Guard, or Public Health Service certifying that you are receiving disability-retirement benefits

WIFE: The wife of a disabled veteran must submit the same documents required of the disabled veteran. If the veteran is retired from military service, the official statement should contain information concerning the nature and extent of her husband's disability. This statement will be issued by the service department at the veteran's request.

WIDOW: A widow files the following information: Preference Form 15; proof of her husband's honorable separation from the armed forces.

When the claim is based on service in a campaign or expedition for which a campaign badge has been authorized, she must file with the Civil Service Commission the veteran's official notification of the award by the military organization in which the service was performed.

She is not required to furnish proof of death except under these special circumstances: If he died in line of duty, she must submit the official notification. If he has disappeared and his death cannot be established she must submit two or more affidavits certifying that he has not been seen or heard from for at least seven years.

The mother of a disabled veteran must submit the same documents required of a disabled veteran.

The mother of a deceased veteran files the following information: Standard Form 15; official notification of the veteran's death in line of duty.

FEDERAL JOBS OVERSEAS

INTRODUCTION

United States citizens are employed by the Federal Government in Alaska, Hawaii, United States territories, and in foreign countries. They are found in almost every occupational field. They are construction and maintenance workers, doctors, nurses, teachers, technical experts, mining engineers, meteorologists, clerks, stenographers, typists, geologists, skilled tradesmen, social workers, agricultural marketing specialists, and agricultural and other economists.

Current needs of agencies with jobs to fill are generally limited to highly qualified and hard-to-find professional personnel, skilled technicians, and, in some cases, stenographers and clerical and administrative personnel. A few agencies are seeking experienced teachers, librarians, nurses, and medical personnel. However, a few vacancies occur in most fields from time to time because of normal turnover in personnel.

This section explains how jobs are filled, discusses conditions of employment, indicates the kinds of skills agencies use, and lists addresses to which inquiries may be sent.

HOW JOBS ARE FILLED

In Alaska, Hawaii, and United States territories, most vacancies are filled by the appointment of local eligibles who qualify in competitive civil-service examinations which are announced and held in the local area. Normally, there is a sufficient local labor market to fill the needs and examinations are not publicized outside the local areas. Some positions, however, may be filled by transferring career Government employees from the United States mainland.

When a vacancy is to be filled in a foreign country, determination is made whether to recruit from among persons in the area where the job is located or to seek qualified applicants residing in the United States. If the position is to be filled locally, the appointee may be a United States citizen residing or traveling in the area, the wife or dependent of a citizen employed or stationed in the area, or a foreign national.

In most instances where United States installations are established in foreign countries, either formal or informal agreements have been drawn up assuring the host government that local nationals will be employed wherever possible in order to be of maximum assistance to the economy of that country. Furthermore, it is almost always to the economic advantage of the United States to employ foreign nationals at local pay rates without responsibility for travel costs and overseas cost-of-living allowances. Positions held by foreign nationals are in the excepted service and are not subject to the competitive requirements of the Civil Service Act and Office of Personnel Management rules.

COMPETITIVE SERVICE POSITIONS

However, there are many thousands of technical, administrative, and supervisory positions in which United States citizens are employed in foreign countries. These positions are usually in the competitive service, and as vacancies occur they are filled in most cases by transferring career Government employees from the United States. This is the case in the Department of Defense, the largest employer of overseas personnel, and in most other agencies having overseas positions. When Government employees are not available for transfer overseas, and qualified United States citizens cannot be recruited locally, these vacancies are filled through the regular competitive examining process.

Approximately 30 examinations now open on a nationwide basis are being used, as recruiting needs require, to fill overseas positions. The examinations cover a variety of business and economics, engineering and scientific, medical, social and educational, and trades positions. Qualified persons interested in overseas assignments in these fields should establish eligibility under appropriate examinations. Applications and copies of examination announcements can be obtained from Federal Job Information Centers.

EXCEPTED SERVICE POSITIONS

Some positions are excepted from the competitive requirements of the civil service rules and regulations. Included in this group are positions in the Foreign Service of the Department of State, dependents' schools teachers, positions in the attache offices, and most positions of clerk-translator, translator, and interpreter. Applications for these positions should be made directly to the agency in which employment is desired.

A description of the principal agencies which employ personnel outside the United States, with should be sent appears later on in this section.

CONDITIONS OF EMPLOYMENT

Physical Requirements

Applicants for most overseas positions must be able to pass rigid physical examinations, since employees may be required to serve under extremely difficult living conditions and, in some areas, at posts where complete medical facilities are not available. Physical standards are applied which are suitable for the location and occupation involved, and may include standards of mental and emotional stability and maturity.

Any physical defect which would make the employee a hazard to himself or to others, or prevent efficient performance of the duties of the position, is disqualifying. Conditions which require periodic medical care, hospitalization, special foods or medicine may be disqualifying for some areas.

Accompanying dependents may also be required to pass rigid physical examinations.

Tour of Duty

Individuals selected in the United States for overseas employment generally are required to sign a transportation agreement for a definite period of service, which is usually for a minimum of 36 months. In certain areas the minimum period is 12 or 24 months.

Investigation

All appointments are subject to satisfactory security, character, and suitability investigations. Applicants considered for appointment are carefully screened, and only those possessing suitable qualifications are selected for overseas employment.

Since most Federal jobs overseas are filled by local residents or by the transfer of people who already work for the Government, opportunities for appointment to an overseas position are extremely limited.

GENERAL INFORMATION

Qualifications

Generally, the qualification requirements are the same as those established for like positions in the United States. Applicants may, however, be required to meet certain additional or higher standards. A foreign language capability, while not required in all, or even most, Federal jobs overseas, would obviously be a valuable qualification.

Dependents

For middle and upper-level positions in what may be broadly termed "professional occupations," most agencies permit employees to take their families with them. In certain other job categories, and in accordance with an established system of priorities, it is usually possible to arrange for dependents to follow from several months to a year after the employee has arrived at the overseas post.

For most clerical and secretarial positions abroad, agencies prefer single persons without dependents.

Appointments of both husband and wife are very infrequent, since there rarely are simultaneous vacancies in which their qualifications could be appropriately utilized at the same post. However, in foreign countries with a large American presence, both governmental and private-industrial, qualified U.S. citizens are sometimes needed for a variety of job openings. In the majority of cases, dependents of U.S. Government employees overseas are given priority consideration for such employment.

Salary

Generally, overseas white-collar workers are paid the same base salaries as Federal employees in the United States occupying similar positions. In addition, where warranted by conditions at the post, they receive a post differential or cost-of-living allowance. In foreign areas, the wages of blue-collar workers are based upon continental United States rates plus, in some cases, a post differential or cost-of-living allowance; in United States areas overseas, their wages may be set in a similar way or they may be based on local rates.

Quarters Allowances

In foreign areas, employees are sometimes housed in Government quarters. If Government housing is not provided, a quarters allowance is paid which covers in large part the cost of rent and utilities. In most United States areas, Government quarters are not provided and no quarters allowance is paid.

Federal Employment Benefits

In general, Federal employees are entitled to such liberal benefits as paid vacations, sick leave with pay, and retirement coverage. They are eligible for life insurance and health benefits partially financed by the Government. Employees serving overseas also normally receive special benefits such as free travel for themselves and their dependents, free transportation or storage for their household goods, and additional paid vacations with free travel to their homes in the United States between tours of duty. Also, the United States Government operates dependents' schools in many areas and provides educational opportunities for children which are comparable to those offered in the better schools in the United States.

Veteran Preference

Veterans must be given consideration by appointing officers in the filling of overseas positions in accordance with the provisions of the Veterans' Preference Act.

AGENCIES EMPLOYING OVERSEAS PERSONNEL

This section indicates the kinds of positions for which these agencies may be recruiting and lists addresses to which inquiries about employment opportunities may be sent. (Persons who have never worked for the Government should also contact the Office of Personnel Management for information about competitive examinations.)

The largest employers of overseas personnel include the Departments of State, Army, Navy, Air Force, Interior, Commerce, and Agriculture, the International Communications Agency, the Agency for International Development, and the Panama Canal Company-Canal Zone Government.

Department of Agriculture

The Foreign Agricultural Service assigns agricultural attaches and secretaries to staff its offices at foreign posts. These personnel analyze and report on production, trade and consumption of agricultural commodities and work to develop foreign markets for U.S. farm products. Professional positions normally are filled by Department of Agriculture employees trained in agricultural marketing and agricultural economics. Appointments are initially made from the Professional and Administrative Career Examination and examinations for Agricultural Economist and Agricultural Marketing Specialist. Secretarial positions are generally filled by transferring persons already employed by the Department of Agriculture; otherwise, vacancies are filled by appointment from the Office of Personnel Management's list of eligibles in the clerk-stenographer examination, followed by a training program in Washington, D.C. Additional information may be obtained from the Personnel Division, Foreign Agricultural Service, Department of Agriculture, Washington, D.C. 20250.

Department of the Air Force

The Air Force uses the Department of Defense Overseas Employment Program (OEP) as the primary source of candidates in filling its overseas positions. Although first consideration is given to qualified employees currently serving at Air Force installations in the United States, employees of other Federal agencies are also considered if sufficient well-qualified candidates are not available within the Air Force. Government employees or former employees having reinstatement eligibility and interested in registering in the OEP should contact the Civilian Personnel Officer at the nearest Department of Defense installation. When well-qualified employees are not available through the OEP, vacancies are filled from the appropriate civil service register through the regular competitive examining process.

Department of the Army

Overseas positions are normally filled through the reassignment of Army career employees from the United States. Information about positions with the Department of the Army overseas, which require highly unusual or scarce skills, may be obtained from the Department of the Army, Civilian Management Field Agency, Attention PECM, Forrestal Building, Washington, D.C. 20314.

Department of the Navy

Vacancies are principally filled through the assignment of well-qualified Navy and Marine Corps career employees desiring to serve overseas. Primary recruitment sources are Department of the Navy career programs and the Department of Defense Overseas Employment Program (OEP). When recruitment from other sources is necessary, it is mainly for positions in engineering, science, skilled trades, accounting and auditing, and administration.

For information about appointment or assignment to overseas positions, see the Civilian Personnel Officer at the nearest Navy or Marine Corps installation.

Department of Defense

Employment opportunities are available for educators with the Department of Defense Overseas Dependents Schools.

The Department of Defense maintains a school system from kindergarten through grade 12 for the dependent children of military and civilian personnel stationed abroad. School year salaries for educators are comparable to the average rates for similar positions in school systems in U.S. Districts having a population of 100,000 or more. Transportation and housing or a housing allowance are also provided. Qualification requirements include completion of a baccalaureate degree with a minimum of 18 semester hours in the field of professional teacher education and 2 years of actual teaching experience within the last 5 years. For information about teaching positions overseas, write to the Department of Defense, Office of Overseas Dependent Schools, 2461 Eisenhower Avenue, Alexandria, Va. 22331.

The Department of Defense also maintains a central registry of individuals interested in overseas employment. This program covers most positions for which overseas recruitment is conducted, by any branch of the Department of Defense. Individuals with civil service status should contact the civilian personnel office of the nearest Department of Defense installation for further information and registration in this program. Those without civil service status should apply under appropriate examinations, as indicated in this pamphlet.

U.S. Department of Commerce

National Oceanic and Atmospheric Administration—Overseas positions are available for persons with meteorological or electronics backgrounds at weather stations maintained in Alaska, Puerto Rico, Mexico, Hawaii, Wake Island, Guam, Johnson Island, American Samoa, the Trust Territories, and Antarctica. Positions exist for persons with appropriate education or experience in geophysics at observatories located in Alaska, Puerto Rico, Hawaii, and Guam. There are a few research positions available in the Antarctic for scientists with specialized experience or background in aeronomy, radio sciences and upper atmosphere-ionospheric physics. Qualified persons interested in any of these positions should address inquiries to the Personnel Officer, National Oceanic and Atmospheric Administration, Washington, D.C. 20852.

The United States Travel Service (USTS), is the national government tourist office of the United States. Its mission is to develop travel to the United States from foreign countries. It works with the travel industry: international agencies; city, State and foreign governments; and other Federal agencies to encourage and facilitate inbound passenger traffic. Through its eight regional offices abroad, USTS provides information and assistance to the foreign travel trade segments which sell travel to the U.S. It carries out extensive publicity and advertising campaigns in foreign media to stimulate interest in U.S. travel destinations.

Positions exist for persons with appropriate international sales and promotional work experience in the field of travel and tourism. Academic background: Marketing, advertising, international economics, business administration, marketing research, and public relations and mass media communications. Positions abroad require fluency in language of country to which assigned.

Job locations abroad are London, England; Paris, France; Frankfurt, Germany; Mexico City, Mexico; Toronto, Canada; Buenos Aires, Argentina; Sydney, Australia, and Tokyo, Japan.

Send inquiries to:

Personnel Officer, Operations Division, Office of the Secretary, U.S. Department of Commerce, Washington, D.C. 20230

Department of Transportation

Federal Highway Administration—Highway design, planning, construction, maintenance, and bridge engineers and specialists with experience in the administration and supervision of the operation and repair of highway construction equipment provide technical assistance to countries in connection with the Government's overseas technical aid program. Experienced persons interested in overseas employment should send inquiries to the Office of Personnel and Training, Federal Highway Administration, Washington, D.C. 20590.

Department of the Interior

Most of the positions are in Alaska. Almost all of these positions have been brought into the competitive service. Vacancies occur from time to time in engineering, metallurgy, geology, forestry, and teaching (elementary) positions. The jobs are usually filled through competitive examinations announced by the Office of Personnel Management. For more information about employment opportunities, address inquiries to the Department of the Interior, Washington, D.C. 20240.

Department of State

The Foreign Service of the United States, administered by the Department of State, recruits personnel for the career Foreign Service Officer Corps. Career Foreign Service Officers fill virtually all professional positions in the over 300 embassies and consulates maintained by the United States in more than 100 countries throughout the world. Officers serve primarily in one of the four functional specializations within the Department of State: Administration, consular affairs, economic/commercial, or political work. The Department of State is interested in personnel with training in diverse fields including political science, economics, public and business administration as well as experience in business, government and organizations involved in international activities. Appointments are made from among those who take competitive Foreign Service Officer examinations. Candidates for these examinations must be at least 21 years of age, except that candidates may apply at 20 years of age if they have a bachelor's degree or have completed successfully their junior year in college. Inquiries regarding these examinations should be addressed to the Board of Examiners for the Foreign Service, Department of State, Box 9317, Rosslyn Station, Arlington, Va. 22209.

There is a continuing need for secretaries and communications and records assistants in the Foreign Service to staff the embassies and consulates throughout the world. Requests for information regarding opportunities and qualifications for employment in positions other than those filled through the competitive Foreign Service Officer examinations should be addressed to the Recruitment Branch, Employment Division, U.S. Department of State, Washington, D.C. 20520.

Agency for International Development

This Agency is the principal administrator of U.S. economic and technical assistance to the developing countries of Africa, Asia and Latin America.

To administer these development programs, A.I.D. relies upon a staff of skilled, experienced men and women from a number of technical and professional disciplines. While employment opportunities vary from country to country and from time to time, the most frequent needs are for economists (MA required, Ph. D preferred), financial analysts, staff attorneys, auditors and accountants to work in Washington, D.C. and the Agency's overseas missions.

The majority of appointees join the A.I.D. staff in mid-level or senior-level positions, but the Agency also has intern positions for accountants, management auditors, economists and financial managers. These are open to young men and women who have majored in the relevant disciplines (and, preferably, have graduate degrees) but have not yet started their professional careers. Training is given in Washington and at overseas missions.

Most appointments are for 2-year tours overseas plus preliminary training and transportation time. Appropriate education and experience are the decisive criteria in the selection of candidates for both professional and intern positions. U.S. citizenship is a requirement.

Requests for information should be addressed to Chief, Recruitment Branch, Agency for International Development, Washington, D.C. 20523.

Panama Canal Company— Canal Zone Government

The efficient operation of the Panama Canal is of vital importance to world trade. Applications are accepted from qualified medical officers, registered nurses, medical technologists, teachers, mechanical and electrical engineers, ship pilots, machinists and electricians. Airmail SF–171 or inquiries to U.S. Recruitment Office, Personnel Bureau, Panama Canal Company, Box 2012, Balboa Heights, Canal Zone.

The Peace Corps (ACTION)

The Peace Corps provides opportunities for skilled Americans to serve in developing nations overseas. Its purpose is threefold: to give help where help is needed, to promote a better understanding of the American abroad, and to sharpen the American's image of other peoples.

Tours of duty are approximately for 2 years, including several weeks of training received before overseas departure. Volunteers receive a living allowance to provide for food, housing, clothing and incidentals, and a readjustment allowance.

While most of the volunteers work in educational and community development programs, there are positions available in more than 300 separate skill areas. A college degree is not required. Beyond teaching and community development, demands are greatest for volunteers experienced in the fields of public health, agriculture, home economics, mechanics, construction, and social work.

Applicants must be at least 18 years of age and American citizens. Married couples are eligible if they have no dependents under 18. There is no upper age limit.

For further information on opportunities for service, and instructions for application, contact the ACTION office in your state or write the Office of Recruitment and Communications, Peace Corps, Washington, D.C. 20525.

International Communications Agency
(Formerly USIA)

Generally, all but a few specialized positions are filled from within the ranks of ICA's career Foreign Service. Entry into the Foreign Service Information Officer corps is open to individuals over 21 years of age under the Junior Officer Program. Candidates must participate in a competitive process involving both comprehensive written and oral examinations. Information about the next examination can be obtained from the Board of Examiners for the Foreign Service, Department of State, Washington, D.C. 20520.

As needed, the Agency may recruit experienced professionals for information and cultural work overseas. They are appointed as Foreign Service Limited Reserve Officers for a maximum of 5 years. They are eligible to apply for career status (FSIO) after 3 years in the Limited Reserve.

Candidates for the Foreign Service must have a knowledge of American foreign policy and international relations, and a solid background in the historical, political, economic and cultural development of the United States. They must possess an ability to communicate convincingly and tactfully, both orally and in writing. A good working command of a foreign language and an ability to learn foreign languages are useful. Candidates must be willing to serve in any country and at any post.

Opportunities for serving overseas also exist for secretaries. Applicants must be at least 21 years of age, be able to take shorthand at 80 words per minute, type at 50 words per minute, and have 3 years secretarial or stenographic experience or 2 years of business school or college.

For additional information, write to the Recruitment and Examining Division, International Communications Agency, 1776 Pennsylvania Avenue, Washington, D.C. 20547. Standard Form 171 (Personal Qualifications Statement) should be submitted to this address when applying for a position with ICA (except for the Junior Officer Program; see above).

FEDERAL JOB INFORMATION CENTERS

The Office of Personnel Management offers Federal employment information through Federal Job Information Centers located in several major metropolitan areas across the country. They are listed under "U.S. Government" in the white pages of local phone directories. In addition, Federal job opportunities are posted in local State Job Service (or State Employment Security) offices.

A call can save you time and unnecessary effort if you want to obtain application forms, announcements and other general types of information.

For specific information on possible openings in overseas areas, you should write:

For Pacific areas:

> Honolulu Area Office
> Office of Personnel Management
> 1000 Bishop Street, Suite 1500
> Honolulu, Hawaii 96813

For Atlantic area:

> Washington Area Office
> Office of Personnel Management
> 1900 E Street, N.W.
> Washington, D.C. 20415

PATRONAGE AND "EXCEPTED" JOBS

The U.S. Civil Service Commission has been abolished since January 1, 1979 and its functions have been divided between two new agencies, the Office of Personnel Management (OPM) and the Merit Systems Protection Board (MSPB). The Office of Personnel Management has taken over many of the important responsibilities of the Civil Service Commission, including examinations and other employment matters, personnel investigations, personnel program evaluation, and training. The Merit Systems Protection Board is a separate and independent agency responsible for safeguarding both the merit system and the rights of individual employees in personnel matters. The addresses and telephone numbers for the new agencies remain the same as they had been under the Civil Service Commission.

ALTHOUGH the merit system for selecting employees is talked about a good deal, it is not practiced throughout the government. Patronage and political considerations control selection of certain public employees, particularly those in the more responsible and higher-paying positions. Patronage, or the spoils system, is not all bad. Employees and officials chosen by this method are frequently competent and often display a freshness of approach which some authorities maintain is not a common characteristic among competitive employees.

The 14 percent of Federal positions that are excepted from civil-service requirements number 347,-800. Of them, 136,400 are excepted by statute and the remainder by action of the Civil Service Commission. Some people believe that all of these are patronage positions; actually, relatively few are true patronage jobs. The Federal Bureau of Investigation and the Central Intelligence Agency for example, are not likely to be touched by the breath of patronage. And many thousands of temporary positions, and others filled for special duties outside the range of civil service requirements, must be maintained in order to uphold the continuity of government functions.

Examples of positions excepted by statute are those in the Foreign Service, on the Atomic Energy Commission, in the Library of Congress, and with the Tennessee Valley Authority.

Nevertheless, there are still left a considerable number of jobs under the spoils system. Several hundred top jobs are open whenever a new regime proceeds with its "housecleaning." A new cabinet is selected, Presidential assistants, various agency heads and sub-heads. The chiefs of commissions and boards are appointed to serve definite terms, but little difficulty is usually encountered if a new President should wish to oust some of these individuals and make room for his own appointees. A quiet Presidential request for resignation is likely in most cases to be honored.

We have seen in "Working for the U. S. Postal Service" that postmasterships are traditionally plums for the party in power; and in "Legal Positions," that all attorneys in the government are under patronage. The Civil Service Commission has no control over such positions. The lawyer who wants a government job must get it by knowing his political leader or someone else who has political pull; many of the positions go to party workers. Not all the party workers selected for patronage positions are incompetent "clubhouse boys." The leader usually submits several names to the appointing officer, who then has a choice. And it is not common today for the name of a thoroughly incompetent person to be submitted.

The recommendation of college deans, professors, and prominent public figures with "contacts" in Washington are also helpful; knowing an official in an agency is often useful, since he may bring the applicant to the attention of the agency chief.

Appointments in the legislative branch of the federal government are not subject to civil service requirements. These appointments include all the workers in the Library of Congress, which hires di-

S1904

rectly, and the various aides—researchers, lawyers, secretaries, messengers, pages, clerks, and guards—to senators and congressmen. Those who want such jobs should get in touch with their representatives in Congress, or talk to their political leader.

Judicial positions in federal courts are not under civil service. These positions include not only those of appointed judges, but marshals, bailiffs, court reporters, referees, probation and parole officers, auditors, and clerks. Here, too, "influence" counts.

RULE VI ("EXCEPTED" APPOINTMENTS)

There is a special rule concerning "excepted" appointments, that is, jobs which are not filled through the usual civil service methods. The rule sets down the kinds of positions which may be filled without examination. Rule VI states that certain positions shall be excepted from competitive service "because of their confidential or policy-making character, or because it is not practicable to make appointments through competitive examination." When it is decided (by the Civil Service Commission) that a position should be "excepted," the title of that position is published in the Federal Register. At the end of each fiscal year the Civil Service Commission submits to the White House a list of the jobs which have been thus freed of competitive requirements. An "excepted" position does not acquire competitive status.

Excepted positions (a long list of them) include all those which were excluded from competition by the original Civil Service Act of 1883, positions excepted by executive order of the President, positions which may be filled under personal service contract, and positions in government corporations. Veterans are entitled to preference in these positions, as in others, and each agency is supposed to set up proper standards for every excepted position, so that it is not filled by incompetents.

Positions excepted by action of the Civil Service Commission are placed in 1 of 3 schedules—A, B, or C—after a study of all pertinent facts (such as the duties, pay, and location of the positions) has been made by the Commission.

Schedule A is for positions for which it is not practicable to hold any examinations. Examples are: Chaplains, professional and technical experts for temporary consultation purposes, narcotics agents for undercover work, certain part-time positions at isolated localities, and many positions in foreign countries. There are 108,000 positions in this schedule.

Schedule B is for positions for which competitive examinations are impracticable but for which *noncompetitive* examinations are given. Examples are positions assigned exclusively to Navy or Air Force Communications Intelligence activities. There are about 2,000 jobs in this schedule.

Schedule C is for positions whose occupants serve in a policy-determining capacity to the politically appointed heads of agencies or in a confidential capacity to them and their key officials. It was established to more clearly define the career service by setting apart from it positions properly in the political area. It contains key positions which should be filled by the administration in power with persons who will fully support its political aims and policies.

No examination is required for appointment to Schedule C jobs. Departments and agencies have authority to assign duties to any position. They may recommend to the Commission that a position be placed in Schedule C if they feel the duties assigned are either policy determining or require the incumbent to serve in a confidential relationship to a key official.

FOR FURTHER STUDY

ARCO BOOKS FOR MORE HELP

Now what? You've read and studied the whole book, and there's still time before you take the test. You're probably better prepared than most of your competitors, but you may feel insecure about one or more of the probable test subjects.

Perhaps you've discovered that you are weak in language, verbal ability or mathematics. Why flounder and fail when help is so easily available? Why not brush up in the privacy of your own home with one of these books?

And why not consider the other opportunities open to you? Look over the list and make plans for your future. Start studying for other tests *now*. You can then pick and choose your *ideal* position, instead of settling for the first *ordinary* job that comes along.

Each of the following books was created under the same expert editorial supervision that produced the excellent book you are now using. Though we only list titles and prices, you can be sure that each book performs a real service, and keeps you from fumbling and from failure. Whatever your goal. . . Civil Service, Trade License, Teaching, Professional License, Scholarships, Entrance to the School of your choice. . .you can achieve it through the proven Question and Answer Method.

START YOUR CAREER BY MAILING THIS COUPON TODAY.

ORDER NOW from your bookseller or direct from:

ARCO PUBLISHING INC. 219 Park Avenue South, New York, N.Y. 10003

Please Rush The Following Arco Books (Order by Number or Title)

....

....

....

....

....

....

☐ I enclose check, cash or money order for $_____(price of books, plus $1.00 for first book and 25¢ for each additional book, packing and mailing charge) No C.O.D.'s accepted.

Residents of N.Y. and Calif. add appropriate sales tax.

☐ Please tell me if you have an ARCO COURSE for the position of ....

☐ Please send me your free COMPLETE CATALOG

NAME_____

STREET_____

CITY_____STATE_____ZIP # _____

Every Arco Book is guaranteed. Return it for full refund within ten days if not completely satisfied.

CIVIL SERVICE AND TEST PREPARATION—GENERAL

Able Seaman, Deckhand, Scowman	01376-1	5.00
Accountant—Auditor	00001-5	8.00
Addiction Specialist, Senior, Supervising, Principal	03351-7	8.00
Administrative Assistant—Principal Administrative Associate	00148-8	8.00
Administrative Manager, Turner	04813-1	8.00
Air Traffic Controller, Morrison	04593-0	10.00
American Foreign Service Officer	04219-2	8.00
Apprentice, Mechanical Trades	00571-8	6.00
Assistant Accountant	00056-2	8.00
Assistant Civil Engineer	01228-5	8.00
Assistant Station Supervisor	03736-9	6.00
Associate and Administrative Accountant	03863-2	8.00
Attorney, Assistant—Trainee	01084-3	10.00
Auto Machinist	04379-2	8.00
Auto Mechanic, Autoserviceman	00514-9	8.00
Bank Examiner—Trainee and Assistant	01642-6	5.00
Battalion and Deputy Chief, F.D.	00515-7	6.00
Beginning Office Worker	00173-9	8.00
Beverage Control Investigator	00150-X	4.00
Bookkeeper—Account Clerk	00035-X	8.00
Bridge and Tunnel Officer—Special Officer	00780-X	5.00
Building Custodian	00013-9	8.00
Bus Maintainer—Bus Mechanic	00111-9	8.00
Bus Operator	01553-5	5.00
Buyer, Assistant Buyer, Purchase Inspector	01366-4	6.00
Captain, Fire Department	00121-6	10.00
Captain, Police Department	00184-4	10.00
Carpenter	00135-6	6.00
Case Worker	01528-4	8.00
Cashier, Housing Teller	00703-6	6.00
Cement Mason—Mason's Helper, Turner	03745-8	6.00
Chemist—Assistant Chemist	00116-X	5.00
City Planner	01364-8	6.00
Civil Engineer, Senior, Associate, & Administrative	00146-1	8.00
Civil Service Arithmetic and Vocabulary	00003-1	5.00
Civil Service Course, Gitlin	00702-8	5.00
Teacher's Manual for Civil Service Course, Gitlin	03838-1	2.00
Civil Service Handbook	00040-6	3.00
Claim Examiner—Law Investigator	00149-6	8.00
Clerk New York City	00045-7	4.00
Clerk—Steno Transcriber	00838-5	6.00
College Office Assistant	00181-X	5.00
Complete Guide to U.S. Civil Service Jobs	00537-8	3.00
Construction Foreman and Supervisor—Inspector	01085-1	8.00
Consumer Affairs Inspector	01356-7	6.00
Correction Captain—Deputy Warden	01358-3	8.00
Correction Officer	00186-0	8.00
Court Officer	00519-X	8.00
Criminal Law Handbook for Law Enforcement Officers, Salottolo	02399-6	12.00
Criminal Science Handbook, Salottolo	02407-0	5.00
Detective Investigator, Turner	03738-5	8.00
Dietitian	00083-X	8.00
Draftsman, Civil and Mechanical Engineering (All Grades)	01225-0	6.00
Electrical Engineer	00137-2	10.00
Electrical Inspector	03350-9	8.00
Electrician	00084-8	8.00
Electronic Equipment Maintainer	01836-4	8.00
Elevator Operator	00051-1	3.00
Employment Interviewer	00008-2	8.00
Employment Security Clerk	00700-1	6.00
Engineering Technician (All Grades)	01226-9	8.00
Exterminator Foreman—Foreman of Housing Exterminators	03740-7	6.00
File Clerk	04377-6	6.00
Fire Administration and Technology	00604-8	10.00
Firefighting Hydraulics, Bonadio	00572-6	8.00
Fireman, F.D.	00010-4	6.00
Food Service Supervisor—School Lunch Manager	04819-0	8.00
Foreman	00191-7	8.00
Foreman of Auto Mechanics	01360-5	6.00
Gardener, Assistant Gardener	01340-0	8.00
General Entrance Series	01961-1	4.00
General Test Practice for 101 U.S. Jobs	04421-7	6.00
Guard—Patrolman	00122-4	6.00
Homestudy Course for Civil Service Jobs	01587-X	6.00
Hospital Attendant	00012-0	6.00
Hospital Care Investigator Trainee (Social Case Worker I)	01674-4	5.00
Hospital Clerk	01718-X	3.00
Hospital Security Officer	03866-7	6.00
Housing Assistant	00054-6	5.00
Housing Caretaker	00504-1	4.00
Housing Inspector	00055-4	5.00
Housing Manager—Assistant Housing Manager	00813-X	5.00
Housing Patrolman	00192-5	5.00
How to Pass Employment Tests, Liebers	00715-X	6.00
Internal Revenue Agent	00093-7	5.00
Investigator—Inspector	01670-1	10.00
Junior Administrator Development Examination (JADE)	LR 01791-0	7.50
Junior Federal Assistant	01729-5	6.00
Laboratory Aide	01121-1	8.00
Laborer—Federal, State and City Jobs	00566-1	4.00
Landscape Architect	01368-0	5.00
Laundry Worker	01834-8	4.00
Law and Court Stenographer	00783-4	8.00
Law Enforcement Positions	00500-9	8.00
Librarian	00060-0	10.00
Lieutenant, F.D.	00123-2	10.00
Lieutenant, P.D.	00190-9	10.00
Machinist—Machinist's Helper	01123-8	6.00
Mail Handler—U.S. Postal Service	00126-7	5.00
Maintainer's Helper, Group A and C—Transit Electrical Helper	00175-5	6.00
Maintenance Man	04349-0	6.00
Management and Administration Quizzer	LR 01727-9	8.50
Management Analyst, Assistant-Associate	03864-0	8.00
Mathematics, Simplified and Self-Taught	00567-X	4.00
Mechanical Apprentice (Maintainer's Helper B)	00176-3	5.00
Mechanical Aptitude and Spatial Relations Tests	00539-4	6.00
Mechanical Engineer—Junior, Assistant & Senior Grades	03314-2	8.00
Messenger	00017-1	3.00
Mortuary Caretaker	01354-0	6.00
Motor Vehicle License Examiner	00018-X	8.00
Motor Vehicle Operator	00576-9	4.00
Motorman (Subways)	00061-9	6.00
Nurse	00143-7	6.00
Office Aide, Turner	04704-6	8.00
Office Assistant GS 2-4	04275-3	8.00
Office Machines Operator	00728-1	4.00
1540 Questions and Answers for Electricians	00754-0	5.00
1340 Questions and Answers for Firefighters, McGannon	00857-1	6.00
Painter	01772-4	5.00

S-3757

LR—Library Reinforced Binding

Parking Enforcement Agent	00701-X	4.00
Patrol Inspector	04301-6	8.00
Peace Corps Placement Exams	01640-X	6.50
Personnel Examiner, Junior Personnel Examiner	00648-X	8.00
Plumber—Plumber's Helper	00517-3	6.00
Police Administration and Criminal Investigation	00565-3	10.00
Police Administrative Aide	02345-7	5.00
Police Officer—Patrolman P.D., Murray	00019-8	6.00
Police Science Advancement	02636-7	15.00
Policewoman	00062-7	6.00
Post Office Clerk-Carrier	04846-8	6.00
Postal Inspector	00194-1	5.00
Postal Promotion Foreman—Supervisor	00538-6	6.00
Postmaster	01522-5	5.00
Practice for Civil Service Promotion	00023-6	8.00
Practice for Clerical, Typing and Stenographic Tests	04297-4	6.00
Principal Clerk—Stenographer	01523-3	8.00
Probation and Parole Officer	04203-6	8.00
Professional and Administrative Career Examination (PACE)	03653-2	6.00
Professional Careers Test	01543-8	8.00
Professional Trainee—Administrative Aide	01183-1	5.00
Public Health Sanitarian	00985-3	8.00
Railroad Clerk	00067-8	4.00
Railroad Porter	00128-3	4.00
Real Estate Assessor—Appraiser—Manager	00563-7	8.00
Resident Building Superintendent	00068-6	5.00
Road Car Inspector (T.A.)	03743-1	8.00
Sanitation Foreman (Foreman & Asst. Foreman)	01958-1	6.00
Sanitation Man	00025-2	4.00
School Crossing Guard	00611-0	4.00
Senior Clerical Series	01173-4	6.00
Senior Clerk—Stenographer	01797-X	8.00
Senior File Clerk, Turner	00124-0	8.00
Senior and Supervising Parking Enforcement Agent	03737-7	6.00
Senior Typist	03870-5	6.00
Sergeant, P.D.	00026-0	10.00
Shop Clerk	03684-2	6.00
Social Supervisor	04190-0	8.00
Staff Attendant	00828-8	4.00
Staff Positions: Senior Administrative Associate and Assistant	03490-4	6.00
State Trooper	00078-3	8.00
Statistician—Statistical Clerk	00058-9	5.00

Stenographer—Typist (Practical Preparation)	00147-X	6.00
Stenographer—U.S. Government Positions GS 2-7	04388-1	6.00
Storekeeper—Stockman (Senior Storekeeper)	01691-4	8.00
Structural Apprentice	00177-1	5.00
Structure Maintainer Trainee, Groups A to E, Turner	03683-4	6.00
Supervising Clerk (Income Maintenance)	02879-3	5.00
Supervising Clerk—Stenographer	04309-1	8.00
Supervision Course	01590-X	8.00
Surface Line Dispatcher	00140-2	6.00
Tabulating Machine Operator (IBM)	00781-8	4.00
Taking Tests and Scoring High, Honig	01347-8	4.00
Telephone Maintainer: New York City Transit Authority	03742-3	5.00
Telephone Operator	00033-3	8.00
Test Your Vocational Aptitude, Asta & Bernbach	03606-0	6.00
Towerman (Municipal Subway System)	00157-7	5.00
Trackman (Municipal Subways)	00075-9	5.00
Track Foreman: New York City Transit Authority	03739-3	6.00
Traffic Control Agent	03421-1	5.00
Train Dispatcher	00158-5	5.00
Transit Patrolman	00092-9	5.00
Transit Sergeant—Lieutenant	00161-5	4.00
Treasury Enforcement Agent	00131-3	8.00
U.S. Postal Service Motor Vehicle Operator	04426-8	8.00
U.S. Professional Mid-Level Positions Grades GS-9 Through GS-12	02036-9	6.00
U.S. Summer Jobs	02480-1	4.00
Ventilation and Drainage Maintainer: New York City Transit Authority	03741-5	6.00
Vocabulary Builder and Guide to Verbal Tests	00535-1	5.00
Vocabulary, Spelling and Grammar	00077-5	5.00
Welder	01374-5	8.00
X-Ray Technician (See Radiologic Technology Exam Review)	03833-0	8.00

MILITARY EXAMINATION SERIES

Practice for Army Classification and Placement (ASVAB)	03845-4	6.00
Practice for the Armed Forces Tests	04362-8	6.00
Practice for Navy Placement Tests	04560-4	6.00
Practice for Air Force Placement Tests	04270-2	6.00
Practice for Officer Candidate Tests	01304-4	6.00
Tests for Women in the Armed Forces	03821-7	6.00
U.S. Service Academies	01544-6	6.00

HIGH SCHOOL AND COLLEGE PREPARATION

American College Testing Program Exams	04363-6	5.00
Arco Arithmetic Q & A Review, Turner	02351-1	5.00
Arco's Handbook of Job and Career Opportunities	04328-8	3.95
Better Business English, Classen	04287-7	2.95
California High School Proficiency Examination	04412-8	4.95
Catholic High School Entrance Examination	04844-1	6.00
The College Board's Examination, McDonough & Hansen	02623-5	5.00
College By Mail, Jensen	02592-1	4.00
College Entrance Tests, Turner	01858-5	5.00
CLEP: The Five General Examinations	04150-1	6.00
The Easy Way to Better Grades, Froe & Froe	03352-5	1.75
Elements of Debate, Klopf & McCroskey	01901-8	5.00
Encyclopedia of English, Zeiger	00655-X	3.95
English Grammar: 1,000 Steps	02012-1	6.00
English Grammar and Usage for Test-Takers, Turner	04014-9	6.00
The Florida Literacy Test, Morrison	04669-4	4.95

Good English with Ease, revised edition, Beckoff	03911-6	5.00
Guide to Financial Aids for Students in Arts and Sciences for Graduate and Professional Study, Searles & Scott	02496-8	3.95
High School Entrance and Scholarship Tests, Turner	00666-8	5.00
High School Entrance Examinations—Special Public and Private High Schools	04861-1	5.00
How to Obtain Money for College, Lever	03932-9	5.00
How to Prepare Your College Application, Kussin & Kussin	01310-9	2.00
How to Use a Pocket Calculator, Mullish	04072-6	4.95
How to Write Reports, Papers, Theses, Articles, Riebel	02391-0	6.00
Letter-Perfect:The Accurate Secretary, Gilson	04038-6	6.00
Mastering General Mathematics, McDonough	03732-6	5.00
Mathematics Workbook for the SAT, Saunders	04820-4	5.00
National Career Directory	04510-8	5.95
New York State Regents Scholarship	00400-2	5.00
Organization and Outlining, Peirce	02425-9	4.95